PENGUIN BOOKS

THE ENGLISH GARDEN ABROAD

Charles Quest-Ritson read history before qualifying as a solicitor. Some twenty years of travel in search of plants and gardens lie behind this book. At home he writes and lectures regularly on horticulture. Active in the National Council for the Preservation of Plants and Gardens and a council member of the Royal National Rose Society, he is also a Fellow of the Linnaean Society. He works in London as a tax lawyer and gardens in Wiltshire, where his wife runs a rose nursery.

THE
ENGLISH GARDEN
ABROAD

Charles Quest-Ritson

PENGUIN BOOKS

PENGUIN BOOKS

Published by the Penguin Group
Penguin Books Ltd, 27 Wrights Lane, London W8 5TZ, England
Penguin Books USA Inc., 375 Hudson Street, New York, New York 10014, USA
Penguin Books Australia Ltd, Ringwood, Victoria, Australia
Penguin Books Canada Ltd, 10 Alcorn Avenue, Toronto, Ontario, Canada M4V 3B2
Penguin Books (NZ) Ltd, 182–190 Wairau Road, Auckland 10, New Zealand

Penguin Books Ltd, Registered Offices: Harmondsworth, Middlesex, England

First published by Viking 1992
Published in Penguin Books 1996
1 3 5 7 9 10 8 6 4 2

Copyright © Charles Quest-Ritson, 1992
All rights reserved

The moral right of the author has been asserted

Printed in China by Imago

CONTENTS

ACKNOWLEDGEMENTS

The authors and publishers are grateful to Frank Magro and Macmillan Publishers Ltd for an extract from Osbert Sitwell's poem 'Umberto the Gardener' in *On the Continent* and to Kathleen Raine for her poem 'Ninfa Revisited'.

Illustration Acknowledgements

The authors and publishers are grateful to the following: Windsor Castle, Royal Library, © 1992 Her Majesty the Queen, 12, 116, 136; John d'Arcy, 176, 181; Antony Beevor, 117; John Berkeley, 48, 62, 74, 202, 203; Mrs Christina Blandy, 166, 167; the Marquesa de Casa Valdes, 190; Mrs B. Clark, 50; Henry Cocker, 7, 149, 150, 151; Mr and Mrs John Delaforce, 168, 169; Esmond Devas, 205; Clive Dewey and Brenda, Lady Cook, 156, 159, 160, 161, 162, 163; Florence, Berenson Collection, reproduced by permission of the President and Fellows of Harvard College, 125 and the colour photograph of 1 Tatti; Miss Kate Forbes, 88, 89; Lieut-Col. Sir Hanmer Cecil Hanbury, 65, 67, 69; Mrs Joan Heaton and the Revd Cranfield, 86, 87; Mrs Philippa Irwin, 53; John Allan Cash Photographic Library, 164; Sir George Kennard, Bt, 25; Paul Miles, 46, 187, 188, 209, 211; Lady O'Neill of the Maine, 109, 110, 111; Miss Daphne Phelps, 10, 90, 91; Mrs Victoria Philipps and Mrs Mary Thomas, 171; Royal Institute of British Architects, 183; James Russell, 8, 51, 52; Christopher Sandeman, 185; Miss Anne Seagrim, 210; Francis Sitwell, 4, 122; Raleigh Trevelyan, 108, 111; Tony Venison, 192; William Waterfield, 58, 59; Fred Whitsey, 56, 60, 123, 126, 137; Baroness Gabrielle van Zuylen, 212 (photo: author). All the following photographs were either taken by the author or are in the possession of the author: ii, 2, 9, 19, 20, 28, 30, 32, 45, 54, 55, 71, 72, 76, 81, 84, 92, 96, 97, 98, 100, 102, 103, 107, 112, 114, 125, 127, 130, 132, 134, 141, 143, 146, 152, 154, 173, 174, 179, 182, 187, 194, 196, 198, 199, 201, 204, 206, 214, 218, 220, 224.

All the colour photographs were taken by the author with the exception of the photograph of the garden at Villa Roquebrune, taken by Paul Miles.

Illustrations have been taken from the following books: J. H. Bennet, *Winter and Spring on the Shores of the Mediterranean*, 17; Lord Brougham, *List of Roses Now in Cultivation at Château Eléonore, Cannes*, 15; H. Eberlein, *Villas of Florence and Tuscany*, 105, 120; Frederick Eden, *Our Garden in Venice*, 94, 95; *Gardener's Chronicle*, 64, 66; Lady (D.) Hanbury, *La Mortola*, 65; Stéphen Liégeard, *La Côte d'Azur*, 18; Joseph Lucas, *Our Villa in Italy*, 119; N. McEacharn, *Catalogue of the Plants in the Garden of the Villa Táranto*, 1963, 148; Mrs Philip Martineau, *Gardening in Sunny Lands*, 22; Giuseppe Mondada, *Le Isole di Brissago nel passato e oggi*, 138, 139; Iris Origo, *War in the Val d'Orcia*, 129.

Thanks are due to the following people for help with illustrations: Miss Gwyneth Campling, Mrs A. G. Chance, Mrs Constance Cluett Ward, Miss Frances Dimond, the Marquis of Douro and the Duke of Wellington, Valerie Finnis, Mrs K. Ingwersen, Sir Geoffrey Jellicoe, Dr Audrey Le Lièvre, Mrs Alvilde Lees-Milne, Lady Millar, Anthony Norman, Prince William Parente, Lord Rothschild, Vernon Russell-Smith, Miss Anne Scott-James, Sir Reresby Sitwell, Princess Greta Sturdza, Mrs Peggy Synge, Miss Nancy Tennant, Major Eudo Tonson-Rye, Anne, Duchess of Westminster, and Mr W. W. Ellis.

PREFACE

THIS IS A theme-and-variations book. The theme is the history of English gardening for the last 250 years. The variations show how generations of English people living or working abroad, as owners, architects, landscapers or horticulturists, have interpreted the English tradition in a foreign country.

I have concentrated upon those nations that have long had both a substantial community of English expatriates and a robust horticultural tradition of their own: namely France, Italy, Spain and Portugal. Indeed, more English gardens of importance have been made in Italy and on the Riviera than in the whole of the rest of continental Europe.

There are other parts of the world with strong and distinct gardening styles, including Persia, China and Japan, which are outside the scope of this work, as is India, although there is a book to be written on the gardens of the British Raj. By confining myself to Europe and the Mediterranean, however, I have not omitted the important influences of the USA and the old dominions. These countries are strongholds of the English style of gardening and skilled gardeners, designers and owners from them have participated in many of the gardens made by Englishmen abroad. So complete was the English influence that Edwin Lutyens in South Africa thought he found written on the garden wall 'Mene, Mene, Jekyll, Upharsin'. It is only natural that South Africans, New Zealanders, Australians and – above all – Americans should recur throughout this book as exponents of the English style of gardening.

I have used the term English in preference to British primarily for convenience, and not to ignore the contribution of the other inhabitants of the British Isles. Until perhaps quite recently, there was no distinct gardening style of substance in Wales or Ireland. The Scottish tradition – particularly the large-scale planting of rhododendrons in woodland gardens – is represented abroad, but was quickly absorbed into the English tradition. Most of the gardens in this book were in fact made by Englishmen, Anglo-Irishmen or anglicised Scots who thought in the English manner. The English horticultural tradition has tended to predominate both within the British Isles and in those gardens made by Britons and Irishmen abroad.

Some of the people in this book were not born citizens of the United Kingdom: Walburga, Lady Paget, was German, Major Lawrence Johnston came from Boston and Baroness St Leger may have been Russian. All became British citizens, and in some ways more English than the English. Certainly they were as much 'one of us' as Joseph Conrad, Edward Ardizzone or Frederick Delius: the creative consequence of crossing frontiers is the essence of this book. Difficulties can arise when considering a garden made by an English designer for a foreign client, not because an unEnglish garden is outside the scope of this book but precisely because the extent to which English influences were predominant or subordinate is one of the more intriguing themes. The gardens which Joseph Paxton laid out at Ferrières for James de Rothschild and Russell Page made near Villar Perosa for Giovanni Agnelli clearly pass the test of Englishness, but it may be less easy to justify the inclusion of such a designer as Cecil Pinsent, who staged gardens in the Tuscan Renaissance style for his discerning Anglo-American clientele in Italy.

Historians of English gardening have tended to confine their studies to gardens in the British Isles, without realising just how significant were the developments which took place in English gardens abroad. The opportunity for experimentation under foreign conditions in turn accelerated the evolution of garden styles at home. Lessons learned and influences acquired in designing and planting abroad were imported back and then applied in Britain. William Beckford first developed in Portugal the elements that shaped his garden at Fonthill; Gertrude Jekyll was strongly influenced by her sister's garden in Venice; while Russell Page's absorption of the French tradition is in large part responsible for the *potagers* and *treillage* which characterise contemporary chic. On this basis it is fair to claim that a complete history of English gardening cannot properly be written without reference to many of the more important gardens in this book.

IT IS CUSTOMARY to end the preface to a book with the author's thanks to those who have assisted him, and I do so with a grateful heart for the generosity I have received from many. I much regret, however, that the photographic service of the British Library is now beyond the means of many authors and publishers. The illustrations in this book are striking and original: they would have been even better had the British Library not priced itself out of the market.

There are three in the top tier of people to thank: my wife Brigid for her constant support and companionship visiting gardens and gardeners abroad; my son Christopher Blair for his knowledge of nineteenth-century literature, freely shared, and his fierce criticism of my writing; and my editor Eleo Gordon

for her enthusiasm, humour and energetic pursuit of illustrations. All three have contributed immeasurably to the structure and details of this book.

Special thanks are also due to Quentin and Sue Agnew, Betty Molesworth Allen, Daphne Phelps, Nicholas and Marie Kaye, and Lauro Marchetti. All have contributed substantially to my researches. Among the many others who have helped I should mention: Antony Beevor, Tim Bergqvist, Camilla Blair, Sally Blakiston, Patrick Bowe, Chris Brickell, Alexander Bridport, Daphne Butler, Edward Windsor-Clive, Henry Cocker, Joyce Crossley, John d'Arcy, John and Valerie Delaforce, Clive Dewey, Heron Dickson, Francis Egerton, Brent Elliott, Giuseppe Ferrari, Kate Forbes, Martin and Elsie Gibbs, Michael Gibson, Margaret Gimson, Christiane Gutbrod, Nicola Harris, Penelope Hobhouse, Esmé Howard, Gerry Huggan, Walter Kaiser, Janet King, Anthony Lambton, Marie Loder, Margaret Longo, Gerald Luckhurst, Simona di Marco, Michael Marshman, Miriam Masterton, Vernon Maxwell, Paul Miles, Jock Moreton, Anthony and Mary Norman, Patricia Norrie, Jean O'Neill, Benedetta and Donata Origo, Anna Pavord, Guido Piacenza, Franco Pillirone, Carol Primmer, Umberto Quattrocchi, Madeline Quest-Ritson, Bambi Rae, Andrea von Rechberg, Tom and Sue Ritson, Martyn and Alison Rix, James Russell, Vernon Russell-Smith, Lisa Smith, Peter Smithers, Gavin Stamp, Christopher Thacker, Richard and Mary Thomas, Rohays Everard Thomas, Eudo Tonson-Rye, Raleigh Trevelyan, Thomas Tuite, Susana Walton, William Waterfield, Bill Wells, Philippa Wills, Gabrielle van Zuylen.

THE
ENGLISH GARDEN
ABROAD

INTRODUCTION

THE ENGLISH garden at Caserta is a classic
eighteenth-century landscape, the equal of any
in England, save that its rolling grassy hills are
planted with camphor trees and date palms; it was
laid out in 1784 for the palace of King Ferdinand V
of Naples. Seventy years later, Sir Francis Cook,
an English cotton merchant in Lisbon, renewed the
Gothic fantasy garden which William Beckford had
made in the Sintra Hills; despite its Englishness, Monserrate is now a Portuguese national monument, with
the best collection of conifers and ferns in Europe.
Some consider Lady Aberconway's early twentieth-
century English garden among the olive trees and
garrigue of the Riviera to be even better than her
masterpiece at Bodnant in Wales, with its spacious
parterres, stupendous vistas, rare plants and exquisite colour schemes, among drifts of naturalised irises
and cyclamen. English traditions are continued today
by such designers as Gerald Huggan on the Costa
del Sol and such plantsmen as Sir Peter Smithers,
who gardens on Lake Lugano. The modern English
horticultural virtues, the combination of good design
and a quick eye for the colours and forms of plants,
are typified by the exquisite garden Russell Page
made with Lady Walton at Ischia.

Gardening is a discipline at which the English can
claim to have excelled for over two hundred and fifty
years. If the history of other arts in England has
often been dominated by foreign influences, the pre-
eminence of the English horticultural tradition is
universally acknowledged. This achievement extends beyond the shores of Britain. Just as lovers of
painting or music must take into account Rubens's
or Handel's work in England, so too, in order fully
to understand the scope of English horticulture, the
work of English landscapers, garden designers and
horticulturists abroad must not be overlooked.

English gardening, in any case, for all its strength,
has had a natural tendency to look overseas. With a
comparatively poor native flora, when set against
the riches of Asia and the Mediterranean, gardeners
looked to other countries to supply their raw
material – plants. They also turned towards the
warmer climates, which they aped at great expense
in the huge greenhouse ranges of the eighteenth and
nineteenth centuries.

One of the perennial excitements for gardeners
abroad is to discover plants that are difficult to cultivate in England thriving happily. At Villa Gallo at
Capodimonte Lady Blessington raved that 'many of
the plants, to be found only in hothouses with us,
here grow luxuriantly in the open air ... terraces rise
over terraces, filled with flowering shrubs, and giving
a notion of the Hanging Gardens of Babylon'. This
delight at tender flowers outside or at summer abundance in winter appears time and again in English
accounts of visits to the south, from Queen Victoria's
diaries and Queen Mary's letters, to the poems of
D. H. Lawrence and the essays of Lawrence Durrell.
From the seventeenth century onwards, the English
yearning to grow exotics had induced them to build
orangeries and hothouses: sojourn in the Mediterranean offered easy fulfilment of this desire.

English joy at the wild flowers of the Mediterranean perplexed the natives. Gardening in Provence, the Hon. Lady Fortescue recounted,

*One of the iris-lined paths cut through an old olive orchard
by Lady Aberconway c. 1910 at La Garoupe, Antibes.*

In the autumn we had laboriously planted thousands of
bulbs imported, expensively, from Holland. These we

Montegufoni, the princely castle in Tuscany bought by Sir George Sitwell and greatly loved by his sons, Osbert and Sacheverell.

planted under the scornful eye of Hilaire [the gardener] who refused to be interested in them – we wondered why. When spring burst upon us one perfect morning (nothing comes gradually in Provence), I found the grassy terraces under the olive-trees one sheet of tiny blue Roman hyacinths, miniature scarlet tulips, mauve and scarlet anemones, and yellow jonquils. When I exclaimed in delight to Hilaire that our predecessor here had planted lavishly and beautifully, he at first looked blank, and then, when I pointed rapturously to the jewelled grass on the terraces below, he gave it one contemptuous glance and said, '*Ah ça! – sont sauvages, Madame*'.

Despite such attractions few of the people in this book, at least initially, went abroad to garden. Settlers settle where travellers travel. The Reformation had cut England off from easy traffic with the Catholic culture of southern Europe, so eighteenth-century Grand Tours targeted the heritage of ancient Rome instead: for about two hundred years the English tended to see themselves as heirs to the Roman Empire. Such writers as Goethe, one of the exponents of English landscape gardening, stimu-

lated a desire for classical romanticism in the northern races. The young Tennyson provided an English echo of '*Kennst du das Land*' with the lines 'For I have longed to see/ The palms and temples of the South'. Later, during the nineteenth century, increased wealth and improved transport made such foreign travel possible for more and more travellers.

As early as 1830 Samuel Rogers wrote in the introduction to his poem *Italy*, 'Ours is a nation of travellers ... none want an excuse. If rich, they go to enjoy; if poor, to retrench; if sick, to recover; if studious, to learn; if learned, to relax from their studies.' For many it was specifically the pull of Italy that they felt, with all its literary and social prestige. John Addington Symonds (*Sketches and Studies in Italy*, 1879) believed that 'we English live and breathe through sympathy with the Italians [for] the magnetic touch which is required to inflame the imagination of the north is derived from Italy'. Italy was the preferred destination of travellers until the late 1860s, when the appeal of the south of France became paramount.

Even in the early nineteenth century travellers were

also attracted to the Mediterranean by its warmth. Lord Dudley wrote of the Bay of Naples, 'I often think of this enchanting spot when shivering in the rude breeze of an ungenial English spring... I assure you it sometimes requires no little self-control and patriotic feeling, to resist becoming a dweller in some such place in Italy.' The popularity of the Riviera at the end of the nineteenth century was based on the exploitation of its mild climate. Bordighera, Hyères and Menton were created as health resorts for invalids from damp northern countries. English expatriates soon discovered that the weather was at least as suitable for gardening as for the cure of respiratory disorders.

Even in Italy the English community could not be considered as a single unit. As Mr Eager the clergyman snobbishly explained in E. M. Forster's *A Room with a View*, ' "... it is of considerable size, though, of course, not all equally – a few are here for trade" '. In much of the rest of Europe, to be sure, trade was the reason for an English presence. The great trading posts produced gardens every bit as fine as those in the tourist regions, but climate seems again to have been a determining factor, as if there was a limit to British horticultural ingenuity. Certainly the stations at Hamburg, Danzig and St Petersburg produced nothing to match the gardens of the wine trade at Oporto, Palermo and Madeira.

THREE MAJOR developments in the history of gardens are distinctively English. The first is the landscape movement which swept through Europe in the late eighteenth century and acquired universal acceptance as one of the ways of laying out a garden. On the continent, the phrases '*le jardin anglais*' and '*der englischer Garten*' indicate a specifically natural style of grand gardening that is typified in England by Blenheim, Bowood and Stowe. The second unique development in English gardening is horticultural plantsmanship, as distinguished from botanical study: it derives from John Loudon's nineteenth-century insistence on diversity and the collectomania of Victorian amateur scientists. The third innovation, a largely twentieth-century phenomenon, which still dominates sophisticated English gardening, composes gardens from the colour, form and texture of plants – as at Hidcote and Sissinghurst.

English gardens abroad are a quintessence of English gardening history. All the major changes in English gardening fashions over the last two hundred years are present in gardens made by Englishmen abroad, as well as lesser variations: the picturesque and natural styles of the eighteenth century; the gardenesque landscape gardens of the nineteenth century; woodland plantings in the Robinson manner; Italianate gardens – even in Italy – such as Barry or Sitwell would have been proud of; Arts and Crafts gardens; Jekyll gardens; plantsmen's gardens; Hidcote gardens; and school-of-Sissinghurst gardens. The basic struggle between the formal and the informal is also replicated abroad: the altercations between garden designers working on the Riviera between about 1860 and 1940 show in microcosm the debate that was being conducted at home. At the same time the English expatriates contributed to similar debates among the nationals of their adopted countries.

Despite the multitude of forms, it is worth trying to establish the essence of the English garden, those certain qualities that are present whatever the style or period. Grace and elegance would feature high on the list: they are both elements of pure gardening. So too are intimacy, seclusion and convenience; the hint of something beyond and the invitation to explore; and that essential harmony which makes for an easy transition from one feature to the next. On a practical level, Englishmen believe that a garden is primarily a place in which to grow plants. It is not an outdoor room, nor an essay in perspective, nor a study in the use of colour. During the writing of this book it became increasingly clear that the most consistent theme was the English obsession with plants – their shapes, their flowers, their scents, the very fact that they grow. It is a passion that has increased steadily over the last 150 years.

One characteristic of English garden owners abroad is that they expect to work in the garden themselves. This is a perennial idiosyncrasy. Lady Mary Wortley-Montagu wrote in 1748 from her home at Brescia, 'I generally rise at six, and as soon as I have breakfasted, put myself at the head of my weeder-women and work with them till nine.' When Frederick Madden called on the Margravine of Anspach, née Lady Elizabeth Berkeley, at her villa on Cape Posillipo near Naples in 1823, he found the elderly Englishwoman dressed in working clothes and digging with a spade in the garden. Walburga, Lady Paget, typified this willingness to turn a hand at Torre di Bellosguardo, on the hills above Florence: 'I rise every morning at six o'clock, then I go into the garden and settle things there. I lop off the branches myself, dig and do all the other things.' On another occasion she recorded, 'I have been working at this house and garden incessantly for the last two months. Painting, digging, making roads, furnishing. I don't think there is anything I have not turned my hand to. I have even broken stones.' Her visitors were expected to turn their hands too. Wallace, Lord Lamington, staying with her before taking up his appointment as Governor of Queensland, met with her approval. 'Wallace is excellent, simple and true,' she testified, citing as proof: 'he weeded a great many baskets of groundsel and . . . afterwards wrote and said it had been the happiest week of his life.' And Iris Origo recalled how the elderly Constance, Lady Wenlock, would rise early to feed the roses at La Foce with liquid manure from a watering-can 'curiously incongruous in her delicate hands. "Roses are gross feeders," she would say, pinning a full-blown "Crimson Glory" in the soft fichu of her dress.'

This eagerness to get their hands dirty is an English trait that continues to amaze, and sometimes to appal, the continental well-to-do. When the Marquis Ernest de Ganay visited Lawrence Johnston, who had a full-time staff of twelve for his garden in Menton, he noticed how its owner 'comes to greet you in corduroys straight from his terraces, with dirt on his hands like any gardener'. Elizabeth von Arnim's gardening met with such disapproval from her Prussian neighbours that she was impelled to write the story of her German garden, a book that was appropriately very popular in England. The English-born Princess Daisy of Pless, who made several gardens at the castle at Fürstenstein in Silesia, was convinced that a love for gardening was peculiarly English, because 'abroad, the gardens of most of the country houses in which I stayed seemed to have been made by professionals or servants'. It may be argued that this owner involvement is in part responsible for the sustained pre-eminence of English horticulture both at home and abroad.

It is a mistake, however, to suppose that gardens are made only by their owners. Often the layout of a garden, and usually the details, are the work of a designer, contractor or employee; but it is the same the whole world over – the rich man takes the credit. Villa Táranto on Lake Maggiore owes as much to the Kew-trained director Henry Cocker as to its celebrated founder Neil McEacharn. Nor should Judge Arthur Cohen bear the palm for the garden which Harold Peto laid out for him at Villa Sylvia on Cap Ferrat. Cohen himself had no interest in gardening: Peto designed the house, and the garden was part of the package.

English gardens abroad are uniquely fascinating to those interested in the history of gardening. Isolated from the country which produced the style, the essential elements of that style emerge on the continent in clearer relief. And the strength of the English tradition creates results of extraordinary variety and invention as it meets and reacts with such distinct forms as the gardens of the Italian Renaissance or the shady Moorish patios of Andalusia. Just how much of the local tradition is absorbed varies from place to place and from designer to designer. In general, where the climate is closest to our own, as in Portugal or northern France, local influences have tended to be taken less into account. But what has made the English style throughout the years so successful is its capacity for adaptation: pragmatism is the political word for it. Every site has peculiar characteristics. English gardeners hold that these should determine or at least influence the disposal of its parts, and give harmony and variety to the whole design.

English gardeners have customarily surveyed foreign gardens with creative opportunism. They take good ideas but return to English practices when they find the foreigners wanting. This receptiveness sometimes extends to objects. Since the early days of Grand Tours, Englishmen were as keen to acquire as their hosts were willing to part with a classical heritage. Only recently has such trade been considered unacceptable. At the beginning of this century Avray Tipping, visiting Harold Peto's own garden at Iford Manor in Wiltshire, with its huge collection of statues, bronzes and architectural bric-à-brac, wrote approvingly of the architect having amassed 'the spoils of Italy'. A hundred years earlier, Lady Blessington told the story of an 'English lady of fine wealth' who, on admiring the bristling finials and pinnacles of the Pisan church of Santa Maria della Spina, begged her husband, 'Do, pray dear, buy me that beautiful thing and have it sent home, to be placed in my flower-garden.'

Most visitors are critical of the native traditions of formal gardening. Percy Bysshe Shelley wrote of the apotheosis of French gardens at Versailles, 'we saw the palace and gardens . . . full of statues, vases, fountains and colonnades. In all that belongs essentially to a garden, they are extraordinarily deficient.' English visitors to Nymphenburg or Aranjuez have since the eighteenth century complained that these are not true gardens, for they lack flowers. (Now one hears similar complaints about such classic English landscapes as Stourhead.) Occasionally an English traveller appears to approve of a foreign garden.

Henry Cocker in 1939, in front of a ten-year-old Quercus rubra; *it is now over 30 m (100 ft) high. The speed of growth in the lush climate of Lake Maggiore creates problems of spacing and crowding.*

Lady Blessington was most enthusiastic when she was able to rent Villa Gallo in the 1820s: she found the pleasure grounds 'quite beautiful ... presenting all the varieties of hill and vale, with rustic bridges spanning the limpid streams, and grottoes of large dimensions offering delicious retreats from the garish and too fervid rays of the burning sun'. All is explained by the realisation that she is describing an English-style landscape garden. An English bias towards plants is often voiced, even at the expense of a garden's structure. A correspondent of *The Gardener's Chronicle* who visited the gardens of the Villa Pallavicini on Lake Maggiore in 1892 found them 'wondrously rich in giant Camphor trees, Camellias and Tea Shrubs, Bamboo and Palms, but to enjoy these one must endure sham ruins and fictitious monuments and the trick jugglery of water-squirts set here and there as traps for the unwary. Even in the best of these southern gardens,' he pronounced censoriously, 'there is evidence of too much artifice and of imitation, and too little of natural effects.' When he visited Isola Bella he was able to write enthusiastically of the specimens of camphor tree and *Sciadopitys verticillata* but never mentioned its famous architecture, except perhaps obliquely by saying that Isola Madre was 'more natural and pleasing'. Even Hazlitt described Isola Bella as 'a pyramid of sweetmeats ornamented with green festoons and flowers'.

On occasion the English show a disproportionate tenderness for their plants and flowers. Walter Savage Landor, in a fit of rage after a bad meal, threw his cook out of the window of Villa Gherardesca at San Domenico di Fiesole. His subsequent concern was not for the injured man but for the violets in the flower-bed where he had landed. The novelist Ouida was so passionately devoted to the notion that trees and shrubs should be allowed to grow freely that she forbade the gardener who tended the Villa Farinola at Scandicci, which she rented, to undertake any pruning. In consequence, her landlord Marchese Farinola filed a legal action for neglect and evicted her from the property. When the tree in the garden of the British Embassy which was the tallest palm in Rome was holed by a cannon during the siege of 1870, the ambassador ordered it to be strapped with iron where the ball had pierced it rather than cut down.

Fortified by the strength of the English gardening tradition, expatriates often view local efforts with a complacent arrogance. (They are on weaker ground when they also uphold the superiority of English cooking.) Nevertheless such insularity is not necessarily harmful to the making of gardens. Some of the best examples of English gardens abroad have been made by those who choose to ignore the cultural context of their host country – Sir Peter Smithers's garden at Vico Morcote, for example. Even amongst those who are more receptive a pioneer spirit prevails. They present as problems (the climate, the landscape) what in practice they seize as oppor-

tunities. Baroness St Leger made raising eucalyptus in Italy sound as difficult as growing coconuts in Iceland.

Perhaps Englishmen living abroad are more prone to delusions than those who live at home. The assertion that they lack the range of interesting plants to choose from which we enjoy in England is only true if there is insufficient demand to create supply. Residents of the Riviera have always been served by some of the best nurserymen in Europe. There have long been some excellent nurseries in the Italian Lakes too. Victorian Englishmen drooled over their rarities then as much as their descendants do now. Rovelli's nursery at Pallanza was one much-visited place of pilgrimage. English visitors particularly admired the tender species that they could not possibly grow for themselves: *Pinus patula* from Mexico, *Keteleeria fortunei* and *Acacia dealbata*, 12 m (40 ft) high after twelve years' growth. The Giardini Allegra at Catania were offering nearly six hundred varieties of rose late in the 1950s, including such Edwardian favourites as 'Captain Christy', 'Viscountess Folkstone' and 'Prince de Bulgarie', which had long been out of commerce in England. Moreira e Silva of Oporto supplied the wants of the most discriminating garden-owners in Portugal, while the French seed house Vilmorin was as good as any in England.

The English tend to believe that they garden in isolation, without realising that in all the countries of Europe there are knowledgeable and enthusiastic plantsmen who, because they are not English, think of their interest in plants as a botanic activity, not a horticultural one. Few of the nineteenth-century English residents of Tuscany knew that General Vincenzo Ricásoli, a brother of the Iron Baron Bettino Ricásoli, grew 114 species of eucalyptus, 190 acacia species and over 200 varieties or forms of palms and cycads in his garden near Porto Ercole. Marnier-Lapostolle's collection on the Riviera, Juan March's cactus gardens at S'Avall, his house at Son Roig in Majorca, and the private rosarium of Gianfranco Fineschi in Tuscany are all contemporary examples of what Englishmen would regard as an English birthright, pure plantsmanship. Possibly the trouble is that English people living abroad do not find the same general level of interest in flowers and gardens among foreigners that they would at home. Gardening is a national pastime for the English. When the English abroad discover that ordinary Spaniards or Italians have no particular interest in lawns and beautiful herbaceous plants, they con-

Lawrence Johnston's collection of Versailles watering cans at La Serre de la Madone, c. 1950.

Bellosguardo. Florence has long had a large community of artistic and articulate English residents. Gardens tend to remain sternly Tuscan in design but full of English plants and plantings. The extent to which English influences interact with local traditions is one of the main themes of this book.

clude that foreigners in general are horticultural ignoramuses.

Despite the obvious concentration of this book on the best examples, not all Englishmen abroad design their gardens in the best of taste. There is as much sentimentality and vulgarity as at home. Colonel and Mrs George Keppel, who lived at Bellosguardo above Florence in the 1920s, commissioned the architect Cecil Pinsent to design them a garden in the shape of a Union Jack. Baroness Orczy described the garden that she and her English husband made at Monte Carlo in the 1920s when they first acquired the appropriately named Villa Bijou:

There was a huge ficus tree in the wrong place, a pepper tree also in the wrong place, and the angle between house and annexe was just a huge pebbled court where presumably carriages driving through the iron gate were turned . . . Well! that pebbled court is now an Italian garden with – in the centre – a pond and a dear little marble fountain of the Florentine *bambino* hugging a fish – who spouts water to the delight of the wild birds who come to preen their feathers and have their daily bath under its pleasant trickle.

When most of these gardens were made Britain was an imperial power. With the contraction of her overseas influence the communities which produced the gardens in this book have dwindled or died out. Of the Sicilian gardens mentioned, for example, only Casa Cuseni and Villa Racalia remain in English hands. Many surviving gardens are, if you like, relics of horticultural imperialism. In other cases fashion has simply moved on. The Spanish *costas* are the new Riviera and in time will doubtless foster important gardens of their own. But the social changes of this century mean that the colossal manpower which went into the creation and maintenance of such gardens as Villa Victoria, Villa Táranto and Paço de Monserrate are unlikely ever to be available again. The history of any art form is the history of social change.

References and Further Reading

For many years the most popular English guide to gardening abroad was H. F. MacMillan's *Tropical Planting and Gardening* (London); it was regularly reprinted (4th edition 1935, 5th edition 1943, etc). Mrs Philip Martineau's *Gardening in Sunny Lands* (London, 1924) was well known to garden owners on the Riviera, but less used elsewhere. *The Mediterranean Gardener* by Hugo Latymer (London, 1990) stands out from all the packaged pot-boilers on the subject as a useful book based on years of practical experience. Among the memoirs which I have used frequently throughout the book are Walburga, Lady Paget's volumes of diaries, letters and reminiscences, *Embassies of Other Days* (London, 1923), *In My Tower* (London, 1924) and *The Linings of Life* (London, 1927). Of general books, I strongly recommend David Ottewill's *The Edwardian Garden* (Yale, 1989) which combines great research with analytical exposition. John Pemble's *The Mediterranean Passion* (London, 1987) is by far the most scholarly analysis of English travel abroad in the nineteenth century and a delightful book as well as being full of good leads. Lady Blessington's *The Idler in Italy* (London, 1839) is a classic, good on both Italy and the early years of the Riviera. I have also quoted in this chapter from *Elizabeth and Her German Garden* (London, 1898) by Elizabeth von Arnim, Princess Daisy of Pless's memoirs *From My Private Diary* (London, 1931), Winifred Fortescue's sketches of life in the South of France in the 1930s, *Perfume from Provence* (London, 1946), Iris Origo's wonderful *Images and Shadows* (London, 1970), and Baroness Orczy's excruciating reminiscences *Links in the Chain of Life* (London, 1947).

Casa Cuseni in Taormina derives its design from the Arts and Crafts Movement and its plantings from the English love of flowers.

Chapter One

THE RIVIERA

Beginnings

IT WAS THE CLIMATE that first drew English visitors and residents to the south of France. The mild winter weather was thought to be good for invalids, while the bright sun of the Riviera was clearly more pleasant for their families. Sometimes the quality of the light was put to scientific scrutiny. Margaret Maria Brewster in *Letters from Cannes and Nice*, published in 1857, wrote that 'Lord Brougham made a calculation, and found that in *one hundred and eleven* days at Cannes, there were only *three* days in which he could *not* make experiments upon light, while at Brougham Hall, in *one hundred and eleven* days at the same season, there were only three days in which he *could* make those experiments!' Miss Brewster herself found the climate 'wonderfully strengthening and exhilarating'. This is hardly surprising given her further assurance that 'it seems as if at every inhalation one were drinking champagne'. She then went on to praise the effect it had upon invalids.

Winter visitors to the Riviera incessantly remarked on the abundance and variety of both wild and garden flowers. Augustus Hare, who spent a winter at Menton in 1861 before the resort became popular, wrote of an English house, Villa Naylor, close to the present frontier between France and Italy, where 'the heliotrope, hanging in masses from the high walls, is in full flower even in December... the brilliant salvias, plumbagos and roses with which the garden

is filled form a striking contrast to the wild scenery beyond it'. Doctor James Henry Bennet, an early and regular winter migrant to Menton, also noted that flowers which in England died down in the autumn grew perennially in the Mediterranean and were bigger as a result. The petunias and carnations particularly impressed him. Bennet attributed this winter profusion to the absence of frost and went on, 'many of our English garden flowers, which are cut down by the first frosty night, continue to flourish and bloom all the winter through. This is the case, for instance, with the Geranium, the Heliotrope, the Verbena, the Nasturtium, the Salvia and some kinds of Roses, including the China Tea-rose.'

Florists were quick to exploit the climate. In the eighteenth century carnations were sent to London, as Tobias Smollett records, 'packed up in wooden boxes without any sort of preparation and pressed upon one another'. On arrival they were revived by being steeped in water laced with vinegar. Later the area around Bordighera even became known as the Riviera dei Fiori, the Riviera of Flowers. Its prosperity was founded late in the nineteenth century on using the expanding railway system of continental Europe to bring flesh flowers in winter to such northern cities as Budapest, Prague, Warsaw, Copenhagen and even distant St Petersburg.

Given the English fondness for flower gardening, it is scarcely surprising that from the beginning Englishmen who bought property in the south of France should also have made gardens around them. Nobody better described the heady exhilaration of starting on the Côte d'Azur than the American novelist Edith Wharton in 1924. To the flower-lover from the north, she wrote in the introduction to Mrs Philip Martineau's *Gardening in Sunny Lands*,

---

Menton looking across the west bay at the time of Queen Victoria's visit in 1882, painted by R. Lightbody as a royal souvenir. Note the old town on a rocky peninsula and the corniche road stretching away behind towards Italy and La Mortola.

the first months of planning and planting on the Riviera
are in the nature of a long honeymoon. In the thrill of his
adventure he looks about him at other people's gardens,
and sees, growing out of doors, and in unbelievable profusion, the plants he has had to cultivate under glass, or
to coax through an existence of semi-invalidism in the
uncertainty of the 'sheltered corner'; he discovers still
newer treasures in the catalogues of the local nurserymen,
he summons them in consultation, he wanders through
their nurseries; and every visit and every consultation
results in the arrival of a cargo of fascinating novelties.

On the whole, the winter-only residents tended to
restrict themselves to plants with evergreen foliage
and those that flower between November and March.
Unlike most Mediterranean gardens, which were
concerned to manipulate shade and shadow in
summer, Riviera gardens were designed to offer sun
and flowers in winter. Palms were popular for the
beauty of their leaves, for their scientific interest
and because they were symbols of the exotic: they
emphasised the mildness of the Riviera climate.

    Tobias Smollett (1721–71) is credited with starting
the English attachment to the Riviera. Smollett was
a doctor, and his *Travels through France and Italy*,
published in 1766, were immediately and enduringly
popular. Long before the English started to make
gardens there, the countryside itself looked to his
eyes like a garden. Of Nice he wrote:

when I stand upon the rampart, and look round me, I can
scarcely help thinking myself enchanted. The small extent
of country which I see, is all cultivated like a garden.
Indeed, the plain presents nothing but gardens, full of
green trees, loaded with oranges, lemons, citrons, and
bergamots, which make a delightful appearance... roses,
carnations, ranunculus, anemones, and daffodils, blowing
in full glory, with such beauty, vigour, and perfume, as no
flower in England ever exhibited.

He also gave detailed accounts of the variety of fruit,
vegetables and other foods available in the markets.
French historians like to pour cold water on
Smollett's reputation for inventing the Riviera, but
he undoubtedly stimulated its renown among the
English. It is a fact that Nice, Cannes, Menton and
Bordighera would never have developed without
English enthusiasm and English money. By the time
the Promenade des Anglais was built in the 1820s
about a hundred English families were coming to
Nice for the winter. A return of foreigners in the
town in March 1862, shortly after the transfer of the
County of Nice from Savoy to France, showed 473
British families, comprising perhaps 2,000 individ-
uals. By the 1890s Nice was attracting over 100,000
visitors a year, of whom a substantial minority were
British.

    The Countess of Blessington (*The Idler in Italy*)
was not convinced that Nice was a suitable winter
residence for consumptives:

a piercing wind meets one at the corner of every street,
and reminds one that an extra *pélisse* or shawl is very
requisite. Winter after winter, poor sufferers, who crumble
at a breeze in their own comfortable homes ... are sent
from England by the mandate of physicians, who know
little of Nice except its geographical position, to fade and
die afar from the home they yearn to see again.

Lady Blessington's rebuff to Smollett and his profession was taken up again by the Revd Sabine
Baring-Gould in 1905. He put it more cynically:

when a gambler has become bankrupt at the tables of
Monte Carlo, the company that owns these tables will
furnish him with a railway ticket that will take him home,
or to any distance he likes, the further the better, that he
may hang or shoot himself anywhere else save in the
gardens of the Casino. On much the same principle, at the
beginning of the last century, the physicians of England
recommended their consumptive patients to go to
Montpellier, where they might die out of sight, and not
bring discredit to their doctors.

Cruel though this sounds, both Languedoc and the
Riviera were indeed favoured by English families in
search of a cure for tuberculosis. Not for many years
did physicians discover that it was the high alpine air
of the Engadine and not the Mediterranean climate of
the Riviera that offered a real chance of remission to
consumptives. By that time English medical practices
had been established all along the Riviera for the
treatment of the dreaded disease. The two subjects
for conversation among residents of Menton,
Richard Monckton Milnes remarked in 1864, were
'lungs and anemones'.

    Cannes was the next town to become popular
after Nice. Lord Brougham takes the credit for its
invention: on this occasion the French concur. On
his way to Savoy in December 1834, cholera forced
Brougham to break his journey at Cannes, then a
tiny unregarded fishing village, notable only as the
spot where Napoleon first touched French soil on his
return from Elba. Brougham was not so struck by

Château Eléonore, built in 1836 for the 1st Lord Brougham, who popularized Cannes as a winter resort.

the beauty of the place as with its climate, for he was told, and apparently believed, that winters were as mild as at Cairo, and that frost was almost unknown. He decided to build himself a house, Château Eléonore, at which he subsequently spent most of each autumn and spring from 1838 until his death there thirty years later. His enthusiasm for Cannes was supported by the Countess of Blessington, who judged that

of all that I have seen of France, this part of it is by far the most beautiful ... I never saw any scenery that could surpass that which presents itself to the eye on crossing the mountains that lead to Antibes; and the eye is not the only organ of sense that is gratified; for the most grateful odours are inhaled at every step. The arbutus, myrtle, and jessamine grow in wild profusion at each side of the road; and the turf is bedded with wild thyme and innumerable other odiferous plants and heaths that exhale their perfumes.

Brougham's house took the style of an Italian villa; 'very pretty with its light graceful pillars and balustrades, and vases of bright flowers', according to Miss Brewster, who also commented on the orange trees. The historian Jean-Jacques Antier described Brougham as '*stupéfiant les Cannois en créant d'immenses pelouses toujours vertes*': incredible though it sounds, Brougham had the turf brought out by boat from England, and replaced it every year. Villa Eléonore was still worth visiting at the end of the nineteenth century, when Stéphen Liégeard considered it '*belle encore, l'aînée de toutes ces soeurs grandies autour d'elle depuis cinquante ans, mais non la plus belle désormais*'.

Brougham persuaded a number of his friends to imitate his example by buying land and building villas. These residents of Cannes quickly acquired a taste for exotic plants and designed their gardens to integrate and display these previously unknown species. Their houses were almost invariably built at the highest point on the plot, to give a view both of their gardens and of the surrounds. This had the effect of separating the house from the garden and later provoked a reaction from such designers as Harold Peto at the beginning of the twentieth century.

One of the earliest settlers at Cannes was Thomas Robinson Woolfield, who first came in May 1838 and died there fifty years later. Gardens and fruit-growing were among Woolfield's many interests: the sweet potato and the gooseberry, the eucalyptus and the acacia, were among his gifts to the Riviera. Admittedly some acacias or mimosas had been planted earlier in Cannes by a Frenchman called Tripet, but they did not flourish like those which grew on either side of the avenue in Woolfield's grounds and were regarded as such curiosities that visitors came from Nice and Menton to see them. They were said to be 'one of the sights of the season'. Woolfield was an up-market English property developer, 'universally liked and respected', according to Miss Brewster. When he settled at Cannes he bought the Château St Georges from a Lady Taylor and almost rebuilt it: Miss Brewster thought that 'the house and the grounds are the prettiest I ever saw; and, being close to the sea, the views are exquisite'. The gardens were made after 1852 and re-landscaped in 1860 by Nabonnand. They were noted for their araucarias, grevilleas, camphor trees and coconut palms. After selling St Georges (which then became known as Château Larochefoucauld, since names usually changed with ownership), he bought Château Sainte Ursule, (otherwise known as Château du Riou), replaced it with a Gothic fantasy which he called Château des Tours and then sold it to Lord Londesborough in 1858. His garden there was renowned for its collections of bamboos and palms, araucarias and evergreen figs. By the end of the nineteenth century it had become the Hôtel du Parc and was still thought worthy of a visit on account of 'the magnificent trees, the luxuriant tropical vegetation, and the fountains and grottoes'. Woolfield landscaped his properties, just as he built the first Anglican church on the Riviera, to attract good buyers; but he was also a serious horticulturist. His mimosas came as seeds from the Royal Botanic Gardens in Sydney, who also sent him *Eucalyptus globulus*. In December 1863 he wrote to the *Journal of Horticulture* that abutilons, cestrums, correas and many other plants were in full flower in his garden. The most attractive were a scarlet passion flower, *Salvia leucantha*, and yellow 'Chromatella', 'queen of all the Tea and Noisette roses … trained in pyramid form to the height of fifteen feet, and covered with blooms'. Beyond the railway line, down by the shore, he laid out a croquet lawn which became so popular that eventually Woolfield 'felt obliged to set aside one day a week for royalty'. In 1874, after 'the passion for croquet' had subsided, he replaced it with a tennis lawn, the first for some time in Cannes.

The development of Cannes was not without its critics. There was seldom much harmony between the architecture of the house and the style of its garden. Gothic-revival castles were perched above Italianate terraces and Moorish villas set in eighteenth-century landscapes. In 1858 Prosper Mérimée, working as an inspector of historic monuments, protested bitterly at the way the coast was being colonised by the English, 'settled here as if in conquered territory'. Moreover the author of Carmen abhorred their vulgarity: 'they have built fifty villas or châteaux, each more extraordinary than the last, and deserve to be impaled upon the architecture which they have brought to this area' (*Letters*, 17 and 18 December 1856). Mérimée's sentiments are shared by many Spaniards living on the Costa del Sol today. Nor was the resentment of such conspicuous extravagance and waste confined to the French. Walburga, Lady Paget, was a frequent visitor in the 1890s to Château de Garibondy near Cannes, which belonged to Lady Alfred Paget, a distant relation of her husband who spent most of her time digging in the garden. After a visit in December 1895, she noted that

the only flowers I saw were in the gardens of rich people like the Rothschilds, who bed out their roses, wisterias, and laburnums and put them back into houses for the night … Cannes I think detestable; it is a long string of very ugly villas built by millionaires. They all spend enormous sums in keeping up a subtropical vegetation, beds of specimen flowers, artificial lawns which have to be re-sown every year. Everything about these gardens reeks of money. The best of them attain a theatrical effect with huge palms and roses climbing to their top, shrubs with big flowers, fountains, stone balustrades, and a bit of blue sea or blue mountain in the distance. There are no drives or walks or resources of any kind within the reach of a moderate income.

(*In My Tower*, 1924)

Perhaps it was Edward Lear who best understood the paradox of Cannes. As a painter, he loved the 'pale broad graduations of distances, & the lofty olive breadths which make up the middle of the landscape', and wrote in 1870, 'could Cannes have been saved from the VULGAR – it might have really been Paradise'.

Cannes certainly enjoyed royal approval. In the 1890s Queen Victoria visited the south of France seven times. In 1891 she stayed at Grasse and in 1892 at Hyères, but it was to Cimiez, in Cannes, that she returned for no less than five winter visits in all. Attitudes changed after the First World War. King George V and Queen Mary abhorred the Côte d'Azur, even though both had spent happy days there when younger. In the 1920s and 1930s it was sometimes suggested that living in the south of France was at worst dissolute, at best unpatriotic. Queen Victoria's third son, the Duke of Connaught, was forced by ill health to spend much of his time at his villa on Cap Ferrat. His biographer was at pains to explain that, notwithstanding, 'like the Britisher that he is, the Duke thinks that there is no place in the world like England'.

After Nice and Cannes, the next resort to develop was Menton. It was a creature of the railways and, as a result, more middle class in tone than its flashy neighbours. Dr James Henry Bennet (1816–91) was a gynaecologist who first visited Menton for his own health, but when he returned in 1859 it was to offer his skills as a medical practitioner to members of the English colony resident there in winter. Bennet was one of many physicians who believed that the sunny climate of Menton would help invalids suffering from consumption. His book *Winter and Spring on the Shores of the Mediterranean*, first published as *Mentone and the Riviera as a Winter Climate* in 1861 and continuously in print for many years, was largely responsible for the surging popularity of Menton. Bennet maintained that

during the winter the most protected and warmest part of this south-eastern coast of France and western coast of Italy, the undercliff of central Europe, is unquestionably the Riviera di Ponente, or western Riviera, extending from Nice to Genoa . . . I believe that the time is fast approaching when tens of thousands from the north of Europe will adopt the habits of the swallow, and transform every town and village on its coast into sunny winter retreats.

Bennet could with some justification claim Menton as one of the warmest sections of the coast since it alone supported a thriving lemon-growing industry, so lucrative that lemon ground was said to be worth £1,000 per acre.

Bennet became an enthusiastic garden owner and prefaced his chapter on 'Flowers and Horticulture on the Riviera' with this quatrain by Joséphin Solary:

> Si j'avais un arpent de sol, mont, val, ou plaine,
> Avec un filet d'eau, torrent, source, ou ruisseau,
> J'y planterais un arbre, olivier, saule, ou chêne;
> J'y bâtirais un toit, chaume, tuile, ou roseau.

Dr Bennet's approach was empirical. He explained that as he

Dr Bennet thought this pergola gave a particularly Italian character to his garden at Menton-Garavan. The garden was open to the public; a tablet by the entrance greeted visitors with 'SALVETE AMICI!'

When Stéphen Liégeard visited Dr Bennet's garden in 1886 he was duly impressed by its botanic curiosities, including Victoria amazonica, *as well as by its suitability as a picnic site.*

became more familiarised with my winter home, I began to grieve that the precious sunshine, light, and heat, that surrounded me, should be turned to so little horticultural account ... the desire came to see what I myself could do with the gardening lore previously acquired in England. So I purchased a few terraces, some naked rocks, and an old ruined tower, on the mountainside, near Mentone, some 300 feet above the sea, with a south-westerly aspect and sheltered from all northerly winds. Here ... I set to work and ... we think we have done wonders in the course of a few years only.

When Queen Victoria stayed at Menton in March–April 1882 she regretted the lack of privacy afforded by the Hotel that she had rented. Dr Bennet put his garden at her disposal and the Queen and Princess Beatrice were able to stroll and sketch in seclusion. At other times Bennet's garden was open every morning, free of charge, to all comers. A plaque of Carrara marble by the entrance bid the visitor a cosmopolitan welcome: '*Salvete, amici!*'

Bennet's garden was 3 ha (8 acres). The soil was limy, formed by the break-up of the oolitic rock. It was therefore rich in minerals but low in humus. The scanty amount of good earth was supplemented by supplies brought in. Watercourses were diverted, reservoirs dug. According to the writer Stéphen Liégeard, he even succeeded in growing the giant Amazonian water lily *Victoria amazonica*. Bennet's own book was of inestimable use to other villa owners wanting to make an English garden with

plants. Having commenced his garden with well-known and familiar plants, Bennet then began to cultivate flowers of the southern hemisphere, notably from Australia and South America. He observed that chorizemas, kennedyas, ixias and sparaxis came through the winter in good health, but that epacris and cape heaths withered and died in summer: this experience was shared by other horticulturists. Bennet came to the scientific conclusion that the plants which best withstand the sun, heat and drought without irrigation are natives of the Mediterranean: thyme, rosemary, alyssum, lavatera, irises and juniper. He also recommended aloes, pelargoniums, mesembryanthemums and the Cactaceae in general. Embued with true Victorian commercial spirit, Bennet hazarded that the aloes might profitably be farmed on the arid flanks of the mountains of the Riviera, for 'the abundance of strong elastic fibres' contained in their leaves. He went on to list all the various flowers that he had tried and which might successfully be cultivated, indicating whether or not special care or extra watering were needed. For example, he had bought a collection of over three hundred species of cacti from a Parisian grower, M. Pfersdorff, of which more than two thirds had survived. He offered detailed advice on how to grow roses, chrysanthemums, gazanias, daturas, palms, bananas, pines and dasylirions. He found that such bulbs as narcissi, tulips and hyacinths were a success: but he also noted failures. Snowdrops, for instance, tended to die out after a year or two.

Bennet was important as a writer and populariser, but he was not the only early English resident of Menton to make a serious collection of plants. One of several enthusiasts was a Mr Kennedy who made a special study of palms at Villa La Chiusa in Menton-Garavan. Kennedy was particularly interested in classifying *Phoenix* and grew, among other palm species not represented at the internationally famous gardens of nearby La Mortola, *Phoenix argentea, P. senegalensis, Chamaedorea glaucifolia* and *C. alexandrae.*

Over the border, the Italian section of the Riviera was never as smart as the French. San Remo and Bordighera were unexciting but safe: like Hyères and Menton, they were principally health resorts, while Monte Carlo and Nice were frequented by seekers after pleasure. Edward Lear wrote to Lady Fortescue from San Remo in 1872 'there ain't a creature here you would know I think ... we are all humdrum middleclass coves & covesses, & no swells'. Lear's analysis is not entirely borne out by the ostentation and vulgarity of the Victorian villas which to this day line the Corso degli Inglesi in San Remo.

Smollett for Nice, Brougham for Cannes, Bennet for Menton: each claimed that his town was climatically the most favoured, most suitable for invalids, most luxuriantly decked with bright flowers at precisely the time of year when England was coldest and most flowerless. Rivalry was particularly strong among members of the medical profession. In *Meanderings of a Medico*, printed for private circulation in 1928, James Linton Vogle, M D, explained that he had bought the goodwill of a doctor's practice at Bordighera; he then went on to extol the benefits of its particular climate, which made it so favourable as a health resort. He asserted that snow might sometimes lie in winter at Ventimiglia some three miles to the west and also at Alassio to the east, yet for twenty-seven years snow had never lain at Bordighera, so that 'life is not only prolonged, but often saved'. He insisted that another characteristic of the climate was its stimulating and tonic quality, particularly advantageous to those whose vitality was lowered after severe illness or by nervous debility.

Bordighera owed its extraordinary popularity to a sentimental Victorian novel. In 1855 Giovanni Ruffini published *Doctor Antonio* in Edinburgh, where he was a political exile. The novel was written in English and tells how an English gentleman Sir John Davenne and his daughter Lucy were returning from a journey to Italy in 1840 when their carriage had an accident near Bordighera. Lucy broke a bone in her foot and spent some time in the care of Dr Antonio who was not only a medical practitioner but also an exile from Sicily. Mutual affection burgeoned between the doctor and his fair patient, though neither dared to further its cause. Lucy recovered and returned to England with her father. She came back as a widow, some years later in 1848, but did not find Dr Antonio because he had gone south to join the struggle to liberate his island from the wicked Bourbons. She caught up with him at Naples and was present when he was arrested and imprisoned by the secret police. Lucy tried to persuade Antonio to escape, but the authorities heard of the plan and Antonio was moved to another prison. Lucy died of a broken heart. The novel ends with the words 'Doctor Antonio still suffers, prays and hopes for his country.'

Doctor Antonio helped to excite English sympathies for Italy and the Risorgimento. Its romantic descriptions of the coastline near Bordighera were the origin of the town's attraction for the English.

Dr Antonio's romantic encounter at Bordighera with the ailing English heroine Lucy Davenne, as imagined by an Italian illustrator.

This extract is typical:

The silvery track of the road undulating amid thinly scattered houses, or clusters of orange and palm trees, leads the eye to the promontory of Bordighera, a huge emerald mound which shuts out the horizon, much in the shape of a leviathan couchant, his broad muzzle buried in the waters. Here you have in a small compass, refreshing to behold, every shade of green that can gladden the eye, from the pale olive to the dark-foliaged cypress, of which one, ever and anon, an isolated sentinel, shoots forth high above the rest. Tufts of feathery palms, their heads tipped by the sun, the lower part in the shade, spread their broad branches, like warriors' crests on the top, where the slender *silhouette* of the towering church spire cuts sharply against the spotless sky... Earth, sea, and sky mingle their different tones, and from their varieties, as from the notes of a rich, full chord, rises one great harmony. Golden atoms are floating in the translucent air, and a halo of mother-of-pearl colour hangs over the sharp outlines of the mountains. 'There is ample food for your pencil,' said Antonio.

The Moreno garden at Bordighera, whose popularity with English visitors owed much to a supposed association with Doctor Antonio, *the Victorian novel.*

'Bordighera is a little London in winter,' opined a contemporary Italian guidebook. The Italian writer Edmondo De Amicis wrote of it as '*Il Paradiso degli Inglesi*'. There was a saying current at the turn of the century that Cannes, Nice and Monte Carlo represented the World, the Flesh and the Devil: and there was some truth in this. Bordighera, on the other hand, was described as 'oh yes, you know! Intellect'. Its social life centred on the English church. De Amicis commented (1903), 'You just have to see the exodus from the Anglican church on Sunday morning; it is a great river that fills the street, a parade of faces, expressions, gaits and attires that makes you stare in disbelief, and smile inwardly to see how deep is the respect we have for this great nation.' Bordighera had a greater proportion of British residents and visitors than any other town in Italy, less of course in total than Rome or Florence but larger in relation to its size. Bordighera – then, as now – was a middle-class resort. Almost the only members of the aristocracy to live there were the Earl of Strathmore, whose family wintered every year in a villa they later sold to the Queen Mother of Italy,

Margherita of Savoy, and the Duke and Duchess of Leeds who lived at Villa Selva Dolce next door. Even they only lived there 'for warmth and economy', according to Lady Paget.

Botany seems to have been one of the favourite pastimes of middle-class Anglican intellectuals and, in fact, the great Riviera botanist of the day, the Revd Clarence Bicknell, was one of the incumbents of the church in Bordighera. His collections formed the basis of all subsequent botanical study in the region. 'Few countries offer to the botanist and lover of flowers a field of research so rich as Liguria,' wrote Frederick Fitzroy Hamilton in 1883. He boasted that it was possible in the morning to gather palm leaves of the native *Chamaerops humilis* from the scorched rocks of the coast and in the evening of the same day to see the edelweiss on the Col di Tenda. This feat could now be achieved in just over an hour by a speedy excursion up the Roya valley but for the fact that the dwarf palm is extinct upon the Riviera, perhaps as a result of too much gathering. Hamilton himself was aware of the problem. He lamented that it was 'almost impossible to enumerate the number

The formal garden at Les Cèdres in about 1920. It was designed by Harold Peto's French partner, Aron Messiah, but was later overshadowed by the vast botanic collection of the Marnier-Lapostolle family.

of species which have either become rare or entirely disappeared during the last few years, owing to this mania for *collecting*' and mentioned *Tulipa clusiana*, *Pancratium maritimum* and *Anemone pavonina* as among the native plants almost extinct. Our Victorian ancestors were among the first to learn the truth that the easiest way to destroy something is to make it popular.

There were, surprisingly, no outstanding English gardens in Bordighera, although the public gardens of Bordighera were given to the town by a Mr Lowe, one of the churchwardens of the Anglican church, a retired banker from Rowde in Wiltshire. The most famous garden belonged to the Italian Moreno, although part of its attraction lay in the suggestion that it might have been the scene of Dr Antonio's dalliance with Lucy. Frederick Fitzroy Hamilton observed that, apart from its rare plants and shrubs, 'there are certain delightful corners ... worthy of admiration from all who love nature and her handiwork'. And he urged, 'Do not delay then, O painters and brothers of the brush, to visit this garden, for it is unique in Europe.' This is quite untrue, even

though a contemporary Italian account suggested that Moreno's garden would remind visitors of *The Thousand and One Nights*. A later attraction was the Winter Garden at Bordighera, laid out by the German botanist Ludwig Winter around his nursery: Winter had been head gardener at La Mortola.

As Nice, Cannes and Menton expanded, and the villas built on their edges redeveloped, new areas of the coast that had been simple farmland or orchards were promoted as fashionable estates. Cap Ferrat, Cap d'Ail, Cap Martin, Antibes and Juan-les-Pins were all creatures of this property boom, the first of many to engulf the Mediterranean coast. In the mid-1890s King Leopold II of the Belgians bought some land on Cap Ferrat. The collections in his greenhouses at Laeken had long been famous: now he devoted himself to cultivating many of the plants outside. He did not originally plan on building a house in his garden because he so enjoyed living on his yacht. His first cousin, Queen Victoria, described in her diary for 4 April 1898 how 'on our way down to Villefranche we met Leopold of Belgium walking. He had arrived in Villefranche harbour on his yacht this morning.' Leopold was a man of exceptional commercial ability: indeed, his ruthlessness in pursuit of advantage made him very unpopular. When he realised that Cap Ferrat was about to be developed, he bought up almost every part of the peninsula that was offered for sale. His estate became the largest by far on Cap Ferrat. Then in 1900 he acquired the Villa Polonais, a large house above the garden he was making and renamed it Villa Les Cèdres after the cedar trees he had planted. It was to become perhaps the most important garden on the Riviera – for a while greater even than La Mortola – and the most renowned privately owned botanic garden in the world.

One of the houses that belonged to Leopold II's retinue was the Villa Mauresque: it was near the tip of Cap Ferrat, and had originally been built for Mgr Charmeton, the King's confessor. Somerset Maugham bought it in 1928 and lived there until his death in 1965: he described it as a square white house on the side of a hill, and claimed to have bought it cheaply because it was ugly. He had some twelve acres of land and was rich enough to maintain four gardeners even after the Second World War. Maugham's greatest success was with avocado pears, which

he believed were the first ever cultivated in Europe – wrongly, since the Hanburys had grown them at La Mortola for over fifty years. He smuggled the seeds into France in a golf bag. After a few years the trees were yielding an annual crop of 300–400 pears. Roderick Cameron of the nearby Villa La Fiorentina said that Maugham's trees bore such quantities of fruit that he was reduced to inventing new recipes in order not to waste them. One was avocado ice-cream, 'a sweet green mush, and quite tasteless, the cold killing the faint, subtle flavour of the pear'. In the summer of 1940, after spending a while in England working for the Ministry of Information, Maugham returned to the Villa Mauresque. He expected to remain there for some time, and ordered 20,000 bulbs to be delivered to him in September. A few days later, the Germans invaded.

As the newer resorts and estates prospered, the old towns sought to recover the trade they had lost. The authorities in Hyères went nap on date palms. They planted many hundreds along its boulevards, one of which ran for more than a kilometre to the town's railway station. Then they changed the name of the town to Hyères-les-Palmiers. Edith Wharton lived at the Château Ste-Claire above Hyères during the

The novelist Edith Wharton in about 1923 at Château Ste-Claire, still the best garden ever made at Hyères.

1920s and in making her garden displayed all the energy and forthrightness that had made her novels so popular. She blasted the hillside and built up retaining walls for the terraces; she made a splendid pergola and covered it in climbing roses; she planted a walk of orange trees and trained her cypresses into Moorish arches. Olives and agaves were kept as a natural background to her bold schemes. Edith Wharton lined a long straight narrow walk entirely with orange freesias and she made an extensive collection of cacti and succulents, said to have been better than the Prince of Monaco's. And despite her enjoyment of the broad brush, Mrs Wharton was a plantswoman, genuinely interested in rare specimens: she was reputed to be the only person on the Riviera who grew *Acacia catheriana*. One visitor observed 'one gets a feeling everywhere that the plants are grown for a genuine appreciation of their own individual value, and not for their massed effect, as is the usual practice on this coast'.

Everyone who goes to live abroad has to learn to adapt his style of gardening. Each generation has made this discovery for itself, and the point cannot be made too often. Dr Bennet insisted that every English gardener 'though trained in the best English school, must learn his art over again to succeed on the Riviera. Should he fail to sow his grass at exactly the right season, his experience and ability in other climates will count for nothing; he has lost his opportunity.' Frederick Fitzroy Hamilton cautioned that

the peculiar fruit and vegetables which characterise the gardens of the Mediterranean region . . . and the abundance of certain flowering plants difficult to cultivate in the north . . . frequently mislead visitors into the idea that gardening must be child's play in so fine a climate. This is however a serious mistake . . . Continual and often expensive watering is necessary; and this combination of sun and water has naturally the effect of pushing the vegetation on too rapidly . . . High-class gardening becomes an expensive undertaking.

(*Bordighera and the Western Riviera*, 1883)

In 1893 a correspondent of *The Gardener's Chronicle* warned 'a man arriving from the north . . . has to commence gardening afresh . . . to proceed very cautiously until he knows the climate and the different seasons'. Water was not the only problem. Mrs Philip Martineau detailed the problems in 1924: the keen gardener should take great care over the choice of a site for a garden, pay special attention to protection from the mistral, note the different soil types,

Château Ste-Claire, in the late 1920s. Edith Wharton planted the ramparts as garden terraces and lined the paths with avenues of orange trees and mandarins.

consider blasting the surface before laying out his garden and terracing it, make provision for drought and the problem of storm drainage, and supply shade even for such plants as choisyas and camellias that are grown in full sun in England. Growing exciting plants was, of course, one of the pleasures of living on the Riviera but, as Baroness Orczy observed when she and her husband bought the Villa Bijou in Monte Carlo, 'it takes an English amateur gardener some time to learn what will simply *not* be coaxed into luxuriance.'

Every so often there was bad weather to contend with. Prolonged frosts on the Riviera, as were endured in 1901 or 1929, would engender lengthy correspondence in the English horticultural press, just as a bad winter in England does today. Readers would write in from California, South Africa and Australia with details of comparable experiences. There were new pests and diseases to combat too, as well as old enemies. Edward Lear wrote in 1883 to the Hon. Mrs Augusta Parker, 'And my garden is now admirably beautiful, & were it not for the Slugs & Snails would be inimitable. But these melancholy mucilaginous Molluscs have eaten up all my Higher-cynths & also my Lower = cynths.'

English enthusiasm and English money were not enough to make good gardens: trained gardeners were also needed. In the early years of the Riviera colony, English expectations were met with total incomprehension. Dr Bennet was probably the first to note that the French did not share the English interest in ornamental gardening, for he complained of a 'complete absence of the intense love of flowers and ornamental gardens which pervades all classes of society', and asked, 'where do we see the Rose and the Clematis, the Jasmine climbing over the peasant's cottage as in England?' As for the French landowners, 'to spend good money on Roses and Jasmines, unless to make perfumes for sale, passes their comprehension'. There were ignorant super-stitions to overcome, too: Bennet's gardener did not like the scent of gardenias and held that 'their odour is very bad, actually poisoning the garden'. The errors of knowledge were, however, not all on the French side: it was sometimes thought that grass was 'a dismal failure' on the Riviera because local gardeners did not know 'how to manage turf ... mowing and rolling especially', not because English fescues succumbed to a Mediterranean summer.

In 1893 a correspondent of *The Gardener's Chronicle* wrote that the 'native' gardeners were generally labourers who had spent most of their life working in private gardens. They were good at producing ordinary flowers for bedding and would do any manner of manual labour. Anyone who could use a spade and shovel, and worked in the garden, was called a gardener: the same was true in England. Riviera residents expected better, and rich men with an interest in gardening learnt to bring their gardener with them. 'Kew-ites' were well to the fore, as their knowledge of nomenclature and experience of plant cultivation served them well. In 1894 an Englishman called Thornton living near Nice established a train-ing school for young gardeners who were to be 'trained in a thoroughly practical manner and kept under strict and almost military discipline'. It was felt at the time that the school would supply a much-felt want, since no 'native' gardeners were available. By the time Mrs Philip Martineau wrote her book in 1924, it was possible to outline a familiar problem, irrespective of nationality or place.

Perhaps a villa has been acquired, set about with palms and round beds or mounds of cinerarias ... it requires some courage, and considerably more command of a foreign language than a newcomer generally possesses, to induce the old-established gardener of the villa to change his ways, uproot his most cherished convictions (his palms), and make a garden more in accord with modern ideas.

Clearly the French gardeners were thought of as old-fashioned and chary of novelty. When the Eng-lishmen actually got down to gardening, it was not cacti or bougainvillea or mimosa that they most enjoyed growing, but roses. In 1885 Edward Lear added this verse postscript to a letter to Lord Car-lingford:

> And this is certain; if so be
> You could just now my garden see,
> The aspic of my flowers so bright
> Would make you shudder with delight.
>
> And if you voz to see my roziz
> As is a boon to all men's noziz, –
> You'd fall upon your back & scream –
> O Lawk! o cricky! it's a dream!

Baroness d'Orczy grew 'Mme Abel Châtenay', 'Noella Nabonnand' and 'Paul's Scarlet Climber' on one pergola at Villa Bijou in Monte Carlo, and 'La Follette' and 'Mrs Herbert Stevens' on another. She decided not to use *wichuraiana* ramblers because they 'are at their best much later in the spring when we are already on the wing for England, and offer no autumnal blooming'. Château Eléonore at Cannes was famous for its roses, mainly teas and hybrid perpetuals: the garden had been redesigned for the 2nd Lord Brougham in 1865 by Nabonnand and had over two hundred varieties and thousands of bushes. *Rosa gigantea* flowered there in April 1898 for the first time in Europe, having been introduced by Sir Henry Collett from an altitude of 1,500 m (5,000 ft) in Burma. Few would disagree with the 3rd Lord Brougham's assertion that it was 'the most desirable, and by far the finest single rose ... ever seen'. English visitors were fascinated by the size and health of varieties that grew but weakly in England. The tender tea rose 'Marie Van Houtte' was 21 m (70 ft) across at eight years old, while 'Papa Gontier' was nearly $7\frac{1}{2}$ m (25 ft) high. Brougham ascribed this vigour partly to the climate and partly to manuring: he wrote in his 'Opusculum, most gratefully dedicated by kind permission to HRH The Prince of Wales' on roses at Cannes 'the greedy Rose requires artificial food that must be administered regularly and lib-erally before she can be induced to produce perfection

Villa Eilenroc, newly planted on the bare tip of Cap d'Antibes by James Wyllie in about 1880. It is now deeply buried in pine woods.

of flowers or true vigour of growth'. Brougham went on to explain that the 'soup' which he fed to his roses was actually a '*purée de vaches*'.

The English tended to believe that they gardened in isolation: it was a measure of their own insularity. Almost every account of Nice and Cannes in the nineteenth century mentions landscape gardens made with exotic plants: it should be no surprise to learn that the French themselves liked to grow exciting novelties. Botanic gardens were started in 1775 at Aix-en-Provence and in 1786 at Toulon: there was already one at Marseilles. Just as English merchants in India or Jamaica returned to Bristol and bought estates in the West Country, so too the French colonial families came back with the fortunes they had made in the tropics to plant subtropical paradises in the south of France. The Empress Josephine, herself from Martinique, arranged in 1804 for several plants indigenous to New Holland to be sent from her greenhouses at Malmaison to the director of the gardens at Nice, asking him to help her plan 'to naturalise a multitude of exotic plants in French soil'. The diplomat and botanist Gustave Thuret (1817–75) started his botanic research institute at Antibes in 1856. Georges Sand wrote in 1868 that it was the most beautiful garden she had ever seen in her life:

Thuret's sister-in-law gave it to the state in 1877. The English tended to regard such places as scientific stations, not gardens.

The first English gardens on the Riviera all followed the landscape tradition, or the fashionable gardenesque which succeeded it. An extreme example of the English style was the garden of Eilenroc on Cap d'Antibes. It was famous in its day, and open to the public twice a week: indeed, the Swiss botanist and nurseryman Henri Correvon considered it 'unrivalled even by the botanical garden at La Mortola'. The house had been built in 1850 for Hugh Hope Loudon, who called it by his wife's name, Cornélie, spelled backwards. It was designed by Charles Garnier, the architect of the Paris Opera House, whose own palmy garden was one of the sights of Bordighera. Eilenroc's garden was laid out after an Englishman, James Wyllie, acquired the 30 ha (75 acre) estate in 1873. His grandson, Sir Coleridge Kennard, who inherited Eilenroc in 1890 at the age of five, remembered how the garden shone with flowers when, as a boy, 'exploring he found, hidden behind walls, countless pots of roses, destined when they came to bloom, to colour the terraces above the sea'. More extravagant still were the gravel walks bordered by blue cinerarias which led without a break from the house to the water's edge. These spectacles were only achieved by importing earth: millions of tons of it, according to Sir Coleridge's son 'Loopy' Kennard. Big holes had to be excavated from the limestone before any of the thousands of trees at Eilenroc could be planted.

About half the garden at Eilenroc consisted of huge boulders and outcrops, some as much as 40 m (140 ft) high. Wyllie turned these natural features into an extravagant rock garden. He laid out a labyrinth of paths and cut easy steps between the fissures to scale the crags: every cleft was filled with plants. To a groundwork of native cistus, stachys and *Convolvulus althaeoides*, he added species from Australia and South Africa, polygalas, acacias, aloes, agaves. Guy de Maupassant visited it in 1887: Cap Antibes he described as 'a prodigious garden ... where the most beautiful flowers in Europe grow'. Eilenroc itself he considered 'charming and whimsical', while Stéphen Liégeard praised it as the pearl of the Gulf and commented on the double hedges of Bengal roses which led to the house. Unfortunately, Sir Coleridge Kennard spent much of his time at Charles Garnier's other monument, the Casino at Monte Carlo: after a disastrous night at the tables in 1926 he was forced to sell Eilenroc, and died in relative poverty.

Despite occasional pleas that they could not get all they required on the Riviera, the truth is that the desire for interesting plants which most English residents expressed was largely satisfied by French nurserymen. The best nurseries were said to be Charles Huber at Hyères and Nabonnand who started up at Golfe Juan in 1860, specialising in rose breeding and the importation of exotic novelties. The expatriates may have longed for the plants that grew only in England, but home thoughts from abroad did not deflect them from enjoying the plants and plantings of the Riviera. Where they differed from the French was in their search for unusual forms and varieties, and their ornamental treatment of garden plants: the English approach was essentially horticultural, while French plantsmen tended to be botanists.

To this day, the English abroad tend to keep themselves apart from the people among whom they live. Lady (Winifred) Fortescue, in *Perfume from Provence*, told how in about 1930 she and her husband planted two cypresses at the end of her rose garden, one for *La Paix* and the other for *La Prospérité*, as is the Provençal custom, but this desire to follow local lore did not prevent her from adding that the table underneath the cypresses made an ideal place for taking tea. On occasion the Englishman's natural reserve also masked an assumption of superiority, and this was not always confined to such unimportant matters as language, commerce and social habits. Some English residents insisted even upon their national pre-eminence in the kitchen: French food was rather improper. Margaret Maria Brewster said that the cuisine in Cannes consisted of grease, pure and unmitigated, 'so I ... descended into the kitchen with considerable dignity to instruct old Marie in the art of boiling a chicken [which] ... was rather a success'. Miss Brewster established a reputation later in life as a gifted evangelist.

Strangest of all English delusions was the frequent insistence that no one could possibly stay on the Riviera during the summer. The season ended on 21 April, and almost everyone returned home by the end of the month. Drains were the excuse for this misconception: ignorance and fashion were the real reasons. In fact, some Englishmen have always lived on the Riviera all the year round, sometimes for their health, and on other occasions for financial reasons. Edward Lear knew what the fashionable visitors did not. His diary for 31 July 1873 reads, 'A wandering = hithery = thithery day – overlooking the terrace-making etc etc – or visiting various gourds & Passaflorae, or enjoying the 'blue' quiet – for it must be confessed, Summer in Sanremo is divine!' After the First World War, more Englishmen began to live permanently in the south of France: often they did so for economy. The historian Sir John Fortescue moved to Grasse because 'in Provence it is possible to be poor with dignity'. His poverty in the 1930s was such that he sold his surplus fruit and vegetables to an hotel in Grasse. 'I can see John now,' wrote his wife Winifred some years later in *There's Rosemary... There's Rue*, 'clad in blue workman's overalls and the enormous straw hat, conscientiously preparing his vegetables for market, washing them in the great stone *bassin* on the top terrace, selecting carrots, turnips, and onions of the same size, and tying them into neat bundles of ten, in the clean and methodical French fashion.'

By this time the decline in relative wealth affected most members of the English community, and almost all the important gardens on the Riviera had been made. Many were open to the public, and visiting became a social pastime. Nowhere else had such a concentration of good gardens that could conveniently and freely be visited on an afternoon's call by motor car. In the next chapter we shall look at some of them in more detail.

References and Further Reading

John Pemble's *The Mediterranean Passion* (London, 1987) is by far the most scholarly analysis of English travel abroad in the nineteenth century. A jolly introduction to the English colonisation is provided by *When the Riviera was Ours* by Patrick Howarth (London, 1977). Two good sources for the development of Cannes are Margaret Maria Brewster's *Letters from Cannes and Nice* (London, 1857), and J. Mossop's *Thomas Robinson Woolfield's Life at Cannes*, etc. (1892). *Winter and Spring on the Shores of the Mediterranean* by J. H. Bennet (1863) is essential reading for understanding the development of Menton and useful for its observations on many other resorts. Augustus Hare's two works about the Riviera, *A Winter at Mentone* (1862) and *The Rivieras* (1897), are both forthright in style and intermittently illuminating, as is Sabine Baring-Gould's *Book of the Riviera* (1905). Stéphen Liégeard's *La Côte d'Azur* (1887) is stylish, amusing and informative. There is a recent edition of Edward Lear's letters, *Selected Letters*, edited by Vivienne Noakes (Oxford, 1988). Lady Blessington's *The Idler in Italy* (1839), Lord Brougham's *List of Roses Now in Cultivation at Château Eléonore, Cannes* (1898) and Edmondo De Amicis's '*Il Paradiso degli Inglesi*', published in *Pagine allegre* (Milan, 1906) all deserve to be better known. Edith Wharton's garden appeared in *Country Life* (3 November 1928). The most comprehensive modern French coverage of Riviera gardens is now available in English as *The Gardens of Provence and the French Riviera* by Michel Racine, Ernest J.-P. Boursier-Mougenot and Françoise Binet (Cambridge, MA, 1987).

Chapter Two

THE EDWARDIAN RIVIERA

Grand Gardens – Landscapers and Architects

SOME ENGLISHMEN, the really rich ones who bought large estates, made English gardens on the grand scale. Two of them merit detailed study. These are Alice de Rothschild's landscape garden at Villa Victoria near Grasse, which flourished between 1890 and 1920 but has now completely disappeared, and Laura Aberconway's more formal garden at Château de la Garoupe near Antibes, begun in 1907 and still one of the spectacles of the Riviera.

Alice de Rothschild was a formidable spinster, a member of the vast European family that was the quintessence of *haute juiverie*. Indeed, so international was the family and its branching connections in the nineteenth century that it may be wondered why anyone called Baronne Alice de Rothschild, born and bred in Frankfurt, should be considered English. But English she most certainly was, by adoption and naturalisation, and after the death of her brother Ferdinand in 1898 she became the chatelaine of Waddesdon Manor in Buckinghamshire, a county where so many of the large estates were owned by her relations that it was sometimes known as Rothschildshire. Waddesdon was laid out by the French landscape gardener Lainé, but Alice de Rothschild's garden at Grasse in the south of France was utterly English in style.

In 1887, Alice de Rothschild, then aged forty-two, stayed at the Grand Hôtel in Grasse and was taken by the quiet charm of the town and countryside around, so different from the coast, whose vulgar

society she abominated. Next year she began to purchase olive groves on the hillside above the town and to build a house there, to be called the Villa Victoria in honour of the Queen. She continued to buy land until, plot by plot, she had acquired an estate of about 135 ha (335 acres).

Alice de Rothschild was her own garden designer: she listened to others, and she counted knowledgeable landscapers and botanists among her social acquaintances, but she made her own decisions about the form and planting of her garden. She followed the principles of 'natural gardening', which derived from such writers as Loudon and Robinson, and used the existing landscape as a background for exotic plants. Thus most of the olive trees were left within the garden, but terraces, hedges and boundaries that were the relics of agricultural activity were smoothed away. Villa Victoria in due course became not only the largest and most perfectly maintained garden in the south of France but also a vehicle for the enjoyment of wealth. In its love of display, Villa Victoria belongs to the tradition that gave us such spectacular English gardens as Shrublands and Westonbirt. Harold Nicolson once remarked that 'a garden is intended for the pleasure of its owner, not for ostentation': Alice de Rothschild would not have understood the distinction.

With the olive trees as a natural background, Alice de Rothschild built up impressive collections of exotic plants: clumps of palms, cacti and winter-flowering aloes, for instance. Citrus fruits were arranged in drifts, each of one variety – bitter orange, sweet orange, lemon or mandarin – to give the impression that they occurred naturally. All the available species and hybrids of mimosa were acquired, so that there was a continuous display from

---

This view of the Spanish garden at Villa Fiorentina exemplifies the simplified lines – almost pastiche – which Ferdinand Bac referred to as 'Spain, without complications, without boursouflure'.

The tea house which Alice de Rothschild built near the top of her vast garden at Villa Victoria, near Grasse. Its roof tiles matched the colours of the Rothschild livery, which all the gardeners were required to wear.

November to May. Every year 1,500 Parma violets and dog violets were put under the olive trees to freshen up the Virgilian landscape. The garden's most famous feature was its carriageway 3 km (2 miles) long, winding up the hillside to the top of the estate through a landscape that turned more carefully wild until the olives themselves became sparse and merged with the evergreen oaks and pines of the *maquis*. Alice de Rothschild's cousin Lady Battersea wrote, when it was extended for a royal visit in 1891: 'as a surprise for the Queen, she has just ordered another mountain road to be levelled and widened, and this is to be done in *three* days, which means building up small walls, picking out huge stones, covering the smaller ones with Macadam and *turning a stream*'. At the top she built an imposing tea house, in the style of an English cottage, which had two drawing-rooms, a pink one for ladies and a green one for gentlemen. An artificial stream ran down the hillside: its watercourse, and the plantings on either side of it, were given a succession of different treat-

ments as it descended. Full-sized trees were transplanted within the estate, or brought from far away, to create instant effects: Alice's brother and cousins did likewise at Waddesdon, Ferrières and Mentmore.

Baronne Alice had a good eye for the effects of colour. The bulbs or annual plants that lined the walks and carriageways were chosen both for harmony within a group and for contrast between one group and the next. She maintained that difficult colours could be blended together by the addition of white or yellow. Many would agree that white is a useful mixer for other tints, but would need convincing that yellow is equally suitable. But Alice de Rothschild had strong views on most subjects. She was a martinet, too, a perfectionist who would shout and scream if a weed were found in her lawn. Lady Battersea recounted her own experience at the hands of her autocratic cousin: 'I was warned by Alice never to put my foot upon the *grass* anywhere in her domain. Fancy, in a fit of abstraction, I did so right under Alice's eyes, which sent her into a violent passion.' Nor was it only careless young relations who felt the sharp edge of Alice de Rothschild's tongue. When Queen Victoria visited the garden, she bent forward to inhale the scent of a rose and inadvertently set a royal foot upon the flower-bed. 'Come off of there!' bellowed her hostess. The Queen jumped back in alarm and invariably referred to Alice de Rothschild afterwards as 'the All-Powerful One'.

Alice de Rothschild was fiercely competitive. She wanted to have the best of everything, even to the extent of instructing her gardeners not to reveal to visitors the names of rare varieties or the origins of recently acquired novelties. One day her head gardener returned from a flower show in Italy, where he had encountered some particularly fine pinks. Why were they so extraordinary, she asked. Why were they better than hers? The gardener replied anxiously that the soil in Italy was much more suitable for their cultivation. Alice de Rothschild exploded. 'Have I ever forbidden you to buy soil? Send a cart off at once and grow me some extraordinary pinks! I will not allow anyone to have them more beautiful than I have!' Such extravagant and capricious behaviour may be difficult to understand nowadays, but it would not have been unusual in England at the time, nor would her insistence that all the gardeners should wear uniforms in the heraldic colours of the Rothschild coat of arms. Life in service at the Villa Victoria was probably not too dissimilar from Woburn, Windsor or Welbeck.

Alice de Rothschild's striving for perfection was

actually a little unEnglish. Landscape gardens from Repton to Robinson had a more casual charm. Lady Battersea thought her cousin's garden 'exquisitely kept, but a little too formal and precise for my taste'. There was no *abandon* of nature, she said. 'I long for a little disorder. There is not one leaf or weed to be met with on the paths.' Nevertheless, as an example of the English garden abroad, the Villa Victoria has no peer for size, scale or excellence. Its very grandeur also explains its transience, for neither the house nor the garden survived its creator. No one, not even a Rothschild, could continue to function on such a scale after the Great War, let alone the Second World War. Alice de Rothschild employed fifty permanent gardeners at Villa Victoria and thirty or forty extras to prepare for the season from October to March, although, when she was in residence, members of staff were supposed to be invisible and all work was laid aside during the hours of her daily promenade. After she died in 1922, Edmond de Rothschild gave the estate to the municipality of Grasse. It was promptly carved up into hundreds of small building plots. Here and there still can be seen a tall palm or lofty conifer, isolated witness to the opulence of a vanished domain.

THE GRANDEST Edwardian garden on the Côte d'Azur to have survived almost intact is Château de la Garoupe on Cap d'Antibes. It is of special interest because Garoupe is twinned to one of the grandest modern gardens of Britain: Bodnant, in North Wales. Both were designed and planted in the early years of the twentieth century by Laura Aberconway, who spent seven months of the year at Bodnant and five at Garoupe. There is a close family resemblance between the two. Each was built in a commanding position, chosen for its view. Bodnant looks down forested hillside and over the River Conway to the outline of Mount Snowdon: Garoupe has a long broad prospect down through the *garrigue* and across a rocky bay to the promontory tip of Cap d'Antibes. Each has a grand garden, conceived on a grand scale, to partner a grand house.

The house at Château de la Garoupe is built of white marble in the Italian Renaissance style, but long and thin like a seventeenth-century French château, dominated by its great central *salon*. The entrance in the north façade is matched by a large door on the south side. Each has sliding inner doors of glass and the sight axis of the garden passes through them. It runs up from the promontory

beyond the rocky bay, across the sun-baked southern terraces, through the twin glass doors and down the gentle northern slopes to a distant view of the Alpes Maritimes: the siting of Château de la Garoupe is nothing if not dramatic.

Garoupe was laid out as a garden for winter and spring, the period from Christmas to Easter when Lord and Lady Aberconway were in residence. Much of the original planting was of spring flowers: the grove of Judas trees and tracts of German irises under the olive trees in the north garden date from its early years, as do the wisterias which are a feature of the sunny side. Freesias and *Cyclamen persicum* have naturalised throughout and can be counted like the descendants of Abraham in hundreds of thousands.

The formal outlines of the garden have changed little since it was first made: the terraces, walks, lawns, pergolas and summerhouses remain as they always were. The geometry of the garden derives indirectly from French and Italian precedents but, in the English fashion, it merges with the natural landscape around. The Aberconways set a rectangular terrace on the south side of the house and a broad flight of steps to connect the arcaded front to a lower terrace. Here a gravel path leads sideways to lawns, well watered in summer, which set off the colours of echiums and large regal pelargoniums. Below this is one of the most impressive features of the garden: two vast parterres each radiating out in triangular sections from a handsome stone urn. But despite their size and intricacy, you are always aware of the long descent to the sea which draws the eye down towards a distant stone seat, perched above the rocky inlet where the sea crashes on to the promontory below. The steps are marked with cone-shaped pittosporums on either side and sun-loving succulents, including yuccas and aloes, interplanted with clumps of *Amaryllis belladonna*. Just at the moment when the pull of this vista becomes irresistible, an alternative axis cuts across it: a broad avenue some 300 yards long, terminating at either end in *trompe l'oeil* pavilions, classically proportioned but modelled in fretwork to designs by Felix Kelly. The tension set up between the walk to the sea and the sideways pull towards the pavilions is intensely dramatic.

After Lady Aberconway's death in 1934, Garoupe passed to her daughter Lady Norman. She in turn expanded the plantings so that there were flowers in summer and autumn. The estate has since passed to her son, Anthony Norman. Garoupe was nearly destroyed at the end of the war, not by actual fighting

Anthony Norman's modern parterres of santolina, box and lavender at Château de la Garoupe, Cap d'Antibes, are easy to maintain but worthy successors to the Edwardian formal garden which they replaced.

but by the Germans' preparations for an allied landing on the Côte d'Azur. Norman managed to pay a flying visit to Garoupe while he was still on active service and found that the retreating troops had planted over 2,000 land mines on the property. But the efficiency of the Germans also saved Garoupe, for they had meticulously sent plans of the minefields to Berlin where, by a stroke of luck, they were later discovered by Norman. Ironically, it was German prisoners of war who were used to clear the mines. The ammonium nitrate they contained was used to fertilise the orange trees.

The war also brought social changes to the garden. Where his grandmother had twelve gardeners, Norman has two and a half. Much has been simplified, but without losing the overall grandeur, because the effect of the garden at Garoupe depends upon broad sweeps of colour and texture. Anthony Norman's gradual, thoughtful alterations to the garden respect his grandmother's ideas. In about 1970, inspired by a design he had seen in the Piazza del Popolo in Rome, he replanted the parterres in front

of the house. He experimented with the planting before choosing big blocks of rosemary, box, *Lavandula dentata*, *Santolina chamaecyparissus* and *S. virens*. They are all trimmed to approximately the same height, but not quite. A French writer sums up the success of this ingenious and satisfying way of updating a labour-intensive parterre: 'the vastness of the design and its elegant tranquillity are a perfect foil to the grandiose views of sky and sea'.

Anthony Norman considers that the secret of good colour planting is to use plenty of white. He has made a charming shaded garden entirely in green and white by mixing pale variegated evergreens with white flowered shrubs: thus *Hydrangea* 'Mme Émile Mouillère' and the grand old lilac 'Mme Lemoine' are underplanted with *Euonymus fortunei* 'Silver Queen'. The garden is small and intimate. It has an octagonal pool in its centre and stately papyrus in the shallow water. Around the outside are tall orange trees. The green and white and the shade impart a sense of coolness that is important in summer but which was not required when the rest of the garden was first laid out. Another modern development is the swimming-pool, set in an English-looking lawn and surrounded by English-looking borders, where all the plants are in fact exotics which flourish in the Mediterranean climate but would never grow outside in England. It is the manner of their planting that is so English: a mixture of shrubs, herbaceous plants, bulbs and annuals placed with the care for harmony and contrast of colour and form that characterises the Jekyll tradition. Clumps of arum lilies and *Chrysanthemum frutescens* provide a pale foil for the deep pinks and reds of pelargoniums. The shrubs include several species of datura grown as standards, a scarlet *Iochroma coccinea*, and pairs of the crape myrtle *Lagerstroemia indica*, a small tree that comes so late into leaf that one of its chief attractions is its handsome mottled bark. Growing shrubs as standards, which means training them to single stems, is a tradition of the garden at Garoupe: the rose mallow *Hibiscus rosa-sinensis* is also grown in this manner, as is the evergreen *Magnolia grandiflora*. 'Much prettier,' says Anthony Norman.

Between the green and white garden and the house is a delightful formal enclosure or *jardin de curé*, where pink and white bedding plants are grown in myrtle-edged beds: stocks in winter and petunias in summer. Each quadrant has a clipped orange tree, and an armillary sundial fills the centre where the paths meet. A small arbour is wreathed in the silvery foliage of *Pyrus salicifolia* 'Pendula'. Norman's most ingenious innovation however has been his treatment of the long transverse axis that runs between the two fretwork pavilions. In his grandmother's day, this was intensely bordered by bedding plants, but he has chosen to fill the sides of this broad walk with a choice of shrubs that blend with the natural vegetation beyond. Just as at Bodnant the exotic rhododendrons are backed by naturalised *Rhododendron ponticum* and the wild oaks of the hillside, so too at Garoupe the horticultural forms of rosemary, cistus and lavender merge with the native species of the *garrigue* and the pines beyond. The principal cistus are 'Silver Pink', *ladanifer* and *purpureus*, none native to Cap d'Antibes, but matched by such truly wild types as *Cistus albidus* behind. The lines of the walk are emphasised by a widely spaced avenue of Italian cypresses. The trees are trimmed to extreme narrowness by cutting off the fruiting cones, lest they weigh down the ascendant branches and render the outlines ragged and open. The shape of these elegant cypresses contrasts with the billowing crowns of the natural stands of Aleppo pine *Pinus halepensis* behind: the effect is rather Italian.

Anthony and Mary Norman recently planted a golden garden at Garoupe to commemorate their golden-wedding anniversary. It contains such yellow-leaved plants as *Robinia pseudoacacia* 'Frisia', *Gleditsia triacanthos* 'Sunburst' and *Physocarpus opulifolius* 'Dart's Gold'. All have grown quickly. It is always interesting to discover which plants take successfully to the Riviera; planted in the right conditions, none of these three has suffered from the scorching that sometimes disfigures golden-leaved forms. The robinia grows so much better than in England that it has been planted elsewhere at Garoupe with the foil of dark cypresses for a background: mimosas are used in a similar way, as sunlit masses against the grey olives.

The gardens on the north side are approached by a broad path that descends between huge multi-headed cycads, a male plant on the left and on the right a female whose apricot-coloured fruits resemble loquats and ripen at the beginning of May. Cycads are a favourite of Riviera gardens. For Anthony Norman some of their appeal lies in the belief that they have remained untouched by evolutionary developments for a hundred million years. Clumps of *Beschorneria yuccoides* border the top of the walk, their $1\frac{1}{2}$ m (5 ft) stems, the colour of forced rhubarb, contrasting with the green and yellow flowers which hang like an English bluebell. In spring, the lower part of the walk down the northern slopes is entirely composed of pink and white flowers. Much of the effect is created by billowing spiraeas and a double form of exochorda, the purest of all white flowers, contrasted with the pink of such Japanese cherries as 'Shirofugen' and the modern crab apple *Malus × hillieri*, which has the unusual habit of flowering along its stems instead of on just the spurs. Later in the year the dominant colours in these borders change as such roses as the orange and yellow 'Chicago Peace' take over. More roses are planted in the olive orchard at the bottom of the slope, all varieties from the nearby Meilland Nurseries, including 'Stefanie de Monaco' and 'Victor Hugo'. Some of the walks through this olive wood are flooded with tracts of German irises, seemingly straight from an Impressionist painting. The idea for this planting may have come from Villa Maryland at Cap Ferrat. The olives themselves are not pruned as they would be if cultivated for their fruit, but allowed to stretch up and grow tall, so that the long, dark limbs contrast not so much with the grey leaves but with the irises, cyclamen, paper-white narcissus and freesias under-neath. A garden owner in England could copy the effect by using holm oaks: it is especially striking after a storm has wet the trunks of the trees.

By the standards of the Riviera, Garoupe is not a great plantsman's garden, although it contains many plants that are uncommon in France. Broad sweeps of colour and bold swathes of a single species typify the planting. Mrs Martineau's verdict on Garoupe is as accurate now as it was in 1924: 'its peculiar charm lies not so much in its rich collection of plants, or even in its wealth of colour and beautiful situation, as in its excellent proportion and design, the rightness of the relation between house and garden, the beauty of the stairways and stone terraces', and she con-cluded that 'it is this artistic sense of fitness and the relation of each part to the whole which alone can create the perfect garden'.

Those principles, of course, were also applied at Bodnant. At both gardens the effects were achieved within a woodland setting, since Garoupe is cut out of the pines and olives of southern France just as Bodnant was won from the oaks and firs of north Wales. Garoupe has the lighter touch. Perhaps this lightness can be explained by physical factors: the limestone rocks are pale, the background shrubs are grey-green or grey, and the sky is naturally brighter, so that Garoupe seems altogether prettier and jaunt-ier than Bodnant. Visually, it is just as satisfying: intellectually, superior. Sumptuous is the adjective which most Riviera residents find to describe it. The aesthete Roderick Cameron once compared Garoupe to his own house and garden, La Fiorentina on Cap Ferrat. He wrote that they were the 'showcases of the Riviera'. The truth is that Garoupe is incomparably greater: and Cameron's self-promotion contrasts with the shy but generous hospitality of Anthony and Mary Norman.

GARDENS CONCEIVED and executed on so large a scale as Villa Victoria and Château de la Garoupe do not need to blend with the landscape beyond their bounds: they *are* the landscape. Most gardens on the Côte d'Azur, however, were smaller and, like the houses that went with them, constructed in an increasingly bizarre variety of styles. In 1910, Avray Tipping, *Country Life*'s influential editor, complained of the poor design of Riviera gardens. 'We find serpentine walks twisting aimlessly about mild imitations of English lawns dotted haphazardly with African palms' and 'great paths bisecting areas of rough grass in which flat masses of bedding-out plants are inserted in rounds and ovals and stars'. It was a common complaint, and many will have agreed with his conclusion that no one had solved the problem of how house and garden should be assim-ilated to the Mediterranean landscape better than Harold Ainslie Peto (1854–1933).

Peto had trained as an architect and entered into partnership with Ernest George in 1876: Edwin Lutyens and Herbert Baker were among the many able assistants who worked for them. When the part-nership was dissolved in 1892, Peto was restricted from practising in England for fifteen years and set up on the Riviera instead. He was a lifelong collector of furniture and architectural salvage; after moving to Nice, he developed a further interest in interior design and garden-making. Peto also studied the art and history of Italy, so that he planned his gardens in the Italian Renaissance tradition while he planted them in the contemporary English idiom.

Peto was part of a larger movement. The gardens painted by such neo-classicists as Alma-Tadema, Lord Leighton and Sir Edward Poynter had helped to inspire a revival of interest in Italian and classical precedents. Arthur Acton began to restore the gardens of Villa La Pietra at Florence in 1902 and Cecil Pinsent to create new Italian gardens for Bernard Berenson at Villa I Tatti in 1910. An import-ant Italian garden was made for William Waldorf Astor at Hever Castle in Kent in 1904, though its opulence owed as much to the Beaux Arts tradition as to the Italian Renaissance. Indeed, the Beaux Arts movement was a specifically French response to the same search for classic style. Naturally, there were also Riviera precedents for houses and gardens in the Italian style. The Villa Arson (1810) in Nice was the most famous, while Villa La Fiorentina at Cannes was also something of a cynosure. It was built in 1881 for Sir Julian Goldsmid, MP (1838–96), with cinquecento frescoed galleries and white marble stairs indoors. The garden was strewn with classical gazebos, an Istrian well-head, a magnificent cloister of squat Romanesque design, and more white marble overrun by roses, wisteria and sweet-scented climbers. Goldsmid's wife had been brought up in Florence.

This revival of interest in Italian architecture and gardens brought Peto some excellent commissions. Although the English on the Riviera continued to build in any architectural style from Scottish baronial to Art Nouveau, there was an increased demand for classical grandeur, especially from the really wealthy.

There were good reasons for this. The newly rich Edwardian English compared themselves to the merchant princes of the Italian Renaissance: it was natural that they should turn to the villas of sixteenth-century Italy for architectural inspiration. Their longing for the Italian style was all the stronger for the problems posed by such houses and gardens in Britain. The high priest of the revival of formalism, Reginald Blomfield, was unequivocal: 'Our climate and the quality of light in England make it impossible to obtain the effect which is actually attained in great Italian gardens.' Gertrude Jekyll concurred: 'I think the true Italian character is only suitable or completely possible in a corresponding climate,' she wrote. Moreover, the Italian style which Peto developed was dimly perceived as historically correct. The Riviera had once been Italian: therefore it was proper to build in the Florentine Renaissance style.

Many a late Victorian garden was a mismatch for both its house and its setting. Writing in *Country Life*, Tipping complained that architects had too little regard for siting: 'the garden wound its gravel paths, extended its mixed shrubberies, dotted its specimen plants, set its lobelia and calceolaria circles, stars and crescents about the lawn without worrying itself where the house stood and what features it was going to make in connection with it'. Jekyll was the best-known English advocate of unity between house, garden and setting. In France, Edouard André had emphasised its importance as early as *L'Art des jardins*, which he published in 1879, while Marchais, head gardener at Villa Thuret, could write in *Les Jardins dans la région de l'oranger* (1884) that the aim of a landscaper should be *'faire paraître grande une petite propriété, étendre ses horizons, les perdre dans l'éloignement, établir ainsi une sorte d'harmonie avec les objets éloignés'*. It was a lesson that Peto took to heart. The virtue of his schemes was that they were always well grounded in the greater landscape around – the trees, rocks, mountains and sea. This became a central point of Edwardian aesthetics, common to both the Arts and Crafts movement and the neo-Italian school: Peto's own training, as we have seen, was in both traditions. At his gardens in England too – Wayford Manor and Iford Manor, for example – Peto was able to create something that came from the Italian tradition and yet seemed to develop naturally out of the English landscape. Moreover, he believed that a site should be treated as a whole, which corresponded with another development in Edwardian thinking: a reaction

Villa Sylvia, Cap Ferrat. Peto's open arcade, inspired by the Italian Renaissance, marks the growing popularity of the Riviera as a summer resort.

against the Victorian practice whereby the architect of the house and the designer of the garden worked independently of one another.

Peto designed the whole scheme and every detail, from the dining-room furniture to seasonal bedding schemes. Three gardens on Cap St Jean Ferrat illustrate his mastery of site, materials, design and planting: Villa Sylvia (1902), Villa Maryland (*c.* 1904) and Villa Rosemary (*c.* 1908). In the balance they achieved between plants and architecture, nature and artifice, they were the forerunners of the modern compartmentalised style of gardening which was brought to perfection at Hidcote Manor in Gloucestershire and Sissinghurst Castle in Kent.

WHEN PETO designed Villa Sylvia for Mr and Mrs Ralph Curtis, he had to make the most of a small plot, a long steep strip which ran down to the sea on the western side of Cap Ferrat. Peto put the house at the highest point, against the road – the main road that connects the promontory to Beaulieu – so that he could use the rest of the site for the garden.

The Florentine loggia on the western side of the house was decked with climbing plants, including the pink *Rosa × anemonoides*, the Cherokee rose *Rosa laevigata* and *Bignonia tweediana*. The only architectural feature given to the garden itself was a none-too-broad terrace which ran in front of the house from a carved well-head at one end to a fountain surrounded by callas at the other. The rest was left half wild and dropped down to Villefranche Bay among olives and overhanging pine trees. The natural woodland was thickened up with flowering trees and shrubs, including magnolias and tree paeonies, and on either side of the broad grassways were planted great colonies of crocus, narcissus, anemone and irises. Villa Sylvia was the least architectural of Peto's gardens.

As the garden developed, so did its owners' interest in gardening. Scarlet *Bougainvillea brasiliensis* (syn. *B. sanderiana*) and purple *Hardenbergia comptoniana* grew to cover the walls of the house. In 1924, Mrs Martineau found pink cherries, spiraeas, *Prunus triloba* and white irises in the woodland garden with scarlet anemones flowering through them. Five years later, the American writer Rose Nichols noted mimosas, camellias and Malmaison carnations. Blue echiums grew against a background of the white broom *Lygos monosperma* and mingled with white wisteria: a contrast not only of colour but also of form, for the tall spikes of the echium stood proud in front of the loose showers of broom and the solid pattern of the wisteria. The brown and grey flowers of *Iris susiana* were planted beneath the olive trees: this Oncocyclus species was commonly grown in Riviera gardens before it became susceptible to virus diseases. Just below the terrace, double nasturtiums trailed down the hillside among orange nemesias and marigolds. Later the colour scheme was modified to incorporate more salmon pinks, coral penstemons and blocks of apricot snapdragons mixed with flowers in various shades of blue. Lower down, a planting of crimson cyclamen and cherry-red nemesias was balanced by velvety black ranunculus and purple hardenbergia. Nemesias became so popular as bedding plants during the 1920s that Suttons & Sons, the seedsmen in Reading, published a small guide to *Gardening on the Riviera* to promote

Villa Rosemary on Cap St-Jean de Ferrat was designed by Harold Peto as a unity. House, garden and all the details – even the rich planting in this photograph, taken in about 1920 – were subordinate to the whole.

these and other good selling lines – schizanthus and cinerarias. Thousands of plants were grown from seed every year at Villa Sylvia. It was perhaps the most English of Peto's gardens, not least because Mr and Mrs Curtis practised the theories of colour blending and segregation which were gaining currency at that time among English garden owners.

PETO DESIGNED Villa Rosemary for Arthur Cohen on a cliff above the sea. It was another difficult commission. First the house and garden had to be accommodated within a 1 ha (2½ acre) rectangle on the barren, rocky soil of Cap Ferrat. Then it was necessary to safeguard the owner's privacy but at the same time to preserve the magnificent views along the Riviera to the east which were the property's main asset. Just as he had maximised space at Villa Sylvia by siting the house right at the top of the plot, Peto placed the house at Villa Rosemary on a small summit at the furthest point from the sea. It was Italian Renaissance in style, connected to the formal garden below by wide marble steps. Peto at once understood that the garden would have to be treated as a whole and not divided into small enclosures. His final design was a spacious rectangular formal garden, bounded by the cliff on the left, a pergola on the right, and a loggia at the far end. Although conceived as one garden, it was treated in three sections: the ground was levelled so that only a short flight of steps flanked by 'Général Schablikine' roses led from one area to the next and the planting was kept low, so that one saw over the flowers to the end of the garden and beyond. Flowers in any case came second to the design, and were limited to the central section. Annuals and bedding plants were displayed in small beds around a permanent planting of grevilleas, rhaphiolepis, *Templetonia retusa* and more 'Général Schablikine'. Peto's original scheme included carnations and *Viola cornuta*. The colours were selected and arranged for harmony, to avoid clashing contrasts at all costs. Mrs Nicholls in 1929 noted coppery stocks, lavender godetias, salmon-pink snapdragons and blue forget-me-nots, 'the soft pastel shades that can be gay without becoming riotous'.

The outer sections at either end were simple grass quincunxes edged in stone and had a blood-orange tree in each quarter. The one closest to the house was called the Roman garden: it was not intended as an archaeologically correct reconstruction, but at least the name suggested imperial grandeur. Orange trees were used to create a theme and to take the place of flowering trees in an English garden. They were required to give shade without growing so tall, as cypresses would, that they might interfere with the view. The pergola was simple, Tuscan in style, with plain stone supports and wooden horizontals, backed by a clipped cypress hedge. Halfway along was a semicircular bay that led down broad steps to the central section of the formal garden. They were important: seen from below, these steps suggested a spacious garden entrance.

Peto called his loggia a *squiffa*, and based it on the arcade in the garden of the Riadh at the heart of the Generalife in Granada. This long and spacious construction, raised upon a terrace of its own, had a dual purpose. It served to terminate and enclose the formal garden and, at the same time, because it was airy and open, its arches framed the view in all directions – Peto had noticed how the beautiful windows of the Generalife improved the prospect of Granada. 'It is in touches like this,' declared a laconic contemporary, 'that the garden of the Villa Rosemary differs from the average.'

The design is one of great skill and charm. It contains every element that was then considered proper – colour, shade and a balance between architecture and wildness: the firm lines of the garden were appropriate to the rugged site and the immense views. The slopes of the cliff were covered in scarlet *Linum grandiflorum* and wild or naturalised annual flowers, which were encouraged to run down to the water's edge. At the far end of the pergola, a small piece of pine woodland was interplanted with magnolias, flame-coloured azaleas and *Sparmannia africana*, and underplanted with golden narcissi, red and blue anemones, irises and Spanish bluebells, on a groundwork of grey santolina and gnaphalium. Somehow Peto also managed to fit in a garage, a tennis-court and a kitchen garden. Fifty years later there would also have been a swimming-pool: one wonders where Peto would have put that, and how he would have worked it into his overall design.

Peto's squiffa, a graceful Arab-Romanesque loggia, makes an irresistible focal point at the end of the formal garden at Villa Rosemary (1910).

In time, the trees and shrubs at Villa Rosemary grew up to alter the balance that Peto had established between house, garden and sea. Flowers were of secondary importance to the architect but not to the owners, and Villa Rosemary became increasingly known as a garden for plants. The bushes of 'Général Schablikine' grew to 3 m (10 ft) high. The house itself began to disappear under climbers and creepers: wisterias, holboellias, stauntonias, *Thunbergia grandiflora* and, of course, roses.

VILLA MARYLAND is perhaps Peto's masterpiece. Mr and Mrs Arthur Wilson's brief for Peto was to oversee every detail from planting the gardens to furnishing the interior: this gave unity of style to the whole, and harmony of detail to its parts. Avray Tipping declared in 1910 'every piece of the puzzle has been deftly lodged where it exactly fits and the picture presents no flaw'. The site of Maryland was another awkward one, for it had a lane running through the middle, not exactly a thoroughfare but a public road nevertheless. Peto took it in, and made it a feature of his scheme: he built the house immediately along one side of it, on the highest point of the four-acre site, which enabled him to make best use of the land on either side for the garden.

The house was an opulent Renaissance-style villa, so full of detail as to appear almost a pastiche: loggias of tiburtine and malachite, terracotta rondels and imitation Della Robbia bas-reliefs, all swathed in climbing roses and honeysuckle. The entrance from the road gave directly into an open two-storey cloister, not unlike an Andalusian patio. Broad steps led up to an arcaded upper walk where one door opened into the entrance hall of the house and another into the formal gardens. Just inside the garden wall was one of Peto's favourite features: a concave semicircular seat, perhaps copied from the marble *exedrae* on which classical maidens disport themselves in the paintings of Alma-Tadema. Peto usually placed this characteristic detail at a vantage point on the edge of a garden or as a focal point at the end of an axis: a good example can be seen at Iford Manor, his own garden in Wiltshire.

Peto built a straight walk along the boundary of Villa Maryland, high above the road, for the whole length of the upper garden, more than a hundred yards. Prostrate rosemary, *Lotus berthelotii* and trailing ivy-leaved geraniums such as 'Mme Crousse' were planted to cascade down the wall, so that the garden's plants were seen to enclose the road itself.

Halfway along this rampart stood the shell of an old tiled fisherman's cottage: Peto kept the external structure but gutted the interior and drove wide arched openings through its walls on either side to secure the terrace walk. The first part of the walk was kept open, the next section was framed by a light pergola, while the final stretch beyond the fisherman's cottage was spanned by an arcade of clipped cypress. This long boundary walk gives a great sense of space and size to the garden. It is, however, no more than a boundary walk: more interesting features lie within.

Peto designed the formal garden at Villa Maryland to fill as much of the site as possible. He placed a garden house in the shape of a small temple at the furthest end: its pairs of Ionic columns supported an arch between two pediments and echoed the arcading of the house. Peto went counter to the French tradition, which preferred to place the more ornamental or architectural features of the garden near the house and to allow the garden to become more natural further away. Instead, he connected the house to the temple by a wide walk across a sunken garden, through an area shadowed by old olive trees, past a thickly planted parterre with an old Roman corn jar at its centre, to a pool enclosed by the semicircular colonnade that flanks the temple. One of these wings connects to the rampart walk and the other to the wild garden. This feature, an arcade on either side of the garden temple, was another favourite of Peto's: an example can be seen at Bridge House in Weybridge in Surrey. The design of the temple itself is similar to the one that Peto built at Hartham Park in Wiltshire, while the lofty central arch and steeply pitched roof were based on the twin pavilions by the water staircase of Villa Lante at Bagnaia. There was a hint of imperial Rome in the lines of the temple and its pool, which was amplified by rows of antique busts on marble columns. The parterre was sometimes called the Roman garden: again this was not intended to be an accurate description but to imply a connection with the splendours of ancient civilisation.

Peto planted the parterres as a scheme of gold and white: dwarf mimosas, orange trees, azaleas, westringias, white paeonies, dicentras and lilies. Throughout the garden he chose soft colours or blending tones, in contrast to the bright kaleidoscope that most Riviera residents preferred. Where oranges and yellows were used – large clumps of montbretias, for example – he contained them within plantings of white and grey. He kept many of the old olive trees

The classical temple which terminates the main axis of the formal garden at Villa Maryland was based on designs from Villa Lante near Viterbo.

in the parterre: their branches stretched over the colonnades and gave a sense of instant maturity, and thus of ancient occupancy. In another part of the garden the olive orchards were left as a background to the wild garden, as Peto had done at Villa Sylvia. Wisterias were planted among the trees to arch over the winding grass paths; they were underplanted with tulips, narcissi and anemones but, most notably, with irises in such concentrations that the whole area became known as the Iris Field. Lady Aberconway planted the iris walks at Château de la Garoupe at about the same time, while Villa Salles, and La Léopolda above Beaulieu too, had similar massed

The main axis of the grand staircase at Villa Maryland, seen from the temple at the bottom of the garden in 1910.

plantings: it would be interesting to discover who first took to the Riviera the Tuscan idea of underplanting olive terraces with a crop of Florentine irises, grown for orris root.

Peto threw a stone arch across the lane to a belvedere on the other side. The single axis of the garden on the southern slope was revealed at once. The eye was drawn down a long gentle staircase lined with cypresses to a circular pool and beyond the garden temple to the Mediterranean sea. The steps were edged with marble, but patterned in brick, and the borders on either side filled with lavender and echiums, a mixture of pastel purples, greys, and blues. Peto surmounted the pool by a fountain with two small bowls, and the temple – no more than a pedimented shelter – held another of his semicircular seats. A brick pergola planted with roses and other climbers led off to the side, but it only went to the

Villa Maryland (1910). The arcade of clipped cypresses which Peto designed to run along the rampart.

kitchen garden, greenhouses, sheds and staff cottages. The view was everything: there was no real need to penetrate further than the belvedere at the top.

Villa Maryland was larger than most of Peto's commissions and he allowed some parts of the garden to be developed distinctly while retaining an overall unity of style. Some owners, lost for identity, wanted to include representative gardens of several styles and periods. Nearby Villa Île de France and Villa Champfleuri at Cannes boasted gardens in the Japanese, Florentine, Spanish, English, Moorish and French styles, but the houses were invariably set off by spacious formal gardens in an Italianate sort of style, while the other incidents were hidden away. A later and somewhat extreme development of this interest in different traditions can be seen at Compton Acres near Poole, where a sequence of several styles becomes the whole point of the design. A French authority explains the phenomenon as a fashion for garden history. The English historian David Ottewill interprets it as a tendency to view the garden as 'a

succession of outdoor rooms, each affording fresh delights for the visitor'. Whatever its cause, Peto believed too firmly in the importance of treating the house and garden as an architectural whole to indulge such fancies, except as an occasional sideshow. In fact he inserted a Japanese garden behind the classical colonnade at Iford in Wiltshire, although some consider it a little uncomfortable so close to his collection of Byzantine bits and pieces. When garden-makers forgot the importance of siting the house in an appropriate setting, and began to treat the different parts of the garden disjunctively, it was natural that they should emphasise contrasts of scale and style, rather than seeking unity. This gave rise in turn to the late-twentieth-century gardening fashion which uses a series of unconnected incidents to build up a world within itself, set apart from both the house and the wider landscape. It is worth remembering that Peto's success derived in part from a reaction against similar mistakes in the late nineteenth century.

Mrs Arthur Wilson, Peto's client at Villa Maryland, was widely perceived as a pioneer. One of her strengths was archly described by a French contemporary as an ability to 'ignore budgetary considerations'. She was *very* rich, and could afford to plant and maintain every part of the garden intensively. The luxuriance of the planting gave the garden unity, so that visitors often remembered the overall effect more than its parts: a strange outcome for a garden so full of architectural excellence. Cecil and Dorothy Hanbury used to come from La Mortola to study the use of colour at Villa Maryland, and it was partly from Peto's grand design that they took inspiration for the architectural improvements made to La Mortola in the 1920s. The principles that Mrs Wilson applied to Maryland were new: it is clear that she was gardening in what later became known as the Hidcote style. She introduced and distributed many untried novelties to the Riviera and used them with an eye to harmonies of colour and contrasts of form, but Peto taught her the importance of good design and the need for architectural harmony between house and garden. English gardens of the late twentieth century owe as much to Peto's skills – and especially the layout and planting of Villa Maryland – as they do to the writings of Gertrude Jekyll or the English tradition of plantsmanship.

Peto demonstrated his ability to connect a garden both to its house and to the wider landscape even in those commissions where he was required to design only part of the scheme. Shortly after Baron van André built himself the palatial château of Isola Bella at Californie near Cannes in 1909, he bought a large tract of olive orchards and orange groves to extend the garden down the slopes beneath the original plot. Peto was then asked to integrate the old and the new: his solution was to build a garden house on the mound where the two holdings joined. It was in effect a spacious double-cube room, surrounded by a marble arcade, reminiscent of the *squiffa* at Villa Rosemary. Not only did it match the Italian magnificence of van André's palace, but it was positioned to be visible from the bottom of the hill. The link was therefore made, and Peto ran a stately staircase from the garden house to the garden below. Its centrepiece was a huge colonnade of white-veined marble around a spacious oval pool, its monolithic white shafts capped by Ionic capitals and reflected in the water. The columns rose from low plinths on which Peto placed pans and pots of lilies and hyacinths. Clearly, no expense was spared: apart from using vast quantities of white marble, Peto

planted an avenue of instantly mature cypresses 10 m (30 ft) tall and 30,000 irises.

Peto's practice flourished on the Riviera and his commissions in the south of France are perhaps more significant than his work in England. His popularity among English residents was such that many gardens were directly inspired by Peto's work at Cap Ferrat and elsewhere on the Côte d'Azur. His influence may be detected, for example, in the Italianate cloisters, Doric temple, Tuscan pergolas and long stone stairways that Thorpe Wilson built for Villa Rosmarino at Menton-Garavan. Peto's views on design then gained currency among French garden architects and during the 1920s became the accepted orthodoxy. By that time, ironically, his structured style was at odds with the re-emergence of natural gardening in England: there was neither the mood nor the money available for Italianate fantasies among the rock gardens, rhododendrons and ground-cover plants that characterised English gardening after the Great War. Peto thus had a more obvious influence in France than in England, where his significance has even now not been properly appreciated. In France

Peto made a woodland garden in the olive grove at Villa Maryland, swathing the trees with wisteria and roses, and underplanting them with irises and annuals.

tastes were different, partly because such designers as Ferdinand Bac and J.-C. N. Forestier had also increased the demand for traditional forms.

Forestier's most imaginative work was undertaken in Spain and Provence rather than on the Côte d'Azur. Bac worked only in France. In some respects he was a French Peto, although neither would have appreciated the comparison. Both disdained the vulgarity and worthlessness of the Riviera houses of the international rich; both were occupied by the search for style and found inspiration for it in the classical and Renaissance traditions; both collected elements from all around the Mediterranean and mixed the best features into a new pan-Mediterranean style that was predominantly Italian in spirit. Peto admired Hadrian's Villa at Tivoli: so did Bac, and used it at Colombières. Bac admired the Generalife: so did Peto, and used it at Villa Rosemary. Both revered the cypress and regretted its association with cemeteries. They differed completely in their attitudes to decoration. Peto used plants as elements of ornament: he enjoyed composing with their forms and colours. Bac was more austere. Plants had little place in his garden except for their shapes and tones: space and light meant more than colour. Nor did Bac approve of embellishments. He 'stripped the Moors of their Arab calligraphy the better to appreciate their use of space'. As for the Romanesque, which Bac used extensively in his garden architecture, he wanted it to recall Spain, 'but a Spain without complications, without *boursouflure*'.

One of the leading admirers of Peto was the French landscape architect Octave Godard. When in 1920 he articulated the most modern principles for making gardens on the Côte d'Azur, he emphasised that the rocky nature of much of the coast made vital the proper use of geometry and management of level. Like Peto, Godard insisted that the garden should be able to take in a view of the mountains or the sea, and merge with the natural vegetation. Indigenous plants of the *maquis* or *garrigue* should not be removed but incorporated into the design: on occasion he even imported heather, cistus, myrtle, arbutus, rhamnus, broom, juniper, rosemary and lavender to settle the garden more firmly into the landscape. Godard railed against the nineteenth-century fashion for planting palms and insisted that the

Ferdinand Bac, France's Harold Peto. Self-portrait aged seventeen. Bac was the grandson of Napoléon I's brother, King Jérôme of Westphalia.

Italian cypress was more correct. Indeed, he declared that it was the only Mediterranean tree in harmony with the character of the region. After the Great War the cypress tree became an object of veneration: like the olive and the carob it was a symbol of traditional values and stability for a ruling class shaken by the winds of change. Above all, Godard declared that he was an enthusiastic partisan of the Provençal tradition of garden-making. The trouble was that no such tradition existed: in practice he advocated a neo-Italian formal style of gardening and cited Peto as one of its great exponents.

A MINORITY of garden owners on the Riviera, even in the 1920s and 1930s, eschewed architectural formalism and clung firmly to the principles of natural gardening. Dr Axel Robertson Proschowsky of the Jardin d'Acclimatisation at Fabron near Nice was a vehement advocate of what he called the 'English or natural style in gardening that is the imitation of the most beautiful scenes of free Nature'. He argued that it was the only rational and therefore truly *aesthetic* style of gardening, in that it allowed the owner infinite opportunities to develop whatever

Villa Isola Bella (1910–11). Quite the most stunning architecturally of Peto's garden designs, the marble colonnade surrounds an oval pool, its sides lined with lilies in pots.

talent he might possess. Proschowsky reviled topiary, geometry and artificial shapes: he considered them the negation of natural beauty, besides requiring too much work. He wrote in 1926 'to such vandalism is now added a new horror, namely the so-called *style provençal*, which is the ugliest style of gardening ever invented'. He complained that everywhere on the Riviera he saw clumsy pillars carrying a kind of heavy ungraceful scaffolding, plants in ugly vases placed at regular intervals, and paths that were quite straight without any of the graceful curves which were the charm of English gardening. Proschowsky continued to advocate the creation of tropical scenes 'thus allowing persons to contemplate in a few hours' journey from the capitals of Europe what they would otherwise have to travel thousands of miles to see'. His ideas were so out of date by the 1920s that they began to be sympathetically received again, not on the Riviera but in England itself, where the tide was

Roderick Cameron was especially proud of the effect he obtained by painting the trunks of the orange trees at La Fiorentina.

flowing back towards naturalism in the garden.

One example will bring the story of the formal garden on the Riviera up to date: Villa La Fiorentina on Point Saint-Hospice, a small peninsula jutting out from Cap Ferrat. Aron Messiah worked on it for Comtesse Robert de Beauchamps between 1915 and 1919. Messiah was a Niçois architect who had collaborated with Peto on several projects in the years before the Great War. Bac had a hand in the landscaping: he designed the Japanese garden and a garden cloister. La Fiorentina itself was a pastiche of a Florentine villa. In 1939, the Anglo-American Roderick Cameron's much married mother bought it and rebuilt it in the Palladian style. Cameron described the garden that Russell Page made around it as predominantly 'a green and white garden with its main axes clearly laid out, and within the classical frame a series of separate compartments or rooms walled in behind clipped hedges'. In short, it was a neo-French garden of the modern school: Hidcote without the plants.

The garden at La Fiorentina did, of course, contain plants, but they were subordinate to the design and the colour schemes. Cameron was not a plantsman and, indeed, the chapter of his autobiography, *The Golden Riviera*, which deals with Riviera gardens manages to misspell almost every botanic name. Cameron considered the *pièce de résistance* at La Fiorentina to be the broad shallow grass steps leading down to the sea: 'along the descent, on both sides, are planted tapering twenty-foot cypresses. Below these tight green columns grow dusty clumps of the Canary Islands blue-flowering echium. They advance in waving lines on to the steps, and mixed in with them come a small white-flowering convolvulus and the deep blue Corsican rosemary'. It was theatrical, if not original: ever since Peto designed Villa Maryland there had really only been one way to lay out and plant a steep descent. There were, however, also lavender terraces enclosed by hedges of rosemary, a pergola, box parterres with red sand in some segments and bare earth in the others and a plantation of oranges. The orange trees were lime-washed on their trunks and lower limbs, not as a commercial protection against parasites but for purely decorative effect, to give a luminous glow to the light that filtered through the dark leaves of the trees and was reflected in the waxy white arum lilies beneath. 'I have never seen this done before,' declared Cameron 'and we were rather proud of the result.' Cameron was a garden decorator.

Gardening in the grand manner is not possible for

everyone. Few have the resources to plan and plant on the scale of a Lady Aberconway or an Alice de Rothschild, or to employ a garden architect of the calibre of Harold Peto. Many good gardens were made on the Côte d'Azur by members of the upper middle classes, seldom rich or titled, who thought of a garden as a place for working with plants. They are in a way more typical of the gardens that Englishmen have made on the Riviera and throughout the Mediterranean.

References and Further Reading

The garden at Villa Victoria is charmingly described in *Les Jardins de la Fortune* by Marcel Gaucher, whose father was head gardener to Baronne Alice de Rothschild. Constance Battersea's *Reminiscences* were published in 1922.

Garoupe is poorly documented but there was a good account by Fred Whitsey in *The Garden* in January 1988. Mrs Philip Martineau's *Gardening in Sunny Lands* (1924) and Octave Godard's *Les Jardins de la Côte d'Azur* (1927) are both classics, while the whole period is authoritatively handled by David Ottewill in *The Edwardian Garden* (New Haven, CT, 1989). *Ferdinand Bac* (1859–1952), by G. de Diesbach (Paris, 1979), is a good short account of his life and work. The Peto gardens are thoroughly described in a series of *Country Life* articles: Villa Sylvia on 16 July 1910; Villa Rosemary on 30 March 1912 and 14 January 1928; and Villa Maryland on 3 and 10 December 1910. The magazine is helpful too on Isola Bella (1 April 1911), La Fiorentina (17 December 1927), Villa Rosmarino (5 December 1925) and La Léopolda (19 January 1929). There is also a useful article 'Les Jardins et Les Architectures de la Villa Maryland' in *L'Illustration*, 25 March 1922.

Chapter Three

THE RIVIERA IN MODERN TIMES

Plantsmen's Gardens

THERE WAS a colony of English plantsmen-owners around Menton in the mid twentieth century: the names of Lawrence Johnston, Norah Warre, Maybud Campbell and Humphrey Waterfield are still honoured along the whole Côte d'Azur. The first Englishwoman to buy a house on the Riviera specifically because she wanted to grow Mediterranean plants was Ellen Willmott of Warley Place. She had stayed with the Hanburys at La Mortola on several occasions before buying nearby Boccanegra in 1905. Her tenure there was short: she never revisited it after the outbreak of war in 1914 and then, in 1920, she was forced to sell it, and her house at Tresserve in Savoy too, to save herself from bankruptcy. The house at Boccanegra was modest, almost cottagey: unlike Warley, it and the garden were never intended for conspicuous entertainment but for Miss Willmott's own pleasure.

Boccanegra is built on a hot, steep site. Its 8.5 ha (21 acres) of olive orchards run down to the sea much more abruptly than the garden at La Mortola: Boccanegra gives a good impression of how that garden looked before Cecil and Dorothy Hanbury gave it an overlay of Italianate formality in the 1920s. A greater contrast to the flat pitch of Warley Place than Boccanegra's luxuriant jungle would be hard to imagine. The main railway line from Nice to Genoa ran through the garden and created an immediate problem: Ellen Willmott screened it with fast-growing palms and gum trees. She realised however that the overriding requirement was for irrigation, and she began not by purchasing plants but by making water tanks. But she was unable to exercise such self-restraint for long. It was the pleasure of growing rare plants that had drawn her to the Riviera and she started to buy extravagantly: 100 *Mahonia aquifolium*, 300 cannas and 600 *Tulipa clusiana* were by no means exceptional quantities.

Where the gradient was more moderate at the western end of Boccanegra, Miss Willmott planted a collection of cycads, and a huge *Arbutus andrachne* with pure white flowers, while the path was curved to draw attention to a fine specimen of olive tree. Four steep terraces ran east along the hillside, the slopes covered by such winter-flowering species as *Iris unguicularis*, *Narcissus papyraceus*, clivias, eucomis and freesias. Much of the horticultural effect came from the play of light on the grey olives and the way they contrasted with the spiky architectural forms of aloes and agaves. Apart from cobbled paths near the house, Boccanegra was almost devoid of formal features, likened in 1929 to a wild garden on the west coast of Scotland 'where woods composed of birch and alder reach down a rocky slope to the shores of a loch'. Large olive trees grew right to the walls of the house. Boccanegra still has good collections of eucalyptus, palms and cordylines, and an overgrown hedge of *Pittosporum tobira*, all dating from Ellen Willmott's time. Among the rare shrubs she planted which survive are *Southia latifolia* and both the male and female forms of *Doryalis caffra*, which probably came from her friends at La Mortola. Fortunately the garden is still maintained as a private botanic garden by Guido Piacenza, an enterprising anglophile nurseryman from Lombardy.

Boccanegra, c. 1910. Ellen Willmott's own photograph of the steps up to a belvedere at the front of the house.

ARGUABLY the most important English garden

La Serre de la Madone in the mid-1920s. Lawrence Johnston bought this postcard view of the bare hillside at Gorbio to show his English friends the site of his future Riviera garden.

on the Riviera was begun by Major Lawrence Johnston of Hidcote Manor when he bought a farm in the Gorbio valley above Menton in January 1924. Hidcote is the most influential twentieth-century garden in England: the Riviera sequel, made with the experience of Hidcote behind it, should be of even greater significance. Edith Wharton wrote to Bernard Berenson in 1933 that the garden at Hidcote was 'incredibly different from the one at Menton' but in fact the two gardens share the same elements of enclosed design, rare plants and inventive plantings. Despite the different climates and circumstances in which they were made, there is an essential unity between them, although the National Trust now maintains Hidcote to a high standard while La Serre de la Madone has suffered some vicissitudes since Johnston's death in 1958.

Lawrence Johnston enlarged and modernised the farmhouse at La Serre de la Madone so that it became, like Hidcote, a gentleman's residence rather than a working farm. The land was steeply terraced and planted with olives and grapes. It faced southwest and had a distant view of the sea. Between 1924 and 1939, Johnston was able to expand the size of his holding by piecemeal acquisitions from nine adjoining owners until it measured 10 ha (25 acres).

La Serre de la Madone was intended as a winter garden, and Johnston lived there between September and April, although it became his main home after Hidcote passed to the National Trust in 1948. As always on the Riviera, the lie of the land determined the design of the garden: it became an exploration of level after level, each treated separately. Some terraces were long and narrow, others broad and wide; most merged into wild woodland at the side; all used their space differently and illustrated a distinct horticultural or architectural theme. Unity was provided by a main axis of successive flights of stairs that ended in a rondel of box in the middle of one of the lower terraces, and also by a spring-fed sequence of fountains and pools. Some of the staircases actually have fountains set into their sides – these terraces have a feel of the Italian Renaissance, which Johnston intensified by placing statues at the ends.

The terrace immediately in front of the house is narrow. From its parapet you look down to some of the garden's best plants: melaleucas and callistemons from Australia and banksias from South Africa, fringed by the winter-flowering *Iris unguicularis* and underplanted with bulbs from the Cape and Mexico. Near by is an enormous bush, 'an astonishing sight' according to James Russell, of the long-leaved, orange-flowered *Mahonia siamensis*, introduced to cultivation in Europe by Johnston from his ill-fated expedition to Yunnan with George Forrest in 1931 – the two plant hunters quarrelled. The biggest and broadest of these terraces is a little further down, almost entirely filled by a rectangular pool, and fronted by a conservatory known as the Winter House. In Johnston's day there were lotus, lilies and papyrus plants in the water, and sculptures around it: the statue in the middle was known as 'Mrs Johnston'. The essence of the pool's design and siting is its sense of openness; it is not overhung by large trees, but free from any suggestion of being enclosed. The whole sky seems caught in the immensity of its reflections. Below it are a green room, a shade garden, and further terraces devoted to single features such as clematis or succulents.

Lawrence Johnston was a good designer, but his enthusiasm for gardening started with plants and he became an active hunter of new species in the wild. He organised collecting expeditions to the Drakensberg, Yunnan and Java, introduced ornamental plants into cultivation and then used them in his garden to good effect. He distributed his best introductions among his friends, particularly to fellow enthusiasts. This interest in plants distinguished La Serre de la Madone from run-of-the-mill Riviera gardens, designed by architects but short on horticultural variety. Unlike the Hanburys at La Mortola, however, Johnston had no ambitions in the world of botanic science: he was essentially an amateur who enjoyed his garden and worked in it.

The boldness and originality of Lawrence Johnston's planting was as exciting at La Serre de la Madone as at Hidcote. Whole terraces were hung with *Beschorneria yuccoides*, while embankments were blue with sheets of agapanthus. Clumps of *Strelitzia reginae* formed a motif throughout the garden: this repeated device both shaped its character and bestowed a sense of coherence. A slope extending to perhaps one dekare (a quarter of an acre) was entirely given to pink *Amaryllis belladonna*, which rose from a groundwork of sky-blue plumbago. The form of *Clivia miniata* which Johnston grew was a dark-flowered selection bred by Charles Raffill at Kew. A parterre, not unlike the fuchsia enclosure at Hidcote, had box edgings filled with the double-

La Serre de la Madone, newly planted in 1930 and showing how Lawrence Johnston devised a long Italian-style axis down the hillside to connect a sequence of terraces, each of which was given different horticultural treatment.

La Serre de la Madone. Lawrence Johnston never married, but this eighteenth-century statue in the big pool was known to his friends as 'Mrs Johnston'.

flowered purple periwinkle, through which grew massed plantings of the red and white lady tulip, *Tulipa clusiana*. La Serre de la Madone was visibly worked in the same idiom as Hidcote. They share a sense of dynamism, and a feeling for theatre, setting up invitations to explore, and offering contrasts between open and shut. In this, and in the series of progressions and repetitions, with their bold use of colour effects and harmonies, the gardens are themselves eloquent and powerful statements of style.

La Serre de la Madone has had a difficult time since Lawrence Johnston died. It was bequeathed to Nancy Lindsay, who despoiled it and sold off the best artefacts. Some of the more important plants were given to the Cambridge Botanic Garden to save, though few survive. Those that remained have flourished and grown to overwhelm the architecture of the garden: the balance between nature and art has altered since the days when Johnston employed a staff of twelve full-time gardeners. In 1960 the house was bought by Sir Charles Baring, who made

several questionable alterations. These included the addition of a Japanese garden and the conversion of the great rectangular basin into a swimming-pool. In about 1970, the estate was sold to a Belgian banker, whose shortcomings gave concern to English residents who remembered the garden in better days. Now it belongs to a Frenchwoman who is reluctant to grant admission to would-be visitors: in the absence of recent reports, one can only fear for its present condition and future prospects. Were it in England, the National Trust would have worked to acquire Hidcote's sequel, which Johnston came to esteem more highly than his 'English baby'. It is difficult to interest the French in the conservation of gardens, particularly a garden that does not belong to their own tradition. Fred Whitsey somehow managed to visit it in May 1986. The excellent but wistful article that he wrote for *Country Life* shortly afterwards may prove to be the last word on Lawrence Johnston's Hidcote in France.

FEW OWNERS can have had such a long and active life in one garden as Mrs George Warre at Roquebrune on the tip of Cap Martin. This promontory had been a shooting reserve of the Princes of Monaco and was not parcelled off until the turn of the nineteenth century, at about the same time that Cap Ferrat was developed. Norah Mosson Warre and her first husband Emerson Bainbridge, MP, bought a 4 ha (10 acre) plot on a steep rough hillside sloping down towards the sea in 1902. She lived there for seventy-five years. Villa Roquebrune enjoyed a particularly warm position, facing slightly west of south, and sheltered by the steep hillside behind: the author Roderick Cameron noticed its almost total immunity from the prevailing wind. There were some drawbacks, however, notably a chronic shortage of water, while the hillside covered with limestone boulders and lack of good soil would have deterred many. When Bainbridge showed his wife the site he had chosen for their house, she burst into tears at her first sight of the unpromising terrain and sobbed 'But I wanted to make a garden!'

Those limestone boulders were cleared from the hillside and broken down to be used for levelling and terracing, and giving a rough edge to the walks. Large loads of earth were imported to supplement the scarce soil; such as there was consisted of limy, heavy clay, the typical *terra rossa* of calcareous formations in the Mediterranean. Year after year quantities of manure were added to keep the soil fertile: visitors always remarked how exceptionally well the plants grew as a result of this treatment. The site of the future Villa Roquebrune in 1902 had a few pines and olive trees, but they were scarce; although fifty years later parts of the garden began to take on an appearance of woodland, this effect was created by the exotic trees Mrs Warre had planted. To start with, a certain amount of terracing was needed: on occasion, because of the slope, the retaining walls ended up higher than the width of the terrace below them. These stone taluses, as much as 4 m (12 ft) high, were then covered with climbers, or shrubs tied in to their surfaces, while plants of lax habit were allowed to tumble down from above. Immediately next to the road at the top, the terrace was wide enough to incorporate a respectable kitchen garden and greenhouse. Large quantities of tender bulbs and orchids were grown here in pots, as displays for the house and replacements in the garden. Here too Mrs Warre grew orange and lemon trees, although she often regretted that her gardeners tended these fruit trees more assiduously than her plants in the main garden.

The garden at Villa Roquebrune was not really designed: it had no association with architects or landscapers and contained few elements of formality. It most closely resembled the artless English cottage garden in which a keen plantsman tries to grow as many interesting plants as possible with little care for structural conceits. Narrow and winding paths predominated. There were almost no straight lines, although the axes along the terraces were clearly determined. Some were surfaced with gravel, others had a sparse covering of grass, but most were no more than beaten earth – very effective in the natural woodland setting as the garden grew up. By the 1960s there was a tree of *Grevillea robusta* 12 m (40 ft) high below the house and 6 m (20 ft) specimens of such shrubs as *Genista monosperma* and *Calliandra tweedyi*, which has startling scarlet bottle-brush flowers like a powder-puff. The trees were underplanted with grey-leaved plants including artemisias, chrysanthemums, gazanias and *Agave americana*, which lit up the shade. From a narrow terrace in front of the unremarkable house a double staircase led to the first of the walks along the side of the hill, underneath a pergola of roses and passion flowers. Among the roses were the hybrids of *Rosa gigantea*, 'La Follette' and 'Sénateur Amic', while the most spectacular passion flower was *Passiflora antioquiensis*. At one end a round pond was surrounded by a stone pergola topped with rustic poles and covered in roses, clematis and other climbing plants;

Norah Warre, who lived at Villa Roquebrune for seventy-five years and made one of the finest plantsman's gardens on the Riviera, seen here as a young woman.

the pergola framed a broad view across the bay of Monte Carlo. Around the pond ixias, freesias and other South African Iridaceae grew in a circular border and flowered throughout the winter, for the garden was mainly planted for autumn, winter and spring effect: throughout her long life, Mrs Warre always returned to England for the summer and so she never saw in flower such plants as *Calodendron capense* and *Amaryllis belladonna*.

Norah Warre was undoubtedly a plantswoman, for whom the pleasure of gardening was cultivation, and she built up an extensive collection of plants at Roquebrune. One of her successes was *Agave attenuata*: she and her friends on the Riviera used to say that the rare flowering of this species presaged a death among their acquaintances. In 1974 no less than four flower spikes appeared in Villa Roquebrune alone, but in the event no one died. To this day, many of the plants at Villa Roquebrune are rare, and defy even the good plantsman's efforts to name them. How much more so was this the case twenty,

A woodland walk at Villa Roquebrune in 1974. It exemplifies Norah Warre's use of pale colours and spiky plants to lighten the underplantings.

fifty or eighty years ago when the garden was still young. Mrs Warre was also fond of saying that she had been fortunate in the generosity of her gardening friends and named especially four individuals: 'Johnnie' Johnston of Serre de la Madone, Cecil Hanbury of La Mortola, Harold Hillier of Ampfield and Fred Stern of Highdown. She grew the form of *Jasminum polyanthum* that Johnston had collected in Yunnan; *Aloe × hanburyana* from La Mortola; *Xanthoceras sorbifolium* from Hillier's nursery; and many tree paeonies from the Sterns, including the hybrid Sir Frederick named 'Mrs George Warre'; with its large, semi-double, pale pink flowers, rather deeper pink at the base of the petals, it gained a First Class Certificate from the Royal Horticultural Society in 1953. She had many other benefactors – *Kleinia dianthioides* even came from Marnier-Lapostolle of Les Cèdres who was notoriously ungenerous – and she was scrupulous in giving due thanks to the staff of Wisley and Kew for plants, seeds, advice and the encouragement that they gave her over many years. She in turn was open-handed with her own plants. Graham Sutherland, who lived in Menton from 1955

to 1980, had not encountered the intensely purple wandering sailor, *Setcreasea purpurea*, before he saw it at Villa Roquebrune in 1973. It was still quite an unusual plant then. Sutherland fell upon it with rapture, and Mrs Warre promptly gave him some pieces to root. 'And, you know,' she used to say afterwards, 'it really is a rather Graham Sutherland sort of colour, is it not?'

THE SAME might have been said of Villa Val Rahmeh in Menton-Garavan, a handsome ochre-washed house in the Provençal style. It was built in 1925 by General Sir Percy Radcliffe and has a stumpy colonnade along part of the front and a corbelled balcony at one end. It suggests a dependable sort of occupant, and indeed for many years was the home of Doctor Campbell, a British medical practitioner in Menton. After Doctor Campbell's death in 1950 his daughter, Miss Maybud Campbell, turned the garden, which already had some good features, into a thickly planted collection of beautiful plants, most of them chosen for horticultural effect rather than

Villa Val Rahmeh at Menton. The simple formal garden was designed to set off the chunky Provençal architecture of the house. Both date from the 1920s.

botanic merit. Miss Campbell was, however, a distinguished botanist of the natural flora of the Alpes Maritimes. Her academic reputation enhanced her standing among the English community as a 'proper' gardener, and gave her the entrée to Kew. No doubt it also helped in her negotiations for the French Government to buy Val Rahmeh in 1956, since the garden is now maintained as 'the exotic botanic garden of Menton', a Mediterranean offshoot of the Jardin des Plantes in Paris.

The house is approached by a closely set avenue of Canary Island date palms, underplanted in the English manner with bergenias, ruscus and the spider plant, *Chlorophytum elatum*, to which the French authorities have since added bedding plants, fuchsias and streptocarpus. Behind the house is a respectable collection of other palms and cycads, also densely underplanted, as indeed is much of the garden. This helps to impart the air of a private garden, rather than a public amenity. This impression, however, is beginning to fade as the original horticultural effects slowly but inexorably disappear. Too much bare earth is now revealed between shrubs in borders

where once there would have been a thick herbaceous ground cover. A collapsed wooden pergola was recently replaced by a structure in tubular steel of the kind that is used for scaffolding.

The ground rises so steeply at the top of the plot that it would not have been possible to place the house at the highest point. It was built some way down on a level platform which holds not only the house but also a wide semicircular terrace to the front. This open area was balustraded with terracotta, whose colour matches the brick of the terrace and the patterned paths. Simple formal beds in the middle have pretty annual Iceland poppies around a permanent planting of strelitzias. This garden is in the shape of a quincunx, a charming concession to the French formal tradition. Sir Percy had made a small pool in one corner of the terrace, and Miss Campbell added a pergola: it and the house were covered with climbing plants, including the blue *Thunbergia grandiflora*, and *Beaumontia grandiflora*, which produces large white trumpets in spring. She chose this terrace for a small collection of citrus fruits, most notably some dainty kumquat

Villa Val Rahmeh at Menton in 1960. The plantswoman Maybud Campbell used giant-leaved house-plants for dramatic effect against the walls of the house.

trees, and planted three species of datura along the edge: white *Datura candida*, red *D. sanguinea*, and the pale orange *D. chlorantha*, which, together with a bush of the Cherokee rose, *Rosa laevigata*, cascades down the wall on the far side of the balustrade.

The original garden at Villa Val Rahmeh extended little beyond the great curving terrace in front of the house. Certainly, the spirit and materials of the garden below are very different. Gravel paths edged with stone follow the lie of the land as much as the contours allow, while rough dry-stone retaining walls support the beds where the plants are grown. The feel is that of a cottagey English plantswoman's garden: elderly spinster rather than serving General. Maybud Campbell exploited the crevices between the stones to grow bromeliads, succulents and bulbs of the kind that need sharp drainage. In the beds today there are vast tracts of *Agapanthus umbellatus* and *Amaryllis belladonna*, evidence that weaker

This arcaded pergola, heavy with wisteria, connects the house at Garoupe to a sheltered garden room.

Above: *Château de la Garoupe, Cap d'Antibes; the servants' wing looks on to this very pretty* jardin de curé, *planted with sweet-scented bedding plants.*

Below: *The sense of richness of Norah Warre's garden at Villa Roquebrune is well portrayed in this view of one of the terraces taken in 1979. Note the rich soil, built up by nearly eighty years of cultivation.*

Opposite: *Villa Val Rahmeh at Menton. A forest of Canary Island palms. Growing exotic palm trees has for long been one of the pleasures of gardening on the Riviera.*

Above: *La Mortola. The formal garden in front of the house. In 1928 Dorothy Hanbury replaced the seasonal displays of cacti and succulents with a permanent planting of sweet-smelling herbs and bright flowers.*

Right: *La Mortola. A view down the cypress avenue, known as the* viale nuovo.

Above: *La Mortola. Bertram Symons-Jeune designed this staircase to curve round a particularly steep part of the vista known as the* viale nuovo; *his sister Dorothy Hanbury planted the wisteria at eye-level along the sides.*

Below: *La Mortola. The lower part of the* viale nuovo, *designed by Bertram Symons-Jeune in the 1920s and originally planted with Australian species; now just a pretty walk through self-sown Judas trees.*

Above: *Clos du Peyronnet, 1974. An arcade of clipped cypresses foreshortens the perspectives in this tightly designed plantsman's garden at Menton-Garavan.*

Above: *Villa Cimbrone, Ravello. The belvedere terrace with its dramatic views of the sea is the lynchpin of the garden's design.*
Below: *A peristyle at Villa Rúfolo, Ravello, built or restored by Neville Reid in the 1860s and originally planted with wisterias and climbing roses.*
Overleaf: *One of the extravagant follies made from architectural salvage which Florence Trevelyan built in her garden at Taormina at the beginning of the century. It is perhaps the most original garden ever made by an English resident of Italy.*

plants have gone to the wall: they underline one of the differences between the Gallic approach to ornamental gardening and the British.

The lowest part is modern, planted by Miss Campbell in about 1950 and reached by a narrow cast-iron bridge over a public footpath. The site is small, but enlarged by the reflection of the sky in an irregular pool of still water. The planting here was given over to some more botanical trees and shrubs: an evergreen *Photinia davidsoniae*, handsome specimens of *Greyia sutherlandii*, a South African shrub with bright red flowers, and a large yellow-flowered *Caesalpinia sepiaria*, which ramps up into the trees around. It should however be said that these are the relics of a thick mixed planting whose character has slowly changed as plants have died out and not been replaced. Most of the survivors are shrubs, including the striking grey-leaved *Solanum marginatum*, which has intimidating spikes projecting upwards from the midribs of its leaves. Clumps of *Pancratium illyricum*, that unusual relation of the daffodil, have flourished here for forty years. There is also a useful collection of hybrid irises, most of them dating from the 1950s, when they must have been the latest horticultural introductions. All have thrived on neglect.

Apart from the formal areas, Villa Val Rahmeh is as English a garden as any, and has that special luxuriance which is common to English gardens on the Riviera. In planning and planting it the cultural needs of the plants were always uppermost. It grew and filled as the plants arrived and a suitable place was found for each of them. That suitability was decided by a plant's willingness to grow in a particular position and the aesthetic effect that one would have on its neighbours, the appropriateness of the planting in relation to other plants. The garden is small, only just over 1 ha (3 acres), and very personal. It contains the accumulated goodies of a knowledgeable plantswoman whose tastes and enthusiasms it reflects. Maybud Campbell obviously had a craze for salvias, and for irises too, but she filled the garden with a wide range of flowering plants. Some are of scientific importance, many are of botanical interest, but all were chosen for their horticultural qualities. The plants one finds in comparable gardens in England are here, but represented by species more adapted to a Mediterranean climate. *Primula × kewensis*, for example, is used as a spring bedding plant in the place of English primroses and polyanthus. There are nice contrasts between plants too. On the edge of the carriage circle, a line of old oil jars is set into a clipped cypress hedge. Spilling from the top are trailing plants of *Lotus berthelotii*, an endemic plant of Tenerife that is almost extinct in the wild, whose scarlet leguminous flowers and grey linear leaves contrast with the glaze of the oil jars and the glaucous green leaves of the cypresses. Near by, plants of plum-red *Tropaeoleum pentaphyllum* thread their way up into the hedge with all the apparent fragility but real vigour of *T. speciosum* as it weaves its way through the yew hedges of Scotland or Ireland. The combination is typically British in inspiration.

Were it in England, Villa Val Rahmeh would be open once or twice a year in aid of the National Gardens Scheme, and the County Organiser would speak of it as one of the most interesting and reliable gardens on his patch. It would be well known among the gardening *cognoscenti* as a source of good plants and good conversation, where a tour in the company of the owner would probably result in a carload of botanical booty for their own gardens. Indeed, it was so in Miss Campbell's day: she was a generous and discriminating garden owner, wary of fools but unstinting of help, advice and plants for those she liked and trusted, one of the pillars of the horticultural mafia on the Côte d'Azur. Villa Val Rahmeh was never a botanic garden, nor even the garden of a botanist. Despite the change of ownership many years ago, it retains the spirit of a private garden, full of English charm.

SINCE THEY accompanied houses that were occupied only for the winter season, the gardens of the Riviera have proved particularly transient. Few – very few indeed – have survived in a recognisable form since the turn of the century. Whereas many of the major Victorian and Edwardian gardens of England are in tolerably good shape, still occupied by the descendants of those who constructed them, only a handful of Riviera properties have enjoyed the same fortune. The structure of life on the Riviera has changed beyond recognition, in a way that country life in England has not. Clos du Peyronnet, at Menton-Garavan close to the Italian frontier, is an exception: it has remained in the ownership of one English family for three generations. It contains the best private garden to be made on the Riviera since the Second World War. The garden is small, perhaps just over half a hectare (1½ acres), and its story is briefly told by the marble inscription set at the top of a flight of steps:

Derick and Barbara Waterfield
and later their son Humphrey
created and loved this garden
1915–1971

Actually, it was Humphrey, rather than his parents, who was responsible for making the garden out of what had been a comparatively simple terraced site with conventional planting. Humphrey Waterfield was a painter, though he used to say that he only painted so that he could sell his work and spend the money on his garden. He also carried out a few commissions as a landscape gardener: best known is the garden he made for Lord and Lady de Ramsay at Abbots Ripton in Huntingdonshire. When he set to work upon his parents' garden at Menton, Waterfield borrowed a variety of features from other gardens and put them together in the Hidcote style. The stone arcade running out from the house to an open focal point is reminiscent of the great pergola at La Mortola, while the cypress arches were derived from the Moorish gardens of the Alhambra, cut neat and narrow but slightly wayward in shape so that they resemble nothing so much as distorted green smoke rings. The two main elements of the design are an ingenious use of water and the construction of long vistas linking together the garden rooms. The most arterial of these sequences ends in a huge framed view of the Mediterranean.

The approach to the house is unexceptional. The carriageway sweeps around an island bed which has

Barbara Waterfield and convalescing officers at Clos du Peyronnet in 1916. The small boys are Humphrey, who remade the garden in the Hidcote style in the 1950s, and Anthony, father of the present owner William Waterfield.

two enormous *Washingtonia filifera* and two *Erythea armata* as its dominant feature. Some young *Jubaea spectabilis* have recently been planted to provide the next generation of palms. Another relic of the pre-war planting near by is a large unpruned bush of the old tea rose 'Général Schablikine', of which Lord Brougham, who lived at Villa Eléonore at Cannes, correctly wrote a hundred years ago, 'this of all roses serves us the most faithfully and generously'. It is, however, immediately clear from the plants and plantings that this is no ordinary *belle époque* Riviera garden. A tall specimen of *Acanthus arboreus* flourishes at the side of the house, beside a spreading 2.5 m (8 ft) bush of another member of the Acanthaceae, *Adhatoda vasica*, with striking white flowers. Soon the cleverness of the design too is apparent. Immediately behind the house a narrow path runs between two stone arches: it has orange trees in long narrow beds on either side, and a double ribbon of irises. The very narrowness of this path and its plantings as they pass from one arch to the other gives an impression of length, and hence size, in what is really a very small space.

William Waterfield, Humphrey's nephew, who now owns Clos du Peyronnet, is another plantsman, but his uncle had a full-time gardener while he has none. A lesser enthusiast might in consequence have been tempted to alter the garden to make it more manageable, or even to sell up and move to an easier pitch. William Waterfield, however, is careful to preserve the structure as his uncle left it, while allowing such plants as irises and cyclamen to seed and naturalise in an informal, romantic, almost exuberant style. This has the further effect of unifying the different parts of the garden. William's own contribution has been to add new plants. He has been responsible, in particular, for placing potfuls of bulbs throughout the garden and has introduced many new species into cultivation from Cape Province. In this way he perpetuates one of the oldest traditions of English gardening on the Riviera, which began with Dr Bennet's experimental imports of plants from comparable climatic zones in the southern hemisphere. Many of the rarer plants growing at Clos du Peyronnet came originally from Lawrence Johnston, Norah Warre and Maybud Campbell, whose gardens once held fine plant collections, but are now impoverished by changes of ownership.

Lawrence Johnston is here in more than his plants, because the sequence of compartments recalls the great modern gardens of England made in the Hidcote style. One enclosure is almost entirely filled by a round basin of still water, very like the tank garden at Hidcote. Humphrey Waterfield's ideas of light and shade, colour and form, balance, texture and mass are all derived from Lawrence Johnston, so that Clos du Peyronnet is not only the best modern garden in the south of France, but also the best example outside England of a garden made in the Hidcote style. In one detail, however, the Waterfields have allowed themselves to go over the top. The house is a pseudo-Italianate villa, with a Doric colonnade along the front. A vast *Wisteria sinensis* has gripped the façade and crushed one of the columns in its stranglehold. Seldom is better displayed the folly of loving Nature more than Art.

PLANTSMANSHIP flourished on the Riviera after the Second World War. Money was no longer available for conspicuous display. Householders learned to cook for themselves, and ate better as a result: gardens improved as owners took a personal interest in the art of gardening. The Hungarian bibliophile and collector Arpad Plesch, of Villa La Léonina at Beaulieu, was an influential friend of English garden owners in the period after the Second World War. His particular interest was tropical fruit: luncheon guests would be offered a choice of different varieties of avocados, custard apples and bananas. He even succeeded in ripening papaya with the aid of plastic shelters. Another influence was Basil Leng, an English plantsman who grew South African bulbs, orchids and *Nelumbo nucifera* in his garden at Antibes. His main interest was said to be 'the palette of hues afforded by flowers and foliage': in other words, he used plants as the material for large colour compositions.

Best known among all plantsmen, however, was Charles de Noailles who started his garden at Grasse in 1947. It quickly became the most perfect example of an English garden made by a Frenchman. Roderick Cameron called it his 'ideal garden ... I can think of no other to compare in taste and ability'. It should be said that Noailles's mother was English. Certainly, his approach to gardening was entirely Anglo-Saxon: indeed he was for many years a Vice-president of the Royal Horticultural Society and numbered Russell Page, Lawrence Johnston and Norah Warre among his gardening friends in France.

Villa Noailles was on a steep slope, and the terraces of old olive orchards provided the garden with its structure. It was formal near the house, less so at the bottom. The sequence ran thus: a lily pool immedi-

Clos du Peyronnet in 1950. The wisteria which graces the colonnade at the front of the house has since crushed one of the columns in its stranglehold.

ately behind the house; a garden with small fountains; a long garden lined with lime trees with an English lawn in the middle, mixed borders at the sides and symmetrical steep-roofed pavilions, a tribute to Hidcote; steps down to a paeony garden with an obelisk at the end; a terrace planted in the natural style, dominated by a gargoyle; the swimming-pool, above the wisteria pavilion; a glade of magnolias irrigated by narrow stone channels and underplanted with narcissi, anemones and fritillaries; metasequoias and bog plants on either side of the stream; a rock garden; a camellia house; an aviary; more water-lily pools; a herb garden; a grove of bay trees underplanted with cyclamen; and finally the long Judas tree arcade which led back to the house. Russell Page suggested that every fifth Judas tree should be the white-flowered form, to contrast with the dark pink of the species. For Noailles it was the presence of water that brought the site to life and unified the parts: 'the most important thing in my garden is the spring from the mountain,' he declared; 'it provides the water supply for the fountains, cascades, streams

Villa Noailles at Grasse in 1970. The winter borders on either side of the lawn were planted with viburnums and wintersweet; the composition does credit to Charles de Noailles's English antecedents.

and water-basins. Some gardens are said to be per-fumed: I would say this one sings.'

The Villa Noailles garden is still privately owned, and now more difficult to visit than during its maker's lifetime, but there is one garden on the Côte d'Azur which was always difficult to get into – Villa Les Cèdres on Cap Ferrat. It belonged to a most extra-ordinary Frenchman called Marnier-Lapostolle, who lived there for about sixty years from the mid 1920s

and was a worthy successor to such botanist plants-men as Thuret. It began as the garden of Leopold II of the Belgians. Harold Peto re-worked the formal garden below the house in about 1911: he enclosed it with balustrading surmounted by swags, urns and allegorical statues. Beyond it, however, the design was more like an English landscape, where a valley of waterfalls created a microclimate unique on the Riviera. Marnier-Lapostolle himself regarded it as a tropical garden 'containing, as it does, some 15,000 different species including large collections of euphorbias, asclepiads, ferns, acacias, Araliaceae, and bromeliads'. He could still afford twenty-seven gardeners as late as 1975. The orchard ran to forty types of citrus fruit and the bamboo plantation numbered thirty different varieties, not to mention the hothouses where such exotic rarities as *Ravenala madagascariensis* and the jade vine *Strongylodon macrobotrys* flourished. Epiphytic tillandsias festooned the olive trees, while *Euryale ferox* and *Victoria cruziana*, as well as the better known *V. amazonica*, were grown in large pools. Despite their gigantic size, all three water lily species are annuals: not only did they flower every year but they also produced ripe seeds.

As a pioneer of plant conservation on the Riviera, Marnier-Lapostolle greatly regretted the passing of the gardens made by such botanist-gardeners as Nabonnand and Prochowsky. He also encouraged the creation of tropical effects, 'graceful in form, flexible and unusual', by using the palms, bamboos, agaves, aroids, bromeliads and banana trees 'which give the Côte d'Azur its individual character'. Marnier-Lapostolle was, however, careful to emphasise the seriousness of his scientific purpose and was not entirely sympathetic to the British amateur tradition. Specialist groups were sometimes admitted to his garden by prior appointment, casual individuals never. He had an almost pathological obsession with privacy. He forbade the taking of photographs and insisted on occasion that writers should not refer to his garden by name. A keen plantsman might be given a spare plant of a desirable rarity, but 'spare' would mean that Marnier had at least five other specimens, and he would probably take some more cuttings off the plant before handing it over. Ironically, among English residents on the Riviera there

was a feeling that he was not a 'proper' gardener. He was too much of a botanist, he did not really *love* plants, they said. He may have had twice as many plants as the Hanburys, but Les Cèdres was not a patch on La Mortola. That was quite different, that was a *true* garden.

References and Further Reading

Until recently, the only account of modern Riviera gardens was an undistinguished potboiler by the Vicomte de Noailles and Roy Lancaster published in English translation (in 1977) as *Mediterranean Plants and Gardens*. A practical modern guide to gardening in Riviera and other Mediterranean conditions is *The Mediterranean Gardener* by Hugo Latymer (London, 1990). A *Country Life* article on 23 November 1929 and Audrey Le Lièvre's short piece on Boccanegra published in *The Garden* in November 1987 are the only accounts I have discovered of this interesting garden. Serre de la Madone is poorly documented: as well as Fred Whitsey's report in *Country Life*, there is a contemporary article by the Marquis Ernest de Ganay in *La Gazette Illustrée des Amateurs des Jardins 1936–37* and the garden gets a bit of a mention in Ethne Clarke's oddly flat study, *Hidcote – The Making of a Garden* (London, 1989). Villa Noailles has been described by Fred Whitsey in *Country Life* on 10 July 1980, and by Paul Miles in *The Garden* in September 1987. The best piece on Villa Roquebrune is by Basil Leng and Patrick M. Synge in *The Journal of the Royal Horticultural Society (RHSJ)* in October 1966. Villa Val Rahmeh has appeared in *Country Life* and the Musée Nationale d'Histoire Naturelle publishes an incomplete *Catalogue des plantes cultivées au Jardin Botanique Exotique de Menton*. My quotations from the thoughts of Marnier-Lapostolle come from a short piece published in the *RHSJ* in August 1958.

Chapter Four

LA MORTOLA

Botany versus Horticulture

N O VISITOR to La Mortola ever forgets his first sight of it. One of the great experiences of a garden lover's life is to pass through the gates of Villa Hanbury and discover the garden spread out below, a great wooded hillside dropping first steeply, then gently down 259 steps to the rocky shore beneath, an enchanted landscape of palms, cypresses, olives, cycads and Judas trees that stretches to the pines by the edge of the sea. The garden displays itself openly and immediately as you enter its portals. As you descend towards the *palazzo*, the views and prospects come and go, but the distant perspective is lost, so that it is the memory of that splendid first overview which urges exploration in all directions at once. That, and the vistas and plants encountered on the descent. Sometimes you drop quickly from one level to the next; sometimes you pass slowly from one end of a terrace to the other, making a leisurely progress. The central structure of the garden is the long straight avenue that always frames a distant view of the sea (all paths ultimately lead down to it) while the botanical and horticultural effects are spread upon the terraces, bidding the visitor to dally among the flowers and take note of their beauty and their names. No other garden offers such equality between the whole and its parts, between the design and the planting.

La Mortola is the first and last promontory on the Riviera dei Fiori, close to the French frontier, 11

km (7 miles) west of Ventimiglia. It was bought by Thomas Hanbury on 2 May 1867, and for nearly a hundred years he and his family lived and made a garden there, the finest ever made by Englishmen abroad. The Hanburys claimed that La Mortola was named after the myrtle that grew wild on the headland, but the locals say that the name means a place of burial, and point to the tall cypresses in the garden as proof of their contention. There is some uncertainty about the size of the Hanburys' garden. A German friend of theirs wrote that it had 20 ha (50 acres) in 1876. Thomas Hanbury himself said that the original area was 40 ha. By 1912, the curator was claiming that it totalled 45 ha, while the present administrators admit only to 18 ha, of which 10 ha are garden and 8 ha are natural woodland. It is known that some additions were made to the estate after 1867, but it is also clear from the papers of Thomas Hanbury's eldest brother Daniel that the whole of the site of the present garden was part of the original purchase. The soil is a nummulitic limestone, heavy and clayey. A small travertine deposit of sandy soil in one part of the garden, although somewhat calcareous, suits such fine-rooted plants as Proteaceae and melaleucas. Roderick Cameron said that he had not seen them anywhere else on the coast, 'and quite a few people I know have tried to grow them, but never with any success'.

Thomas Hanbury was a Quaker who worked in China from 1853 to 1872 as a cloth merchant, buying silk for the European market. He was there at the time of the Taiping Rebellion, a period of crisis during which many rich Chinese made over their properties to him in the belief that there was no threat to the life or property of an Englishman. Hanbury kept them safe until the rebellion had

---

La Mortola in 1905, a photograph taken by Ellen Willmott, whose house at Boccanegra was on the next headland, about a mile away. Note the strong growth of the pine, Pinus canariensis, *on the right, and the climbing rose in the foreground.*

Daniel Hanbury (1825–75), the botanist brother of Sir Thomas, who was largely responsible for laying out and planting the garden at La Mortola in its early years.

subsided and then handed them back to their former owners. This honourable behaviour gave him great renown among the Chinese: they trusted him, and he prospered in business. In 1867, he returned to Europe on extended leave to buy property and find a wife. It was while he was wintering at Menton that he first saw the ruins of La Mortola.

Augustus Hare visited La Mortola in the last years before Thomas Hanbury bought it. He was spending a winter at Menton in 1861 and took a boat trip to Ventimiglia, the birthplace of Julius Caesar. Hare described how, on turning the corner of the promontory 'one reaches a quaint dilapidated building, with a solitary palm tree and some old cypresses beside it, which ... has an open loggia covered with frescos'. On shore, he found that the rooms of the house, then known as Palazzo Orengo, were in the last stage of decay, and that many ceilings had collapsed. La Mortola was a remote spot, for the railway stopped at Nice, and visitors from Menton had to travel by diligence along the old corniche road. Its

surface was rough and perilous, so most travellers first saw La Mortola, as Hanbury himself did, from a boat. Viewed from the east, the ruins of the house stood proud on the promontory, as is clear from some early sketches by Daniel Hanbury. Rather than restore it, Thomas Hanbury built a new villa of white marble, a sumptuous patrician palace to hold his collection of Roman antiquities and oriental treasures. This son of the British Empire was greatly attracted by the history of ancient Rome. He excavated and preserved the remains of the Via Aurelia within the estate; its route cannot be traced beyond the boundaries as it has been infilled and built over.

Daniel Hanbury (1825–75) was a distinguished botanist. He had accompanied Sir Joseph Hooker on a collecting expedition to the Himalayas and had visited the Holy Land to study the effect of excessive grazing on the cedars of Lebanon. In 1874 he published his major work, *Pharmacographia*, written jointly with Friedrich Flückiger of Strasbourg. Daniel Hanbury's energy and enthusiasm and, above all, the contacts he made when he was treasurer of the Linnean Society, are essential to an understanding of how the gardens of La Mortola grew so quickly in size and fame. When Thomas returned with his wife to China, Daniel was left in charge.

Daniel Hanbury remembered the overgrazing on Mount Lebanon and attempted to re-establish the *garrigue* at La Mortola. The estate was stoutly walled to put an end to the raiding parties of peasant farmers and their livestock, who pillaged the hillside for firewood and food. Seeds of evergreen trees and shrubs, including the holm oak *Quercus ilex* and buckthorn *Rhamnus alaternus*, were scattered all round the edge. On his first visit Daniel noticed that no species of cistus grew wild in the grounds of the *palazzo*. He collected seed of *albidus* and *salvifolius* from nearby Mortola Superiore and sowed them in the valley to the west of the house, where they soon became established. Aleppo pines *Pinus halepensis* regenerated spontaneously in the same valley. The famous plant hunter Augustine Henry considered the stand to be proof of the recuperative power of a forest: 'it has grown from a few sparse trees without other care than protection from man and goats, cutting or grazing having been prohibited for many years', he noted in 1912. Down by the shore Daniel planted umbrella pines *Pinus pinaster*, which are now beautiful, rugged trees. In December 1867 he also put in twelve young carobs *Ceratonia siliqua*: fifty years later the tallest was more than 8 m (27 ft) high and 2.5 m (8 ft) in circumference.

The Palazzo Orengo and the site of the future gardens, sketched by Daniel Hanbury in 1867, the year that his brother Thomas purchased the estate.

Daniel Hanbury was a pharmacologist, a partner in the family firm of Allen Hanbury & Barry, with a special interest in medical and economic plants. He grew *Aloe ferox* because it was the source of the aloe drug, and a specimen of *Catha edulis*, an Ethiopian member of the Celastraceae, now 8 m (27 ft) high, because the leaves may be used as an infusion, or chewed, for their stimulant properties. Victorian botanists were attracted to useful plants. Hanbury was able to obtain seed of *Styrax officinalis*, the source of storax, and tubers of the Florentine iris, which yields orris root. He planted the wax tree *Rhus succedanea*, and its close relation *R. verniciflua*, from which Japanese lacquer is made. The blue dye plant *Indigofera tinctoria* and the oil tree of Morocco *Argania sideroxylon* were also successfully established. In October 1871, two trees of the Chilean *Quillaja saponaria*, from whose bark saponine is obtained, arrived from the Jardin Thuret at Antibes; forty years later, they were 15.5 m (50 ft) high. Among the fruiting plants first introduced to Italy and the Riviera at La Mortola for the study of their commercial potential are the passion fruit *Passiflora edulis*, the guava *Psidium dulcis* and the thorny *Dory-alis caffra* from south-east Africa, planted by Daniel in 1872. He also grew several forms of the jujube *Zizyphus sativa*, a popular native of the Mediterranean; the pawpaw *Carica papaya*; and *Pseudocydonia sinensis*, the giant quince, whose fruits were to become very popular on the Riviera.

Above all, the brothers made a collection of citrus fruit. It excited much comment from visitors, since many varieties were thought to have a medicinal or economic use. Through his extensive connections in the Far East Thomas Hanbury was able to obtain stock of all the cultivars then unknown in western Europe; these included forms of mandarin which were later grown commercially, and the citron 'Buddha's Finger', whose fruit is split into several digit-like segments, acquired from an English correspondent in Shanghai in 1880. By 1890 there were more than twenty varieties of citrus fruit in the Hanbury collection, although the coveted cultivar known as 'Bizzaria', a graft hybrid between the orange and the lemon, was not procured until 1908.

When the Hanbury brothers set to planting the garden, they turned to the nurseries of Huber at Hyères and Nabonnand at Golfe Juan. Thomas and

'Buddha's Finger', an aberrant form of citron, drawn in 1890 for The Gardener's Chronicle *from a specimen in the Hanburys' citrus collection. The magazine had a long association with La Mortola, which contributed to its reputation among professional English gardeners.*

Daniel bought in large quantities from the start: 20 callistemons, 40 eucalyptus species and 80 varieties of acacia, for example. Not every introduction was successful. *Howea forsteriana* and *Castanospermum australe* flourish at Menton-Garavan 4 km (2½ miles) away, but not at La Mortola. *Lagerstroemia indica* can be grown at San Dalmazzo di Tenda some miles up the Roja valley, but does not succeed at Villa Hanbury on the coast. Thomas Hanbury tried unsuccessfully for many years to establish two important economic plants, coffee *Coffea arabica* and tea *Camellia sinensis*. Sugar cane *Saccharum officinarum* never really prospered and lychees *Litchi sinensis* were another failure.

As well as local nurseries, plants arrived from botanic institutes and private collections. These included Gustave Thuret's famous garden at Antibes, and the Jardin des Plantes in Paris, which gave Daniel several new plants when he visited it on his way to La Mortola in May 1868. Indeed the list of sources from which plants were obtained reads like a horticultural and botanical *Who's Who* of the Victorian world. Correspondents sent seeds from botanic gardens in Germany and eastern Europe, including Darmstadt, Prague and Tiflis, as well as France, Italy, the Americas, Australia and the Far East. German institutes were always to the fore: Daniel had built close connections with academics in central Europe, and until the First World War the curators and administrators of the garden were usually Germans.

La Mortola owes much to the teutonic tradition of systematic botany and flair for horticultural administration.

The Hanburys were lucky during the garden's early years to have as their head gardener and curator Ludwig Winter, a young German who had started work at the Tuileries but had been sacked by the Empress Eugénie for singing the republican anthem '*La Marseillaise*'. He stayed at La Mortola from 1868 to 1875 and went on to found a large and successful nursery at Bordighera, ending up a Cavaliere of the Cross of the Crown of Italy. His influence was decisive in establishing the design, plantings and systems of work at La Mortola; his contribution to the success of his employers' plans is comparable to that of Henry Cocker at Villa Táranto sixty years later. His departure coincided with the death from typhoid fever of Daniel Hanbury in March 1875. Thomas Hanbury was left to carry on alone the work of establishing a major botanic collection, and returned to Europe for good.

In 1876, Friedrich Flückiger informed the visitor to La Mortola, in language that recalls Smollett's observations on Villa Borghese at Rome, that 'he who looks for fountains, curiously-cut hedges, kiosques, artfully-formed paths, grottoes, and gay ribbon gardening will be disappointed'. Thomas Hanbury's intentions were twofold: first to undertake serious scientific experiments in acclimatisation, and second to make a collection that was both useful and instructive. He saw his garden as a site for the acclimatisation of plants from all over the world: the contemporary wisdom was that subtropical plants might be persuaded to adapt to the temperate conditions of northern Europe if they were first hardened off in the halfway climate of a Mediterranean garden. Acclimatisation was attempted the other way, too. Every year Thomas Hanbury brought fresh supplies of the dainty *Pinguicula grandiflora* from its native rocks in the Roja valley, to plant them at La Mortola on a wet wall. They never survived the transition from alpine to Mediterranean conditions, but Hanbury kept alive the hope that they might adapt to the change.

Early accounts of the garden make clear what pleasure the Hanburys had from their collections of plants. Visitors too made solemn lists of the rarities, detailed their provenance and described their distinguishing characteristics. Collecting proved to be a family weakness: *Caltha polypetala* was introduced from the Vatican gardens by Thomas Hanbury's daughter Hilda in 1902. Since the giant Caucasian kingcup was not then grown elsewhere in Europe, and was said to be closely protected by the Swiss Guard, it would be interesting to know just how she obtained material of this species.

Many of the exotic trees at La Mortola date from the early days of the garden, although most of the eucalyptus were lost during the Second World War, and there is no trace of the famous specimen of *Pinus canariensis*, which by the outbreak of the First World War was over 23 m (75 ft) high and 2.5 m (8 ft) in girth. The collection of cacti and succulents, now rather depleted, which occupies a hot open bank at the top, was for many years the most comprehensive on the Riviera. The displays which used to be mounted on the terrace below the house were dominated by a plant of *Euphorbia abyssinica* which grew to 8 m (27 ft) before succumbing to a hard winter. By 1912 there were no fewer than 112 species of agave and 115 mesembryanthemums. The collection of bright blue, scarlet, and crimson salvias from America was another of the earliest at La Mortola. It was said to comprise over sixty species by 1889: the genus has remained popular with plantsmen on the Riviera. Bamboos were fewer in number, but they gave a lesson in using the gifts of Nature. Guides to the garden, among them Thomas Hanbury's father Daniel Bell Hanbury (1794–1882), would explain the many uses of bamboo for food and fodder, fences, wattle work, baskets, hats, fibre, pipes, rafts, bridges, furniture, houses, rakes, harrows, vessels, weapons and musical instruments. Its protean adaptability appealed deeply to the utilitarian Victorians.

The garden always had certain ornamental features. Most renowned was the main pergola, or *topia* as they called it, using local dialect: it followed the curve of the hill for nearly 300 m (330 yd) and was according to the Hanburys the longest in Europe. Each of its thirty-nine columns was host to two or three different plants. In 1888 these included *Akebia quinata*, *Cantua dependens*, *C. pendulifolia*, and *Quisqualis indica*, whose seeds are used in India as a vermifuge. The pergola gave such an impression of solidity and permanence that by 1893 a correspondent of *The Gardener's Chronicle* referred to the structure as 'very quaint and old'. He further noted that *Tecoma jasminoides* grew not only on one of the columns but also 10 m (30 ft) up the house, and that *Bignonia grandiflora* had climbed to the top of a 12 m (40 ft) cypress.

The names of several plants are associated with the garden. Best known in Britain is a form – possibly a hybrid – of *Rosa brunonii* known as 'La Mortola',

which is widely grown in the south of England. A magnificent example covers the south wall of the neo-Byzantine museum building at Winchester College. Then there are two plants named *hanburyana*, a hybrid aloe which flowers late in the season, and a mimosa which is a cross between *Acacia podalyriifolia* and *A. dealbata*, and makes a small tree, remarkable for its early flowering and profusion. It originated in Ludwig Winter's garden at Bordighera, not in the garden of La Mortola itself. Its hybrid origin shows in its foliage, some leaves being simple and others pinnate. These three plants alone would be sufficient to immortalise La Mortola and its owners.

Scientific experiment was endemic to La Mortola. In the 1890s, Thomas Hanbury introduced from America the moth *Pronuba yuccasella*, which is the only insect able to fertilise yuccas. Unfortunately, as it is so small and only visible at night during a few weeks of the year, no one could ascertain whether

A 1930s view of the house at La Mortola, showing the Italian tower added by Thomas Hanbury, photographed through the branches of a clematis-draped olive tree near the top of the garden.

the moth had established itself. In 1897 and 1898, however, the curator found seed capsules on *Yucca flaccida*, and some exhibited the peculiar holes from which the larvae had escaped. This was thought to be the first time yuccas had set seed in Europe. The Hanburys built a botanical museum, a herbarium and a library at La Mortola. In 1889 Thomas published the first edition of *Hortus Mortolensis*, which included a complete list of the plants in the garden. It was compiled by the head gardener Gustaf Cronemeyer, edited by Professor Penzig of Modena and distributed to all botanic gardens 'with permission to draw upon the collection for scientific purposes'. When the second edition was prepared by the then curator Kurt Dinter in 1897, it listed over 3,600 species. For many years too the *Index Seminum Mortolensis* seed list was circulated to botanic gardens; it contained the names of 557 species when first issued in 1883 and was endorsed with La Mortola's current Wants List. No less than 6,378 packets of seed were sent out free of charge in 1900, 9,331 in 1902, and 13,085 in 1908.

In 1874 Thomas Hanbury sent *The Gardener's Chronicle* the first of many lists of plants flowering at La Mortola during the course of January: it had 103 names. In 1886 the list totalled 516 and he wondered whether it was 'a benevolent act to publish a list of over 500 species of plants blossoming in the open air at a place thirty hours distant by rail, to be read by those compelled to endure the full rigour of a northern winter?' It later became the custom to send the magazine a list of the plants actually in flower on New Year's Day. It was not always printed in full, but the number of species and some of the more interesting plants were always given prominence in the magazine. In a year without frost, the number would be close to four hundred. There were 294 in 1895, 372 in 1896, 405 in 1898, 401 in 1906, 405 in 1926, 265 in 1927, 376 in 1937, and 232 still in 1985. Hanbury often corresponded with English gardening journals and established a special relationship with *The Gardener's Chronicle*. Since most readers were working gardeners rather than garden owners, his willingness to contribute to their magazine gave him and his garden particular prestige among professional horticulturists. La Mortola came to represent much that was best about English endeavour abroad. When it was said that a tree of *Eucalyptus globulus* had attained a height of 17 m (60 ft) and a girth of nearly 1.5 m (5 ft) in a mere seven years at the Hanbury Gardens, no one doubted the truth of the statement.

Meteorological records were kept at La Mortola for many years. The average annual rainfall is about 850 mm (33 in) and there are between fifty and sixty rainy days a year. Cisterns and pipework underlie the whole estate. Sometimes the roots of a eucalyptus find their way into a well or underground tank and burst its walls. As with all Riviera gardens, the occasional severe frost causes losses. In January 1901 $-4°C$ was experienced and $-9°C$ in January 1925. The natural reaction of the garden superintendent was to make a complete list of all the plants that had suffered damage and send it to *The Gardener's Chronicle* for publication so that other residents of the Riviera could benefit from the experience. After the hard winter of 1954–5, Dorothy Hanbury-Forbes wrote that the garden had endured temperatures of $-3°C$ to $-5°C$ for nearly four weeks, with the loss of many plants.

Solandras, all daturas, reinworthias, streptosolens and most of the *Convolvulus* family, especially the lovely hanging *C. cneorum*, and the variety *C. floridus* (of which even the bark is split open by frost) look very sick. The bark of even old trees of *Tecoma stans* is also cracked open by frost. Slopes of *Aster fruticosus* [syn. *Diplopappus fruticulosus*] look as if a fire had swept over them, and the dark glossy leaves of the clivias look like shreds of dirty white paper. Genistas and jacarandas have suffered, too, but will I think recover. Not a single mesembryanthemum is left!

Nevertheless, among the plants that appear to have stood up to this weather were the citrus, a surprising survival, since they were among the most severely damaged in the equally hard winter of 1985–6.

For its first fifty years, La Mortola was an example of Quaker principles put into practice. The Hanburys used their wealth to display the wonders of God's handiwork and to demonstrate the usefulness to man of many members of the plant kingdom. The moral seriousness of their undertaking was emphasised by such inscriptions as the plaque set into the wall at the end of the long pergola which reads 'AUDIVERUNT VOCEM DOMINI DEI DEAMBULANTIS IN HORTO' ('They heard the voice of the Lord God walking in the garden'). There are quotations too from Martial and Dante, among others, on the house and at suitable points in the garden. In accordance with his tenets, Thomas Hanbury used his wealth for public benefit. One of his first concerns was to build schools in the surrounding countryside for the children of those who worked for him, who had hitherto received no formal education. Later he extended this to all the children of adjoining villages. In 1868, Thomas Hanbury was made a Cavaliere, later Commendatore, of the Order of St Maurice and St Lazarus, and in 1885 and 1888 a Cavaliere and Commendatore of the Cross of the Crown of Italy. In 1892 he gave to the University of Genoa land for the endowment of a garden for a botanic institute, a garden that was to make a particular study of medicinal plants. In 1901 he received an English knighthood, and in 1903 he gave the sixty acres of Wisley gardens to the Royal Horticultural Society.

It is commonly said that the Hanburys were responsible for initiating the cut-flower industry on the Riviera dei Fiori. In fact, the Italian growers themselves organised the expansion of the trade in cut flowers, especially carnations and roses, and built the local markets and packing centres at Ospedaletti (1894), Bordighera (1898) and Ventimiglia (1904). Not until 1914 did Thomas Hanbury's son Cecil contribute to the project to construct a regional centre for the cut-flower market at San Remo. It should

however be said that the Hanburys were the leading local benefactors and usually backed any public works that might bring prosperity to the region.

From the earliest years, visitors were welcome at La Mortola. Permission to visit was at first given only on written application but, after a few years, the gardens were opened to all comers on Mondays and Fridays throughout the season. In the winter and spring of 1908–9 there were 7,295 paying visitors, by 1924 nearer 10,000; the takings went to support local charities. Personal callers were treated handsomely. The distinguished gardener Canon Henry Ellacombe (1822–1916) described how, after a lunch party at La Mortola, the porch of the house was filled with cut flowers for the visitors to take away. Soon public figures too began to come to the garden. In 1882, Queen Victoria, during her stay at Mentone, visited La Mortola twice and painted the greys and greens of the trees below the house. In her wake came the Empress Frederick of Germany, Edward Prince of Wales and members of the Italian and German royal families. Books about the Riviera proliferated, and so

The elegant figure of Dorothy Hanbury – she was 6 ft 3 in. tall – in 1927, reclining against the windswept trunks of Pinus pinaster, *planted on the seashore by Daniel Hanbury some sixty years earlier.*

did the variety of superlatives applied to La Mortola. Stéphen Liégeard commented crisply in 1887, '*La flore exotique éclate surtout d'une puissance inconnue. A coups de volonté, de goût et de bank-notes, le Génie de cette solitude y a vidé la corbeille des deux mondes.*' By 1892, the gardens were described by Hugh MacMillan, an Anglican parson, as 'one of the principal show-places of the Riviera'. MacMillan was very much taken by the range of exotic trees and shrubs, but felt that the results imparted 'an appearance so novel and curious that the first feeling in the mind of every visitor is one of absolute bewilderment'. MacMillan sought refuge in the beauty of the site: 'the views of the romantic coast as far as San Remo and of the deep blue far-spreading Mediterranean – seen through the trees and transfigured by a light, crystalline in its purity, which makes even the commonest object a picture – seem like glimpses of paradise'. In 1893 Sir Joseph Hooker, by then Director of Kew, wrote that it was 'a garden of exotic plants, which in point of richness and interest has no rival among the principal collections of living plants in the world'; and when Augustus Hare returned to the Riviera in 1896 he called La Mortola the most important private garden in Europe, 'more beautiful than anything out of the *Arabian Nights*'.

Sir Thomas Hanbury died in 1907, but his widow had an able and devoted curator in Alwin Berger. Lady Hanbury encouraged him to prepare another catalogue of the plants, published in 1912 as the third edition of *Hortus Mortolensis*. It listed about 5,500 taxa and contained botanic descriptions of several new species. Berger could write truthfully and with pride that 'no efforts have been spared to develop La Mortola into an important subtropical botanic garden'. The seed lists, the international correspondence, the acquisitions to the collections, the reports to *The Gardener's Chronicle* and the stream of visitors continued right up until 1914. Lady Hanbury was already back in England at the outbreak of war. Berger returned to Germany.

It was a reduced La Mortola that Cecil Hanbury inherited when his mother died in 1920. Cecil was quite different from his father. He preferred the life of a Dorset landowner on his estate at Kingston Maurwood to that of a Shanghai trader. Only his youngest brother Horace made a career in the Far East: Cecil became instead a figure of the establishment. He abandoned his Quaker upbringing and adopted the Anglican faith. From 1924 until his death in 1937 he was a Conservative Member of Parliament, whereas Sir Thomas had been a Liberal, even

a Radical. These changes of priority affected La Mortola, because while Cecil Hanbury followed a career of public service in England, for which he was knighted in 1935, he left much of the thinking about La Mortola and its garden to his wife.

This transfer of authority might have proved disastrous, because Cecil had married a woman of quite exceptional silliness. Dorothy Symons-Jeune was brave, proud and amusing, but a social and political liability. She treated La Mortola as her personal fiefdom, and used it to attest her own glory. She loved its wild romantic attributes: the yellow Banksian rose which draped itself all over the olive trees, the rollicking masses of multicoloured geraniums, the rocky promontory where in winter the great waves broke in spray 12 m (40 ft) high and splashed the windswept pines – an awesome sight – and 'the nice wholesome smell of fresh cow dung being dug into the earth to enrich next year's floraison'. She had a great admiration for Mussolini, and was proud to be the first Englishwoman given the right to wear the *distintivo*, the badge of the Fascists, and to have joined the woman of Ventimiglia when they gave their gold wedding rings to the state to buy arms for the Italian campaign in Abyssinia.

Dorothy ('Dodo') Hanbury was convinced that pretty flowers made a garden. This conviction has long been common among the English, but in Dodo Hanbury's case it took the form of revelling in a riot of colour and disparaging all botanists, horticulturists, garden designers and possessors of expert knowledge, unless they were related to her by blood or marriage. She upset the botanical friends of La Mortola by declaring that 'most gardens have too many plants' and adding 'yes, botanists and gardeners, I am going to say boldly that there can be too many labels and specimens visible'. Dodo Hanbury did not of course dislike plants, but she thought La Mortola had far too many of the wrong sort, and recalled that one of the things that struck her when she first visited the garden was its very flowerlessness. Many of her ideas were excellent, and much of her work was an improvement to the garden. She redesigned parts to give the garden a firmer and more logical structure; she used colour to considerable effect; and she added a more specifically Italian overlay that increased its beauty. It was the

---

The delicious cupola at the top of the long avenue known as the Viale Nuovo, surrounded by agaves, dasylirions and spiky plants growing on the steep hillside.

manner of her bearing that gave such offence, and her behaviour towards the garden, the staff, the botanists, the visitors, her children and even to Cecil himself. Even now, thirty years after her death, it is difficult to find anyone on the Riviera who has a kind word for her.

Cecil and Dodo Hanbury's structural alterations to the garden solved the problems of levels, perspective and direction which had not been properly tackled by Sir Thomas. Dodo excused him on the grounds that he had not been able to acquire all the estate at once, and therefore had had to design the garden piecemeal, which was not strictly speaking true. Her brother Bertram Symons-Jeune was a competent gentlemen garden designer and cut a new vertical axis through the garden which now serves as a central point of reference. Cecil Hanbury called it the Great Glade, but it is actually a long, straight walk which begins at a point near the top of the garden known as the Quattro Stagioni, where a limestone cliff falls to a steep slope covered with agaves, aloes, opuntias, yuccas and mesembryanthemums. The vista leads from the cupola beneath this garden of succulent plants, down a cypress avenue and along a new path called the Viale Nuovo, to a distant glimpse of the seashore and the Mediterranean. The straightness of this splendid cutting down the hillside gave rise to new problems of level because at a certain point it descended too steeply even for steps. Bertram Symons-Jeune resolved the difficulties by building a curving staircase to the side. It widens as it goes, and is one of the garden's most handsome features. The sides of the steps are bordered with wisterias which run up at a height to make the flowers accessible to eye and nose. One of these plants, a pink form of *Wisteria sinensis*, wraps itself around the old oil jars which are an important detail of both this part of the garden and the Viale Nuovo. But the staircase was originally arched over by Japanese cherries underplanted with Darwin tulips, and the coping covered by pink *Rosa × anemonoides*, a very 1920s combination.

Straightening the main lines at La Mortola had the effect of making it more Italian, reminiscent of the great baroque gardens of Tuscany and the Campagna. This was deliberate. Dodo Hanbury had already added Italianate formal gardens to Kingston Maurwood House in 1918–20 and was keen to dis-

tinguish La Mortola from other Riviera gardens. She Italianised every part by the insertion of long vistas, steps, pools, fountains, balustrading, urns, columns and statues among the cypresses and olives that were the background to the collections. She also made three small formal gardens in the Italian style in the lee of the house, by no means exact copies of original Italian models, but essentially Italian in inspiration. One was a shady garden, sheltered and secret, full of tree paeonies and Madonna lilies in spring and early summer. The second was incongruously planted with members of the South African daisy family in hot colours of scarlet, orange, yellow and brown. The third was an enclosed courtyard with Roman statues and white *Clematis armandii*. On the terrace in front of the house itself, the gardenesque displays of succulent plants which Thomas Hanbury had mounted were replaced by a parterre of sweetly scented plants set within hedges of lavender and rosemary. Most people would agree that the Italianisation of La Mortola in the 1920s was an unqualified improvement.

The botanic character of La Mortola was not entirely lost by the prettifying of the garden. It remained open to members of the public and visits were no longer limited to Mondays and Fridays. Its popularity inspired the Prince of Monaco to build an exotic garden as a tourist attraction on the cliffs above Monte Carlo. The collections were increased and the catalogue of plants in the garden was reprinted as the fourth *Hortus Mortolensis* in 1937. This lists 6,300 species, prefaced by a long and embarrassing introduction by Dodo Hanbury. The *Index Seminum* flourished and included as many as 2,000 different taxa; 13,000 packets of seed were sent out in 1924, and by 1937 the garden staff were distributing 18,000 a year. The garden was also developed as an auxiliary school for young gardeners. Every year, starting in 1927, one or more students from Kew would be sent to study at La Mortola for a period of six months or longer, the time to count as part of their Kew training; a young Italian travelled to England in exchange.

Dodo Hanbury was nevertheless more interested in creating an ornamental garden than maintaining a botanic collection. She observed that La Mortola was full of fine specimens which had been acquired without regard for how they would look when juxtaposed with other plants. 'Things had been planted out one here and another there,' she recalled some years later; 'everything was all mixed and muddled, and planted with no regard for appropriateness.

Part of the collection of cacti and succulents surviving at La Mortola in 1990; the trunk-like trees are Aloe elephantipes.

Papyrus plants around a vase brought from China by Thomas Hanbury, photographed by Ellen Willmott, c. 1905.

Under olive trees would be aloes (and how they swear!). Round the uneven stone edges (looking like decayed teeth) of tanks – one could not call them pools – would be dry and prickly cactus!' Dodo Hanbury set about replanting the garden in accordance with contemporary tastes, grouping and massing plants for decorative effect: she even argued that when such principles were applied to the sub-tropical, succulent and Australian collections they helped to create a more rational botanic display. 'There are three very simple rules to bear in mind,' she wrote in 1937: 'never plant singly, do not mix families of plants which by the laws of nature could never have grown together, and study your colour schemes.' In practice she usually broke one or more of these rules. Typical was her treatment of the Viale Nuovo, which was originally planted with eucalyptus, metrosideros, melaleucas, *Araucaria bidwellii* and other Australian trees. She added wide borders in blue and grey, edged with lavender, ageratum, stachys, iris, artemisias, salvias and the huge blue shrubby *Echium fastuosum*.

Dodo expanded the nursery so that by 1924 as many as 40,000 plants were grown in pots for the

year's bedding out; this included sheets of rich blue cinerarias, backed by orange *Streptosolen jamesonii* and bordered with yellow polyanthus. The grass slopes were re-sown every autumn. Plants were encouraged to naturalise and create drifts of colour, including *Cyclamen persicum*, freesias, and sparaxis (chequered hybrids between *Sparaxis tricolor* and *S. grandiflora*) in scarlet, vermillion, carmine, garnet, violet, purple, rose, lilac and white. Dodo said that she was continuing a tradition started by Sir Thomas Hanbury in whose day cyclamen, *Primula sinensis* and epacris had been grown for bedding out (contemporaries said it was only to satisfy the tastes of the Italian gardeners) and she used to wonder whether her father-in-law would have liked her new schemes. She decided that he would have approved of them, because she knew his object had been the same as hers, 'to beautify this sea-kissed mountainside'.

It must be said that Dodo Hanbury was not only instrumental in changing the garden from a botanic to a horticultural cynosure in the years before the Second World War, but she was also largely responsible for restoring it in the different financial circumstances afterwards. It is undoubtedly to Dodo Hanbury that La Mortola owes its survival. During the war the library, the botanic laboratory and much of the herbarium were destroyed, while the house was reduced almost to ruins and the garden neglected. Lady Hanbury could have broken the estate into building plots, sold up, restored the family fortune and retired to England. She chose instead to move into the head gardener's cottage and to restore, replant and publicise the garden. By the early 1950s La Mortola had recovered some of its pre-war splendour.

Lady Hanbury gave La Mortola to the Italian state in 1960; some say she did so to prevent her sons from inheriting it. It was leased and, in 1964, transferred to the Istituto Internazionale di Studi Liguri di Bordighera, which managed the garden well until 1979, when financial constraints obliged the institute to discontinue its work and even to renounce ownership. There followed several years of total abandonment, a time when the gates were left open and plants stolen or disfigured; even the structure began to collapse. In 1983 the garden was transferred to the University of Genoa, whose botanic faculty Sir Thomas Hanbury had founded in 1892. The university was slow to take action. It is said that during this period of neglect, and partly as a result of severe frosts in 1985 and 1986, the number of species grown at La Mortola sank to less than 1,500. Drought, overcrowding and shading accounted for many of the losses, which particularly affected the collections of aeoniums, echeverias, agaves, aloes, haworthias and gasterias, and even such trees as acacias and melaleucas. The steps, terraces and retaining walls decayed to such an extent that only one third of the garden could safely be opened to the public; it was not possible to obtain public liability insurance for the rest.

Since 1986, however, the *Sopraintendenza della Liguria*, the regional office of the Arts Ministry, has poured money into the garden to make good the essential structure. Walls have been repaired, which has often involved stripping back stone facing and digging out the soil behind; the whole system of irrigation and its pipework have been renewed, as has the electricity supply; the wall around the property has been entirely rebuilt; and work has begun on restoring the *palazzo*, parts of which have been unoccupied since before the last war. Meanwhile the University of Genoa is attempting to replenish the botanic collections, replanting everything that is known to have been lost since the last catalogue of plants was published in 1937.

The English traditions at La Mortola pose a particular problem. The Italians regard the garden as the best botanic collection in the Mediterranean, and they are proud to have it. They appreciate also the 8 ha (20 acres) of *garrigue* which adjoin the garden and form part of the estate, and indeed they value the natural woodland of Aleppo pines which regenerated when Daniel Hanbury excluded grazing animals; the need to preserve these relict populations of the natural vegetation is one that the Italian authorities keenly understand. They encounter difficulties, however, in establishing priorities for planting, in recognising what is rare and what is commonplace, and in deciding what needs to be kept and what should be removed. They prefer the gardenesque displays of succulent plants which used to be mounted on the terrace in front of the house to the scented garden of herbs and sweet flowers that replaced them in Dodo Hanbury's day. This is because the Italians esteem the botanic tradition more highly than the horticultural. Deciding priorities for restoration is seldom easy, but both traditions are uniquely developed at La Mortola and ought to be properly represented in future.

Teaching the authorities to appreciate English horticulture is crucial to the future of La Mortola. The Italians perceive the ornamental overlay which the garden gained between 1920 and 1940 as a puzzling change of direction. They cannot assess its importance, cannot appreciate its aesthetic and cannot put it into an historic context. Moreover, they are perplexed by the passion it arouses in the English. Although the botanic heritage will be preserved and re-created, the ornamental elements are in danger of abandonment. It is likely that the gardens will in future be maintained in the Italian manner. None of the administrators nor any member of the garden staff was reared in a school of horticulture attached to the great botanic institutes of Britain, the Royal Botanic Gardens at Kew and Edinburgh and the Royal Horticultural Society at Wisley. Nevertheless the gardens are undoubtedly safe, and perhaps with their renewed emphasis upon botanical and pharmaceutical studies they approximate more closely now to the original vision of Thomas and Daniel Hanbury. It is difficult to be so optimistic about other English gardens in Italy.

References and Further Reading

Anyone who writes about La Mortola is spoiled for choice of good source material. Above all, the garden was very well documented through the pages of *The Gardener's Chronicle* for over a hundred years; scarcely a year passed without half a dozen reports of plants and plantings at Villa Hanbury. It is often mentioned, too, in the memoirs and biographies of botanical and horticultural worthies who have visited La Mortola – Canon Ellacombe and Ellen Willmott, for example. The first single volume devoted to it was *La Mortola – A Short Description of the Garden of Thomas Hanbury, Esq.* by Friedrich A. Flückiger, privately printed in 1885 but based on the German original published nine years earlier. The various editions of *Hortus Mortolensis* are all worth reading, especially the third edition, for the notes written by Alwin Berger in 1912, and the fourth edition (London, 1938) which has a useful but tiresome introduction by Dorothy Hanbury. Cecil Hanbury wrote an article in *Country Life* (11 February 1928) which has excellent illustrations of the design and horticultural innovations he and his wife were then putting into effect. La Mortola's recent fortunes and misfortunes have latterly been well covered in *The Garden* and *Il Giardino Fiorito* (see, for example, '*Alla Mortola le parole sono pietre*', June 1989). I have relied for family facts upon a duplicated booklet *Gli Hanbury della Mortola e la loro villa* by Paolo Ceschi in the library of the Anglo-Ligurian club at Bordighera. I have also spoken to many of the protagonists on both sides of the modern argument about the past and future of this unique garden.

Chapter Five

ITALY

Garden Paradise of Exiles

EVER SINCE the Renaissance, Englishmen have visited Italy in search of art and antiquity. By the eighteenth century the lure of travel to the classical sites had developed into the ritual of the Grand Tour, which might include visits to other countries but always led inevitably to Rome. For many years too, English merchants, prelates and envoys had travelled to Italy. As Giuliana Artom Treves points out, at times these visits were essential: young men had gone to learn astronomy and mathematics from Galileo. Long before that the most advanced banking systems could be observed only in Genoa and Florence. 'Where else could one study diplomacy so well as in the Vatican? And where archaeology, and architecture, decoration and silk manufacture so well as in Pompeii, in Rome, on the Brenta or up in Como?'

Substantial English communities grew up in Florence, Rome and Naples during the eighteenth and nineteenth centuries, especially after the arrival of the railways, when their numbers were greatly swelled by seasonal visitors. By the 1840s, travel books on Italy were appearing in England at the rate of four a year. John Pemble, the historian of Mediterranean travel, has described how the presses 'plied the reading public with Sketches, Notes, Diaries, Gleanings, Glimpses, Impressions, Pictures, Narratives, and Leaves from Journals about Tours, Visits, Wanderings, Residences, Rambles and Travels in all the quarters of the South'.

Some of the English saw themselves as heirs to the Roman Empire. Lady Eastlake confided after visiting the Colosseum for the first time in 1858, 'I felt proud that my nation was more truly the descendant of that matchless race than any other in the world.' Occasionally they also behaved with imperial superiority, and carried on their social life as if they were still at home. Charles Weld wrote from the Eternal City in 1864 that 'these English parties are so very similar to those given in London during the season that it is extremely difficult to realise that you are in Rome'. His experience is familiar to modern travellers: the English abroad are sometimes more English than at home. It was perhaps such stereotypes that Antonio Gallenga had in mind when he wrote, in *Italy Revisited* (1876):

Men and women go to Paris to shop, they go to the North to fish, to Nice to gamble, to Egypt to stave off consumption, but they come to Italy to idle ... Italy also secures many of her foreign visitors as fixtures, and most of these are not, as in other countries, mere men of business, but remain for many years, and sometimes for their lives, the same idlers they were when they first settled – the same inquisitive, somewhat fussy, but, on the whole, genial and benevolent idlers.

Italy was cheap too, of course, and Englishmen settled there so that they could live better, or not have to earn a living as they would at home, in the same way that their grandchildren would retire to France during the 1920s and their great-great-grandchildren to Spain. Gallenga went on to explain that

---

Villa Cimbrone, Ravello. The temple to Pan built in the garden by the 2nd Lord Grimthorpe in 1910, whose ashes are deposited under the statue.

the intercourse between the Italians and these strangers, whether fleeting or permanent, is, as a rule, not very intimate or cordial; still some points of contact as well as of repulsion between them do exist (were it only community or antagonism of religious creed), and from such intercourse springs occasional intermarriage (usually the exchange of a high-sounding Southern title for a comfortable Northern dowry).

There are many examples of this aloofness. In the hundreds of letters written by Elizabeth Barrett Browning, there is mention of only one Italian whom she met socially, while Lady Blessington observed that 'the English, more than all other people, carry with them the habits and customs of their own country. It would appear that they travel not so much for the purpose of studying the manners of other lands, as for that of establishing and displaying their own.' Francis Toye, the Director of the British Institute in Florence, shared this opinion. He wrote of Col. and Mrs George Keppel, who lived at Villa L'Ombrellino on Bellosguardo hill just outside Florence during the 1920s and 1930s, that

they remained *au dessus de la mêlée*, a timely reminder to the present generation of what a genuine governing class is like, taking themselves for granted, as others without question took them for granted both as regards personal distinction and mode of life. They were neither more intelligent nor more moral than their neighbours: they were just of a different caste. It would never even have occurred to them to doubt the superiority of England, at any rate their England, in everything that mattered.

It follows that the English perception of Italy was often shallow and inaccurate. When Tobias Smollett visited the Villa Borghese in 1765 he commented, 'he who loves the beauties of simple nature, and the charms of neatness, will seek for them in vain amidst the groves of Italy'. Such observations suggest that the Englishman visited Italy with fixed expectations of what he would find there. In the eighteenth century he went in search of classical Rome; in the nineteenth century he rediscovered the Italian Renaissance; not until modern times has he fallen upon the baroque with similar enthusiasm.

It should quickly be said that not every Englishman in Italy remained aloof. There are exceptions to most generalisations, and there has always been a minority of Englishmen who went native; such men gave rise to the Italian saying, first attributed to Pope Sixtus V, that an Italianised Englishman is the devil incarnate: '*inglese italianato, diavolo incarnato*'. In the early years of the twentieth century, for instance, a British diplomat, Sir Edward Capel Cure, became so

attached to Italy, and in particular to the Lakeland region, where he bought an island called San Giorgio near Pallanza, that he wrote a number of novels in Italian under the pen-name of Giacomo della Quercia. His garden of flowers and trees and lawns, however, remained as English as English can be.

Many of the Englishmen who lived in Italy bought or rented old villas with traditional gardens and became enthusiastic garden makers. The fabric of a Renaissance garden would be restored, or at least replaced, by an anglicised approximation of the Italian original. The best-known examples of these old–new gardens were Villa Gamberaia and Villa Palmieri at Florence. There were hundreds more, usually restored in the English Italianate style, which is a loose romantic interpretation of the Italian seventeenth century, overlaid by our national passion for plants. So the parterres would be replanted in a design that owed as much to Nesfield as to Alberti, lined with hundreds of clay pots bursting with sweetly scented flowers and filled with bright bedding plants in the Victorian taste.

This did not prevent the English from appreciating the nature of the Italian tradition. In her novel *Pascarel*, Ouida insisted that 'the delights of an Italian garden are countless. It is not like any other garden in the world. It is at once more formal and more wild, at once greener with more abundant youth and venerable with more antique age. It holds Boccaccio between its walls, all Petrarca in its leaves, all Raffaelle in its skies.' The American novelist Edith Wharton wrote, more learnedly, in *Italian Villas and Their Gardens* (1905) that

the inherent beauty of the [Italian] garden lies in the grouping of its parts – in the converging of the lines of its long ilex-walks, the alternation of sunny open spaces with cool woodland shade, the proportion between terrace and bowling-green, or between the height of a wall and the width of the path ... The great pleasure grounds overlooking the Roman Campagna are laid out on severe majestic lines: the parts are few; the total effect is one of breadth and simplicity.

But in general the English found, and still find, some truth in Tobias Smollett's assessment of the Italian capacity for gardening: 'the Italians understand, because they study, the excellencies of art; but they have no idea of the beauties of nature'. They also insist that Italians are not interested in plants. D. H. Lawrence was dismayed to discover that if he asked an Italian peasant the name of a flower he would simply reply, 'It is a flower,' or perhaps, with more detail, 'It is a flower that smells.' Osbert Sitwell maintained that flowers could only be grown at Montegufoni where his father's gardener could not destroy them –

> ... in the dark umbrageous confines of the garden
> Where the ferns grew and the violets,
> In a mossy stone vase
>> On the top of a tall stone fountain,
>> Safely out of Umberto's reach,
> Arum lilies flowered with magnificent impunity.

To this day, the advertisements for Villa Táranto invite the visitor to 'See the Gardens and the Flowers', which suggests that flowers are not necessarily or even normally part of an Italian garden.

IT IS NOW TIME to examine in detail some of the many gardens made by Englishmen in Italy over the last two hundred years. Separate chapters are devoted to the landscape movement in Italy, and its successor the gardenesque type of garden; two areas where a particular style and concentration of gardens evolved, Tuscany and the Lakes, also have a chapter each to themselves. The remaining gardens, which form the subject of this chapter, nicely illustrate the historical development of English gardening styles and their application by Englishmen to Italian conditions over the two hundred years which begin at the end of the eighteenth century with the English community in Naples.

By the beginning of the nineteenth century, a substantial number of expatriates lived in southern Italy, especially after the restoration of the Bourbons in 1815. In addition to the Actons and Sir William Hamilton at Naples, there was a regular influx of visitors drawn by the city's reputation as a winter resort and by the nearby excavations at Pompeii. In the 1830s, Lady Blessington wrote warmly of such English residents as Sir William Drummond, Colonel Challoner Bliss and especially the Hon. Richard Keppel Craven, who lived on the cape which is now known as Posillipo. Craven's large villa there had been built by his mother, the Margravine of Anspach, born Lady Elizabeth Berkeley, who in about 1825 also laid out the garden as a shady woodland park. Renamed Villa Rae after the English family who have owned it since 1924, the garden owes as much to the English landscape tradition as to the Italian eighteenth-century taste for *boschi* and classical groves.

Elizabeth, Lady Craven, later the Margravine of Anspach, who laid out the garden at the Villa Rae, Posillipo (drawing after Sir Joshua Reynolds).

The Margravine was an admirer of the work of Capability Brown, who had landscaped Coombe Abbey for her father-in-law Lord Craven at a cost of £12,000, but she herself laid out the grounds of Banham Place in Berkshire since she 'thought it unnecessary to be more plundered'. In defiance of the Italian tradition, there is no formal garden at Villa Rae: the Margravine trusted her own preference for an artless garden. 'I had always the satisfaction,' she wrote in her memoirs, 'of observing natural beauties, the graces of which I particularly studied.' Although the garden is not open to the public, the natural layout still survives: hedges and walks under a shady canopy of pines and ilex, paths that run down to the rocky cove, and stupendous views of the city and Bay of Naples. In Lady Elizabeth's day there was also a grotto, of which only traces remain.

In the early twentieth century the leading English resident in Naples was Lord Rosebery, one of Gladstone's protégés, who had served briefly as prime minister in 1894–5. He was a lifelong lover of the city, which he had first visited as a boy of seven in 1854 when he watched King Ferdinand II reviewing his troops. It was the Villa Delahante at Posillipo that Rosebery coveted. As early as 1879, he had written to Sir James Lacaita that its purchase had long been 'the dream of my life', but conceded that it did not seem easy to realise although he would like to own it 'even if I could never see it again'. He was to see it again on a visit with his wife in 1882, after which Rosebery wrote 'we spent an hour of rapture at the Villa Delahante. Hannah was amazed and stupefied by the beauty of the place.' Lady Rosebery died before her husband was able to buy Delahante in 1897 but for many years thereafter Rosebery spent several months at the villa, whose gardens run down to the water's edge. He declared that he appreciated its pleasures more with the advance of years: 'when other amusements leave us from want of strength or aptitude, gardening remains to us an increasing enjoyment and pleasure'.

Sir James Lacaita, a Neapolitan lawyer, had attached himself to the British legation and was extremely useful to the liberal cause during the revolution of 1848. As a friend and confidant of Gladstone's, he later made his way in English politics and launched the Anglo-Italian Bank. Then, in 1869, he bought a large estate called Leucaspide near Táranto, surrounded by olives trees so old that Sir James fancied that Horace himself had once sat under them. Janet Ross visited him one April and described his garden in *The Land of Manfred* (1889): 'the *loggia*, or arcade, running all along the south-west front of Leucaspide, overhangs a garden full of orange trees, wallflowers, stocks, Parma violets, carnations and roses; beyond, an expanse of brilliant green corn grows under the colossal olive trees which arborists declare to be at least two thousand years old'.

Sir James's brother-in-law Francis Neville Reid worked at the British legation in Naples. He was an amateur archaeologist and a good botanist: a form of *Crocus imperati* from the Lattari hills south of Naples, with rose-pink flowers, white spots at the base of its segments and brown lines on the outside, is called var. *reidii* after its discoverer. In 1851, Reid bought a ruin at Ravello on the Amalfi coast. Villa Rúfolo had been famous for many centuries and even contained traces of a palace built by the Saracens. Boccaccio's description in the Second Day of the *Decameron*, written in 1349, still gives an accurate picture of life in this corner of Italy: 'the coast of Amalfi overlooks the sea and is dotted with villages, gardens and fountains, and inhabited by very rich men … among the villages is one called Ravello which, as nowadays, was inhabited by men of great wealth … the richest of them all was Landolfo Rúfolo by name'.

Reid engaged Michele Ruggiero, who had superintended the excavation of Pompeii, to restore the house and garden. His brief was to be as scrupulous as possible. He was to leave intact or restore features from every important period in the palace's history – Saracen, Norman and Gothic. The result is a unique house and a unique garden, which made a big impression on Richard Wagner when he visited it in May 1880. Although Richard Strauss considered Pena Palace at Sintra in Portugal to be the garden of Klingsor, Wagner could have told him otherwise. The inspiration for the magic garden music in Parsifal came from Villa Rúfolo.

The garden at Villa Rúfolo is laid out on two levels around a colonnaded courtyard or cloister whose graceful arabesque arcades and carved stonework find a living complement in the details of the garden. The plants, leaves and roses on the stone capitals are echoed by the palms, shrubs and roses outside. Lady Paget wrote in *In My Tower* (1898) that it was the most enchantingly romantic place she ever trod:

dim, Norman, Saracenic cloisters with richest tracery, almost lost in climbing roses and ivy, surround several courts. Vaults and stairways with flowers clustering all around them lead to mysterious vaulted chambers or oleander-shaded terraces. High walls encircle the gardens on all sides, excepting towards the sea, where terraces with fountains, steps, and flowers lead down into the orange and olive orchards.

On the lower terrace Reid put not a Norman or Saracenic garden but a Victorian parterre: that was what he thought proper. The permanent planting still contains the sort of plants that would have formed the centrepiece of tropical bedding schemes in contemporary England: cycads, cordylines and palms. Near by are mahonias, evergreen viburnums and bergenias, all popular in England at the time the garden was made. There are some fine conifers and a good example of *Sterculia populnea*, but nothing to suggest a botanist's interest in exotic trees. Reid's respect for historical accuracy required him to use plants only as an adjunct to architecture to create a garden that he considered appropriate to his fabulous palace.

Villa Rúfolo was eventually inherited by Charles Lacaita, Sir James's son, and then remained in the family's ownership until bought by the Salerno Ente per Turismo in 1974. It is the beauty of Villa Rúfolo's position which enchants visitors, not the cleverness

Villa Rúfolo. This conventional-enough Victorian garden was considered 'exotic', 'Norman' and 'Saracenic' by visitors in the nineteenth century. Richard Wagner found the inspiration for Parsifal's garden of Klingsor here.

of its design nor the richness of its planting. The American Rose Nichols wrote in 1929 that the garden, 'no matter how well planted, would shrink into insignificance beside the matchless view of wild romantic mountains and the rock-bound sea dashing against the precipitous cliffs below'. It must, however, be said that classic colonnades and terraces which terminate in a breathtaking view have always had a particular appeal to the German temperament, and to that extent there is something slightly unEnglish about Villa Rúfolo. It is not surprising that the garden should have appealed so strongly to Richard Wagner. But the best German gardens are made by Germans: had Wagner visited Karl Faust's intensely romantic garden at Blanes on the Costa Brava, he would have found inspiration for any number of Klingsors.

Villa Rúfolo was not the only English garden at Ravello. Lord Grimthorpe, a rich banker, bought a large area of hillside on the town's western promontory in 1904 and spent nearly twelve years laying out the gardens of Villa Cimbrone there. He chose

not to employ an architect, but a local man called Niccolò Mansi, who was variously described as a waiter or tailor. Whatever his training, or lack of it, the inevitable result is that when the exuberant and eccentric Villa Cimbrone is compared to the dour but correct Villa Rúfolo it is found wanting in historical authenticity. Neville Reid was careful and meticulous where Lord Grimthorpe was extravagant and capricious. Yet the gardens of Villa Cimbrone are more inventive than Villa Rúfolo, and very much larger and more varied too. The Italian influence is strong, although the gardens could only have been made by an Englishman. Lord Grimthorpe's descendants sold the villa in 1960 to a local hotelier called Marco Willeumier. He, unusually for an Italian, has continued to maintain the English character of the garden.

Villa Cimbrone is dominated by a long straight walk past pergolas, pots and plinths to a circular temple which shelters a statue of Ceres. The temple opens on to a belvedere terrace lined with eighteenth-century busts and perched 300 m (1,000 ft) above the

Villa Cimbrone, Ravello, c. 1934. The long walk to the belvedere dominates the design of this remarkable garden; note the different enclosures to the right of the walk.

sea. The effect is breathtaking: 'the jewel is worthy of the setting,' declared Geoffrey Bret Harte in 1929. This walk dominates the garden, and is the first feature to catch the eye as the visitor passes through the massive wooden gates of the entrance. It runs from north to south, so that the Temple of Ceres appears as a portal of the sun. The dynamism of the design is emphasised by symmetrical walks on either side. On the eastern slope a long lawn lined with flowering shrubs leads to a wild garden where a path meanders past viburnums, yuccas, cypresses and acacias until a grove of arbutus trees brings it up to the temple. Below runs another terrace, this time of clipped cypress, with recesses for statues and traces of old topiary. These long open walks – the ruins of a third can be seen further down the hillside – run like Renaissance galleries in parallel along the hillside to draw the visitor towards the belvedere. The view, the drama, the position and the effect are everything.

The terraces on the western slope of Villa Cimbrone are wooded and sheltered. Close to the house is a neo-Byzantine pavilion, which is said to have

been Lord Grimthorpe's favourite place for drinking tea, although the Italians are so convinced of the English passion for it that they will believe almost anything to have been consecrated to tea drinking. There is a collection of bronze reproductions from Pompeii and Byzantine columns in front of the pavilion: the effect is worthy of Peto. The formal garden which holds these antiquities was designed with geometric beds and planted with standard roses; now there are pansies and begonias. At the far end, a Latin inscription above a basin in the wall exhorts 'Scatter roses: I hate the hands that will not scatter', and leads naturally into the main rose garden beyond. This centres on a sundial and is in effect a garden within a garden, because it is enclosed by a decorated wall or balustrade inset with curious tiling. The inner rose garden is also slightly sunken, which increases its sense of detachment from the rest of the garden. All the beds are outlined in a curious terracotta piping that is trefoil in section. Lord Grimthorpe filled the outer rose garden with eighteenth-century casts of classical figures and put up a plaque with a quotation from FitzGerald's *Rubáiyát*:

Ah, Moon of my Delight that know'st no wane,
The Moon of Heaven is rising once again:
How oft hereafter rising shall she look
Through this same Garden after us in vain.

Behind the Byzantine pavilion a path leads down to the next terrace along the western side of the garden. It passes through a circle of brick pillars and under a pergola covered in Banksian and other roses, with hydrangeas underneath. There follows a dramatic rock garden of dolomitic limestone shaped into shady ravines and grottoes, a copy of one of Donatello's statues of David, a wisteria arcade which runs up to the rose garden, a serpentine walk edged with box, and avenues of cedar trees and umbrella pines which lead to a small circular temple. On the next level, a natural wood of chestnuts and oaks is underplanted with *Rhododendron ponticum*, apparently growing on a limestone hillside at what must be its most southerly sea-level station in Italy. Further down, a bronze statue of an athlete, said to be Hermes, occupies the focal point at the end of a hedge of hebes surrounded by huge arbutus trees. To one side, a stone set in the wall reads:

Lost to a world in which I crave no part,
I sit alone and commune with my heart;
Pleased with my little corner of the earth,
Glad that I came, not sorry to depart.

A little further down a temple of Bacchus stands at the end of a short avenue of cypresses and a straggly lavender hedge. The temple has eight rough Ionic columns and a cupola; in it is a copy of the School of Praxiteles Dionysius from the Museo Nazionale in Naples. And underneath the statue are buried Lord Grimthorpe's ashes. On the frieze of the temple a famous quotation celebrates Catullus' love of home:

O quid solutis est beatius curis?
Cum mens onus reponit, ac peregrino
Labore fessi venimus larem ad nostrum,
Desideratoque acquiescimus lecto.

Still further down in a natural cave in the side of the hill known as Eve's Grotto lies a white marble figure naked on a tuffet of fig leaves. The unorthodox attitude is explained when you know that, far from depicting the mother of all mankind, this statue by Todolini represents a classical nymph. When D. H. Lawrence stayed at Cimbrone in March 1927, he remarked of this statue, 'she is too bleached out and pale, altogether too demure after her fall. I'll give her a touch of colour,' and began to rub earth on to the statue's face. Not content with the effect, he continued until the entire body had endured a mud bath, black from head to foot. Then he placed a cluster of green leaves in her hair and announced that the result was perfect. His fellow guests were much amused. Evidently the gardeners were not: by next morning Eve was as pale as ever.

The gardens at Villa Cimbrone are remarkable for their size, and the sheer verve of their design. They are both dramatic and decorative. No feature in any other garden, English or Italian, has such a pull as the walk to the belvedere, while the ornamental work around the rose garden is without precedent or sequel in the history of garden design. Full use is made of the site to contrast the open terraces on the eastern side with the intimate woodland on the western face. The former uses the grey limestone mountains as a backdrop scarcely less dramatic than the sea below the belvedere, while the other relies on natural stands of oak and chestnut for effect.

Some of the most important trees are umbrella pines *Pinus pinea*. A long line was planted, originally to provide a visual boundary between two levels, but they have grown to an impressive size and now give this part of the garden the character of a sacred wood. The disposition of classical follies within the woodland is reminiscent of eighteenth-century English landscapes, which draw the visitor gently from one delight to the next. Villa Cimbrone has also a good collection of plants: the planting is an essential part of the design, and illustrates the importance which English gardens attach to variety. Almost every part of the garden is grassed, which means that considerable irrigation is needed, and there remains a strong herbaceous underplanting. The wild plants include *Crocus imperati* and *Cyclamen repandum*, while *Iris unguicularis* has naturalised itself throughout the hillside.

Villa Cimbrone does not belong exclusively to the English or Italian tradition of garden design. It has elements of each, and many that are unique to itself. There is none of the austerity of Cecil Pinsent's contemporary work in Tuscany at Villa Cimbrone, nor does it belong to the Robinson–Jekyll school that was in the ascendant when it was made. Compared to Villa Rúfolo, it contains much eccentricity and self-indulgence: it lacks the fidelity and measure of Neville Reid's Saracenic palace. It is perhaps closest to the prodigy gardens of the Riviera, whose rich

owners could indulge any style that took their fancy, and often did so with a panache that was matched only by their absence of taste. Such strictures do not apply to Lord Grimthorpe. Villa Cimbrone is original, exciting and harmonious all at once and, as such, one of the greatest examples of the English garden abroad.

The only other place in Italy where the raffish international style of gardening practised on the Riviera became popular was Capri, which D. H. Lawrence called 'a gossipy, villa-stricken, two-humped chunk of limestone, a microcosm that does heaven much credit, but mankind none at all'. In the early years of the twentieth century the island was rather louche: it attracted the fast international society portrayed in such books as Norman Douglas's *South Wind* and Compton Mackenzie's *Extraordinary Women*. A few were more conventional and some, such as Lady Algernon Gordon-Lennox, were enthusiastic garden owners. Most were content to leave the design and planting of their gardens to a fashionable local designer and devote themselves to other pleasures. Mimì Ruggiero made gardens for the Wolcott-Perrys at Villa Torricella and for E. F. Benson and Somerset Maugham at Villa Cercola. It was an international style of gardening, that suited the mixture of English, American, German and Swedish expatriates who found life on Capri to their taste. Lord Algernon Gordon-Lennox acquired the Villa Monte San Michele on Capri in settlement of a gambling debt incurred by its former owner, a Prince Caracciolo. Lady Algernon fell in love with the property, so they rebuilt the house in 1904 and began to make the extensive garden described in 1928 by Thomas Mawson as among the best-known modern gardens in Italy. Faith Compton-Mackenzie thought that the garden was successful 'partly because it is an entire mountain, but chiefly because [Lady Algernon] has given years of intelligent devotion to it ... she really worked in the garden. A crowning advantage over all other gardens in Capri it was bound to have – plenty of water; for under the terraces were cisterns of vast size, built by the Romans probably in the time of Tiberius.' Lady Algernon herself introduced many garden plants to the island; one of them, the blue shrubby echium from the Canary Islands, is now naturalised through-

Villa Cimbrone, Ravello, 1990. Part of the rose garden with Lord Grimthorpe's parabolic balustrading and the Byzantine tea house behind.

out Capri. When Lady Algernon died in 1945 Villa Monte San Michele passed to her daughter the Duchess of Portland, who gave it to her daughter Lady Margaret Cavendish-Bentinck. It now belongs to her son William Parente, the fourth generation of the family to garden upon the steep slopes of the villa with its walks, balustrades, terraces and flights of steps.

NO ENGLISH family, however, owned land in Italy for longer than the Dukes of Bronte, heirs of Viscount Nelson, on whom King Ferdinand I of the Two Sicilies had bestowed an estate on the lowest slopes of Mount Etna around the ruined monastery Castle of Maniace. Although Lord Nelson told his friend Captain Hardy that he was 'determined to reside there in peace', he died without seeing his Sicilian estate, and Bronte with its 16,200 ha (40,000 acres) was instead administered by an agent. The first administrator, recommended by Sir William Hamilton, was the botanist and landscape architect Johann Gräfer who had helped Hamilton to make the English Garden at Caserta. No member of the Nelson family actually visited the property until the 1830s when the admiral's niece, Charlotte, Lady Bridport, Duchess of Bronte, arrived in a sedan chair slung between two mules. She was horrified by the primitive nature of the accommodation, and declared on her departure that she would never return 'unless there were a revolution in England and even then I would probably go elsewhere'. This contrasts with the delight of William Ewart Gladstone, who was struck during his visit in 1838 by the resemblance of the natural woodlands at the base of Etna to an English park, 'very picturesque ... with its old oaks and abundant fern'. Nevertheless, Lady Bridport's son, the first Viscount Bridport, began to visit Maniace regularly in the 1860s, and in 1873 established his fourth son there, the Hon. Alec Hood, to manage his interests in Sicily.

For the next sixty years Alec Hood spent nine months of every year at Maniace. With his father's encouragement he modernised the estate. He built a 5 km (3 mile) carriageway from the highway between Bronte and Randazzo, established extensive orange orchards, imported the Pedro Ximenes grape from the Duke of Wellington's estate in Spain, planted woodlands and brought out a 10 h.p. traction engine made by Clayton & Shuttleworth. The house was restored to look like a 'good-sized, rambling, half-fortified old monastery', according to the novelist F.

Castello di Maniace, Lord Nelson's house in Sicily, 'a rambling half-fortified old monastery' with a Victorian garden.

Marion Crawford, who made it the scene of action for his novel *Corleone* (1895). He described how the castle looks down 'from a gentle elevation in the high valley on one side, having a deep gorge at the back, through which a torrent tumbled along over dark stones during three-quarters of the year' and thought that 'Etna's enormous cone rose above a dark blue eastern sky like a monstrous, streaked sugar loaf'. The torrent became a feature of the garden which Alec Hood laid out and was much admired by the many who came from England to receive his lonely hospitality. The indefatigable Lady Paget came here and noted a little unfairly that the house had no architectural merits. She was, however, correct to pronounce that 'the two remarkable things are the church ... and a natural rock garden which borders for half a mile the rushing stream'. Visitors were fascinated by the retention of *carabinieri* to fight the brigands who were a blight on travel in Sicily, and by the isolation of Maniace's position. Mrs Lynn Linton, a Victorian three-volume novelist, wrote in 1883 of 'the wildest, bleakest-looking mountainous

region you can imagine ... it is the very acme of desolation, grandeur and awfulness'. Yet it was the contrast between primitive Sicily outside and civilised comfort within Maniace which most impressed Alec Hood's guests, even a hostile D. H. Lawrence: Frances Elliott (in *The Diary of an Idle Woman in Sicily*, 1881) summed it up when she wrote 'all is so strangely English, yet so foreign – a comfortable mansion, evolved out of a mediaeval monastery, with that mountain desolation outside'.

What sort of garden did Alec Hood, the benevolent English nineteenth-century landlord, make around his fortified Norman monastery in the wilds of inland Sicily? Naturally enough, an English Victorian garden. He started in 1876, and continued to develop it until well into the 1930s, by which time he himself had become The Hon. Sir Alexander Nelson-Hood, 5th Duke of Bronte. First he laid out a formal garden on a flat site immediately in front of the house: the area is walled on all sides, and perhaps just over 0.5 ha (1 acre) in extent. A central pergola, planted with vines, led between two formal box-edged gardens, each in the shape of a rhomboidal quincunx, filled with roses and bedding plants. By the time Frances Elliott visited Maniace two years later, she was able to write that 'tulips and hyacinths, violets and daffodils, snowdrops and turkshead, crowd into beds of antique patterns'. Hood's interest in gardening increased with age. Outside the walls are plane trees planted to celebrate Queen Victoria's jubilee in 1887 and others which commemorate family events and the visits of friends. Four palm trees, now in their prime, were added to one of the quincunxes in 1912. In common with many English garden owners in the Mediterranean, Alec Hood was certain that things grew better for him than anywhere else. 'At no other place have I seen such growth of roses ... the La France [and] Paul Neyron varieties being the best,' he declared. The walls of the house and the enclosed garden were planted with 'Maréchal Niel' and 'Fortune's Yellow', but bedding roses were continually replanted as new varieties were introduced, and a substantial order for French varieties was delivered by Pernet-Ducher in 1922. None of these remain. Indeed, the only roses now left in the garden are *Rosa banksiae* and some recently planted hybrid teas and floribundas. The house is covered only by Virginia creeper, with bushes of *Chaenomeles speciosa* against the walls to flower in early spring.

The best feature of the garden at Maniace was the lower garden or wilderness, described as a '*grande parco selvaggiamente suggestivo*' (Beltrandi, *Castelli di Sicilia*, Milano, 1955) and in effect an English natural garden planted along the stream where once had been a mass of thorns and rocks. Hood reclaimed this woodland and planted palms, conifers, shrubs and bulbs to give a succession of interest in different seasons. The flowering began early in spring when the almond trees blossomed. It reached a peak in April when the pink and white hawthorns, purple-leaved prunus, irises, paeonies, primroses and violets all combined to enchant the senses. When the novelist William Sharp visited Maniace in 1903, he wrote of the 'floating fumes of roses and violets, of heliotrope and the long-clustered spires of medlar and lemon-scented verbena ... an invisible smoke of sweet odours' and asked 'is there anything in Europe finer ... or anywhere is there another Enchanted Garden like that Giardino Selvaggio of the Castle of Maniace ... surrounded by giant poplars, vast tremulous columns of shaken but unfallen gold?' High praise indeed. But the wild garden was not entirely without artifice. At the top of it, near the gate that leads from the walled garden, stands a sandstone column,

Castello di Maniace. The formal garden seen from the upstairs windows. The parterres were designed by the Hon. Alec Hood in the 1870s and at first filled with bedding plants; Vernon Russell-Smith replaced them with shrub roses for the 4th Lord Bridport a hundred years later.

crowned by a Corinthian capital. It came from Egypt as the first instalment of an Egypto-Roman temple which an enthusiastic but somewhat demented agent wished to erect on the top of Mount Etna as a memorial to the great Lord Nelson.

In the 1970s the garden was overhauled by the 4th Viscount Bridport, with plantings devised by Vernon Russell-Smith, who described Maniace as one of the most romantic places that he had ever known. The Victorian parterres were then somewhat neglected, and those nearest the house were cleared away to create an open lawn. The opportunity was taken to install irrigation and floodlighting, and the area immediately below the house was extensively replanted. A hot border in full sun was filled with lavender, rue, caryopteris, cistus and ceanothus, while a shadier bed was put to soft, cool colours – silvers, pinks, mauves, greys and whites. *Senecio greyi, Teucrium fruticans*, artemisias, white

Florence Trevelyan, whose magnificent gardens at Taormina are now in public ownership, photographed with her husband Dr Cacciola (c. 1895).

The size of the Bronte estate was reduced over the years by two of the historic hazards of life in Sicily: private litigation and public expropriation. The last 4,200 ha (10,250 acres) and the Castello di Maniace itself were sold to the Comune di Bronte in 1981, and the garden has quickly reverted to the standards of simplicity that Italians expect. The *giardino selvaggio* is more wilderness than garden. The herbaceous underplanting in the quincunxes has disappeared under the blades of a cultivator but the palms, magnolias and cypress trees planted by Alec Hood have survived, as have the box edgings. Almost the only relic of Vernon Russell-Smith's inspired replanting is an immensely handsome pair of deep blue *Rosmarinus officinalis*, which came from an Italian nurseryman. There is no trace whatsoever of the collection of old-fashioned roses, though at first they grew apace, flourishing, just as 'La France' and 'Paul Neyron' had many years previously for Alec Hood, in the rich black volcanic soil, which resembles nothing so much as a cinder track. Dust to dust is the story of most English gardens in Italy: at Maniace it is ashes to ashes.

At Taormina, on Sicily's eastern coast, a small but thriving English community grew up after about 1890. Soon there was an English church, its congregation often doubled by naval officers and their families on leave from Malta. The English were not the only foreigners to fall for the town's artistic and historic attractions. 'Taormina,' exclaimed Douglas Sladen in 1905, 'is flooded with Germans. At some hotels they have separate tables for them, because the other nations do not like sitting with Germans.' It was, however, the English who made gardens. Lady Hill's Gothic garden in the old convent of S. Caterina was famous before the First World War. The Hon. Albert Stopford also made a garden in an old monastery, next to the Cappuccini convent. Later he planted a terraced rose garden above the church of S. Giuseppe and distributed an unnamed rose variety as 'Albert Stopford'. But the two best and longest-lasting gardens were Florence Trevelyan's and Robert Kitson's.

Florence Trevelyan belonged to a gifted but eccentric Northumbrian family. Her parents died when she was in her twenties and, as she was their only surviving child, their demise left her comfortably off. She and a cousin, Louisa Perceval, took off together for the Mediterranean; when they arrived at Taormina, Florence decided to settle there and Louisa returned to England alone. Freed from the conventions of Northumbrian society, Florence

hydrangeas, viburnums, deutzias and *Philadelphus* 'Virginal' were among the shrubs used, most of them imported from Hilliers of Winchester or Mrs Desmond Underwood's Colchester nursery. A collection of old roses was made in the quincunxes, including 'Charles de Mills', 'Königin von Dänemark', 'Cardinal de Richelieu', 'Fantin Latour' and 'Blanc Double de Coubert', and interplanted with such herbaceous plants, rudbeckias, delphiniums, lupins and paeonies as might be expected to tolerate the hot, dry Sicilian summer. The beds at the foot of the pergola were planted with early flowering bulbs, to show in the spring before the vines and wisterias came into leaf and fade away as summer approached. Here were little clumps of St Brigid anemones, jonquils, the hoop petticoat *Narcissus bulbocodium*, *Crocus* 'Blue Pearl', *Tulipa fosteriana* and *T*. 'Red Riding Hood'. All these plantings were inspired by the Pre-Raphaelite dream gardens painted by Dante Gabriel Rossetti.

Villar Perosa. The valley garden which Russell Page laid out in the English style for Giovanni and Marella Agnelli in the 1950s

La Mortella. Pools and fountains at the bottom of the valley are linked by a Persian-style channel; these and the spray irrigation give the garden much of its character.

Above: *Crinums in a border of spiky plants at La Mortella on Ischia. Lady Walton's plantsmanship was the perfect foil for Russell Page's design sense.*
Below: *Villa Stibbert, near Florence. The Egyptian temple which Frederick Stibbert built by the lake, perhaps according to designs by Papworth.*

Above: *Villa Malfitano, Palermo, in 1990. Joseph Whitaker's garden has much colour and interest still, but it is badly maintained. The palm trees have not been trimmed for many years, and a dead trunk has not been removed.*
Opposite: *Villa La Pietra, near Florence. Twin columns with broken pediments in Arthur Acton's neo-Tuscan garden. All very classical and correct, but note that the balustrade is garlanded with 'Dorothy Perkins' rambler roses.*

Above: *Villa Gamberaia in 1990. The garden was restored after the Second World War as it had been in the 1890s. The water parterres were much admired by English garden owners, but are not historically correct.*
Opposite: *The Green Garden at I Tatti, Cecil Pinsent's essay in Tuscan correctness for Bernard Berenson, who actually preferred his olive orchards and woodland garden.*

Cetinale. A walk lined with 'The Fairy' rose in the old walled garden.

Trevelyan married a local doctor by the name of Salvatore Cacciola but their only child died at birth. Florence sought solace in long walks, and in making a large garden on the steep slopes below the town walls of Taormina. Much of her work was conventional: she built stone terraces and inlaid pebble pavements; she placed classical statues and huge oil jars at critical points; and she planted trees and shrubs with all the Victorian enthusiasm for rarity and variety. To the native olives, carobs and almonds she added cypresses that have now grown tall, and many exotics new to cultivation in Taormina. She experimented in particular with trees from the southern hemisphere, calculating correctly that they would adapt well to the climate and position: there are now venerable specimens of *Melaleuca armillaris* from New South Wales, hakeas from Western Australia, *Calliandra tweedyi* from Brazil, *Bauhinia aculeata* from Peru, the monkey puzzles *Araucaria excelsa* from Queensland and *A. bidwillii* from Norfolk Island.

Florence Trevelyan's lasting monument, however, was an extraordinary series of tall pavilions. They must have been of particular importance to her, since she built them before the garden was made, and only later did she add the paths, steps and plantings. Her buildings were extravaganzas, made with whatever materials were available. Two of them, known as Casa della Capra and Calverley Cottage (her mother was a Calverley) were built on the foundations of farm buildings, inspired conversions rather than new work: she called the others Campanile and Bagnoli. The designs and details are purely Sicilian in origin, whether Romanesque, Gothic or rococo in style; but the fantastic construction is unique. Florence Trevelyan combined bricks of different sizes and colours, odd pieces of dressed stone or rag, tiles and pipes of every imaginable length and section, and pieces of wood or metal as the fancy took her, to create shapes and effects that are both brilliant and absurd. Corbelled platforms made from drainpipes, and decorative effects obtained by setting cross-sections of roof tiles into the brickwork were among her innovations: the classical urns perched high on cornices, Romanesque marble columns re-used as mullions and wrought-iron balconies brought from long-demolished eighteenth-century palaces were the fruit of an early essay in architectural salvage.

She remains a slightly elusive character. Determined and energetic, creative in many ways, she shared with Gertrude Jekyll an interest in costume, needlework and folklore. Short, unsmiling and fairly plain of feature, she was acknowledged to be the leading English citizen of her day in Sicily. When King Edward VII visited Sicily in 1906 it was Florence Trevelyan who received him at Taormina. The Taorminesi will tell you – most improbably – that she was actually the greatest of the King's mistresses, and that when she died the following year, it was of a broken heart. But the Italians are willing to believe any romantic story. Edward VII's most distinguished mistress was actually Alice Keppel, who went with her husband in the 1920s to live in Florence. Modern visitors to their house on Bellosguardo hill are shown a photograph of Colonel George Keppel and told that he was 'the last of Queen Victoria's many lovers'!

It is widely believed that, after Florence Trevelyan died in 1907, her house in Sicily was inherited by the historian, George Macaulay Trevelyan. The truth is that he was the fortunate beneficiary who received her farm at Hallington in Northumberland, while the Sicilian property was left to his brother Robert. Both were subject to a life interest in favour of Doctor Cacciola and, when he died many years later, it was found that he had so encumbered his wife's estate in

Florence Trevelyan (plus dog) on the balcony of one of her extraordinary garden follies at Taormina (c. 1900).

Taormina with debts that it was effectively worthless.

A plaque in the garden records that it was given to the Comune in 1923 by the Duke of Cesarò. It is unfortunate that he should take the credit for a confection that is exclusively English, and very eccentrically English at that. Recently, however, the local Rotary Club has put up a bust of Florence Trevelyan (1852–1907) to commemorate her achievement. In a land where gardens are seldom looked after in the way their original owner would have wished, it is pleasant to discover that hers is maintained to a high standard by the Comune di Taormina. It is regarded as 'one of our most precious jewels from the touristic point of view', says an elaborate notice. The authorities intend to restore all the plants that once grew in it and to create an educational 'botanic garden', the term Italians use to describe a collection of plants. Comparatively little has changed in the last hundred years. It is true that the focal point is now occupied by the town war

memorial and that the Comune has resurfaced some of the paths with modern bricks. The wonder is that so much of the Giardini Pubblici is still recognisably the same dotty garden that Florence Trevelyan Cacciola made. One corner of the garden has particular poignancy, not only because it is so English in sentiment, but because it suggests that life among the Taorminesi was not always easy. The Dogs' Cemetery includes the sorry inscriptions 'Dear Fanny. Faithful Friend and Companion. Poisoned 27 July 1899. Aged 15 years' and 'JUMBO PERCEVAL (Terrier). True Honourable Loving. Little Friend and Helper. September 3, 1887 – Murdered July 24 1904. Never Forgotten.'

Robert Hawthorn Kitson (1873–1947) was an engineer whose family made locomotives at their factory in Leeds. He first visited Sicily in 1900 at the age of twenty-seven, after an attack of rheumatic fever. The beauty of Taormina and its position were a revelation to him, and when he returned in 1903 it was to settle there for life. Kitson was interested in

Casa Cuseni. English irises in a formal garden at the side of the house in about 1930. The garden is dominated by its view of Mt Etna and the sea.

contemporary British art and was himself a more than competent water-colourist. He loved order, symmetry, repetition, axes and drama; everything about him suggests good taste, mingled with charm and modesty. The house and garden that he made in Taormina are witness to an engineer's sense of proportion, an artist's love of colour and an architect's instinct for dramatic angularity.

Kitson named his house Casa Cuseni. It was not in the historic centre of Taormina, but on a steep hillside outside the walls of the old town. The site of about 1.2 ha (3 acres) faces just west of south, which makes it open in summer to bright light and intense heat. Kitson chose it for the panoramic view of Mt Etna, whose huge cone rising over the bell towers and fortifications of the city gives a stupendous majesty to the setting. The volcano was made integral to his garden. He positioned the house in the middle of the plot, halfway up the hillside; there is no access for cars, so visitors have to walk up from the road below. Kitson gave careful thought to his garden and its development: it was an integral part of the overall design. The house was Palladian in concept: a high-ceilinged *salone* which opens on to a terrace through a loggia is matched by two other principal rooms approximately half its size, a double cube flanked by two single cubes. Kitson's friend Frank Brangwyn designed much of the interior, and some of the garden's features are also said to have sprung from Brangwyn's suggestions. The two artists had a good deal in common: the freshness, vitality and panache displayed at Casa Cuseni could have come from either man. Most of the designs were worked out in Kitson's notebooks over a period of forty years; these included his plans for the planting of trees, shrubs and roses. Brightly coloured bedding plants, notably schizanthus and cinerarias, were an important part of the scheme in early years. When a road-widening scheme demolished his entrance gate in 1931, Kitson designed new rococo gate piers and a sinuous roadside wall; then he planted many of the citrus trees which now shade the lower terraces. His final sketches in 1946 depict these trees and gates again, as well as a new design for a wooden grille in the garage fanlight. Since his death in 1947, the house and garden have been maintained with devotion and fidelity by his niece, Daphne Phelps.

The garden at Casa Cuseni is axially oriented on the house, and ignores the old almond terraces which follow the contours of the hillside. In essence it is a single design, but it can only be clearly understood by reference to the steeply rising levels. They are

Casa Cuseni. The ciottolato *pavement, complex patterns of pebbles in different colours, being laid* (c. 1905).

linked by steps, ramps, paths and staircases, and enlivened by the judicious placing of old oil jars, terracotta pots filled with flowers and other artefacts designed to surprise and catch the eye. At road level, just inside the half-moon gates, is a shallow basin fringed with papyrus and backed by rococo decorations that run to the terrace above. Two paths curl away, through blue echiums and paper-white *Narcissus papyraceus* and up to the fruit garden where grapefruit, mandarins, lemons and sweet oranges are grown as if in an English orchard. The walls are stencilled with profiles of Kitson and his master builder, jolly caricatures in stucco strapwork frames. Twin flights of steps rise to the brickwork terrace, made over one of several reservoirs that Kitson installed to provide the garden with sufficient water through the long dry summer of Sicily. One is on the site of an old Arab cistern and incorporates much of its ancient structure. Another feeds a marble basin deeply recessed between the two staircases, and passes through a sculptured satyr's mask. The main terrace in front of the house is wide and spacious, with a tiled surface. Off to one side, above an iron arcade planted with vines, broken busts bear silent witness to the damage done by the German officers

Part of the ciottolato *garden at Casa Cuseni today. The ornamental tiling which decorates the retaining wall of the terrace above also provides a vertical focus for this level. Kitson brought it from north Africa.*

who occupied the house during the early years of the Second World War. The other end of the terrace projects over a pergola of white wisteria, bougainvillea and jasmine, and leads round to a formal garden edged with lavender and santolina at the side of the house.

The best parts of the garden at Casa Cuseni are behind the house, high up on the hillside. First comes the *ciottolato*, an ornamental patio that illustrates how Kitson used local materials and skills for the detail of his garden: it roots him in the Arts and Crafts Movement, as does his choice of traditional building materials for the house. The terrace is paved with a flowing pattern of tiles inlaid with symmetrical *broderies* of pebble mosaic from which it takes its name, *ciottolato*. The technique flourished in the baroque gardens of the Tuscan seventeenth century, but the intricate patterns developed by such artists as Vaccarini in Catania early in the eighteenth century carried the art to the peak of its development. It is clear from Kitson's notebooks that it was these Sic-

ilian refinements which inspired him to use *ciottolato* at Casa Cuseni, while his contemporaries in Tuscany drew on the Florentine tradition. Both Arthur Acton at Villa La Pietra and Bernard Berenson at I Tatti used black and white pebble inlays to re-create old decorative patterns at the same time as Robert Kitson applied the technique to his garden in Sicily.

A narrow path leads steeply up from the *ciottolato* through cypress, citrus, pomegranate and olive trees, underplanted with luxuriant spurges, acanthus, freesias and antholyza, to Kitson's masterpiece: a deep cube of a swimming-pool, edged by a blue and pink pergola which is festooned with night-scented jasmine. Still on the central axis that begins with the half-moon gates at the roadside entrance, the pool is oriented to catch the summit of Mount Etna; bathers can plunge Empedocles-like, not into the crater but into its reflection. Coolly moonlit, it must have been idyllic.

Kitson has never received the recognition he merits. It is true that Casa Cuseni is not generally open to the public, although Daphne Phelps runs it as a *locanda*, and that Kitson never designed houses and gardens for others. Indeed, much of the interior was Frank Brangwyn's work. Nevertheless, Kitson's own contribution is of outstanding importance. His designs were of a classical nature, owing much to Renaissance principles, rococo witticisms and the type of intellectual ingenuity that Lutyens practised. He deserves to be remembered alongside his Anglo-Italian counterparts in Tuscany, who have become renowned, even notorious, thanks to their literary sons.

IN ABOUT 1880, a rich English invalid went to live in Venice with his wife Caroline: his name was Frederic Eden. A city without noise, flies or dust was what he sought. But he soon became satiated by the very beauty of Venice and remarked, 'I am sick of all this water. I am tired of pink and grey, of blue and of red. I thirst for dry land and green trees and shrubs, and flowers; a garden.' He realised that no such thing would be found in Venice: an Italian proverb speaks of Venice as the grave of flowers. But his gondolier found a garden on the Giudecca, and Frederic Eden bought it early in 1884. He began to plant it at once, while continuing to live at Palazzo Barbarigo on the Grand Canal. When Lady Paget visited them in July of that year, she wrote to her husband, then Ambassador in Vienna, 'The Edens ... have a lovely garden on the other side of the Giudecca, all covered with vine trellises and intersected with shady avenues. One side looks on the open sea; it is a wilderness of flowers, carnations, mignonette, stocks and hollyhocks. Orange and lemon trees in big vases stand round the old wells and broken fountains.'

There was nothing very remarkable about a rich Englishman settling in Venice in the nineteenth century and buying a plot to indulge his passion for gardening. But Frederic Eden's garden is interesting for two reasons. First, because he wrote an exquisite book about it, published by Country Life in 1903, which explained exactly how they set about planning and planting *Our Garden in Venice*; and second, because Caroline Eden happened to be Gertrude Jekyll's elder sister. Indeed the famous garden designer often stayed in Venice during the formative years when she was observing and absorbing the ideas that would one day bring her fame.

The Edens' newly acquired plot was about $1\frac{1}{2}$ ha (4 acres) in extent: a vast area for Venice. It contained a small parterre; four huge cypress trees; some statues and stone vases, most of which had fallen on the ground; two arbours, one of jasmine and the other of honeysuckle; and an orchard of peaches, apricots, mulberries, pears and apples. Rather than spoil the existing structure by imposing a brand-new plan, they decided to make only such changes as were 'needed to utilise and beautify it'. The Edens noted that the English love 'vegetation as nature grows it, rather than as man clips it' but did not consider such a garden appropriate in Venice: it was necessary to have regard for the spirit of the place. They took as their theme the long straight intersecting pergolas which already ran through the orchard and seemed to Frederic Eden in keeping with the spirit of the *calli*, the narrow footpaths between the tall old buildings of Venice itself. The pergolas were of wood, and had to be remade every few years, to support the vines, roses, clematis and other climbing plants. Frederic Eden reckoned that the garden contained more than 550 m (600 yd) of them and that 'in a warm climate there are few things more enjoyable than a stroll, even in August, under a vine pergola': a generous opinion for an invalid who was incapable of walking and would spend the month of August in the Dolomites anyway.

Eden bordered the paths beneath the pergolas with box hedges or old bricks, and laid boatloads of crushed sea shells as a substitute for gravel, which is not found in the Veneto. Then he and his wife set about planting the spaces which the pergolas formed and enclosed. Eden wrote, 'the joy of a garden lies, more or less, in its wealth; one loves to see things grow as if they liked it. To see colour in masses, depth of shade, bloom in profusion, glorious promise, and bountiful flowering – these are the characteristics that the soil ... will give to those who ask it.' This is an entirely English sentiment, and so it is no surprise that the Edens planted English garden flowers: daffodils, anemones and tulips; foxgloves, columbines and larkspurs; peach blossom, forsythias, deutzias and weigelas. Even the so-called Italian Garden consisted of hundreds of plants in pots around the entrance court of the house: tall palms, jasmine and ivy-leaved geraniums trained in pyramids behind; groups of arum lilies, agapanthus, azaleas and Canterbury bells in the middle; and lines of such dwarf plants as begonias, lobelias and musks in front. The list of roses that they planted is particularly impressive. Varieties now lost to cultivation such as 'Comte de Paris', 'Beauté Inconstant' and 'Souvenir de Catherine Guillot' grew among others still known to

us, 'Mme Laurette Messimy', 'Mme Caroline Testout' and 'Souvenir de la Malmaison', while among the many vigorous roses planted on the pergolas were 'Gloire Lyonnaise', 'Reine Olga de Wurtemberg' and 'Crimson Rambler'. But by all accounts the glory of the garden was the thick lines of Madonna lilies that flowered in early June underneath the pergolas. 'The beauty of the garden at this time is beyond description,' wrote Alethea Weil in 1900. 'In every direction the eye is carried along lines of pure white lilies to some fresh vision of loveliness.' It was a planting that Gertrude Jekyll particularly admired, for she used a photograph of it in *Lilies for English Gardens* (Country Life, 1901), while Beatrice Parsons included a water-colour of the Lily Walk which Lady Downe planted at Dingley Park 'with a reminiscence of Mrs Eden's well-known Venetian garden' among the illustrations she used for *Gardens of England* (Black, 1911).

Frederic Eden maintained that the origin of his design was the walled garden of a house they had known in Ross-shire, but he never explained why this improbable source had provided the inspiration. Nor did he name the garden in question. Other elements were taken from the Generalife at Granada, notably the reservoir for watering the garden which was a stone basin nearly 2 m (6 ft) deep: its marble cornice was edged with potted lemon trees. Hedges of old cabbage roses were inspired by others at Battaglia in the Colle Euganee. But, beyond these, Eden gave no indication of whence he derived his ideas. It is tempting to suggest that Gertrude Jekyll had a hand in the planning and planting, but she did not begin to develop her interest in gardening until several years after the Edens had completed their garden. In fact, it is closest in spirit to the Arts and Crafts Movement, which sought to use traditional English materials to create gardens that were in harmony with their surroundings. The choice of pergolas as a unifying theme for the garden is recognisably of the same school, as is the charming substitution of shells for gravel. Then there are specifically Italian elements: pools and fountains, and an abundance of statuary and ornaments. The garden was Italian enough to appear in Gabriele d'Annunzio's novel *Il Fuoco*, which is a *roman à clef* about the patriot's relationship with Eleanora Duse.

Frederic Eden, the brother-in-law of Gertrude Jekyll, in the very English garden he and his wife made on the Giudecca at Venice (c. 1895).

Villa Eden at Venice (c. 1900). A natural winding path lined by fruit trees and bamboos, richly underplanted in the English taste. The inspiration for some of Gertrude Jekyll's most successful plantings may be traced to this garden.

It conveys, however, an abiding impression of Englishness, above all in the importance attributed to plants. The pergolas provided the structure, as the paths of an English walled garden bordered with espaliered fruit trees might do, but the underplanting with lines of lilies, irises and herbaceous plants belongs to the English tradition. So too did the delight of the owners in growing such exotic fruit as pomegranates, loquats and persimmons, all the envy of many a Victorian head gardener in England.

The expression *matti inglesi* ('crazy English') gained currency from such residents of Venice as the Edens, who kept a herd of fifteen cows in stalls in their garden on the Giudecca in 'imperial disregard' of all the city's sanitary laws. Milk from Luna, Perla, Stella and their sisters not only 'found a ready market in the best hotels of Venice' but was also sold to those members of the English community who could not bring themselves to trust the Italian suppliers. And, according to Lady Paget, Frederic Eden spent nine years in atrocious suffering, completely bedridden, until the doctors gave him up. Caroline Eden then administered gout powders made by some nuns in Pistoia, and he made such a miraculous recovery within three months that Lady Paget did not recognise the 'healthy, burly, red-faced man' who rushed into the room and shook her warmly by the hand.

Both Frederic and Caroline Eden died in their nineties, and the garden was then acquired by Princess Aspasia of Greece. It was badly affected by the floods of 1966, when salt water destroyed much of the planting, but the Princess restored it, and the garden was well maintained until her death in 1972. It remains something of a local cynosure which most Venetians praise but few have seen. Predictably they call it the Garden of Eden. Latest reports are that the present owner 'is letting nature take the upper hand' and that 'conceptually, the garden today is much closer to a Japanese model, attuned to the values of simplicity and natural beauty', a euphemism for the neglect which characterises the fate of so many English gardens in Italy.

Villar Perosa, Piemonte. Russell Page built this chinoiserie bridge to link the house and its formal garden to the new woodland valley garden which he designed for the Agnelli.

Frederic and Caroline Eden had another property in northern Italy, a country house at Salce in the Bellunese, where they retreated in August when the heat of Venice became too oppressive. The garden was designed to be enjoyed entirely at that season, just as Sir Philip Sassoon planned the borders at Port Lympne to be seen by his political masters at his house parties during the parliamentary summer recess. The Edens enclosed the garden at Salce with hedges of hornbeam and box, punctuated every so often by green pompoms on top. The parterre in front of the house was planted with bright bedding plants, gaillardias, zinnias, coreopsis and salvias, mixed with scented heliotrope, petunias and tobacco plants. The herbaceous border was said to 'offer a vision of dazzling beauty and harmony', where perennial hostas, Michaelmas daisies, Japanese anemones and delphiniums were padded out (in the approved Jekyll fashion) by tender dahlias, cannas and gladioli, and annual sunflowers and cosmos. There were lawns and arbours and a bowling green, and an open loggia where Frederic Eden, a competent water-colourist, sketched and painted. It was altogether more modest than their garden in Venice, but so completely English that no part of it would have looked out of place in a rectory garden in the shires.

THE WORK of Russell Page pervades modern English gardens in Europe, and is analysed in detail in a later chapter. Much of Page's most lasting work was done in Italy; his long association with the Agnelli family brought some of his best commissions. Early in the 1950s, Avvocato Giovanni Agnelli asked Page to 'rearrange the grounds' around the house at Villar Perosa which had belonged to them for several generations. The problem at Villar Perosa was that the house was positioned sideways on an awkward hillside, and could not be used to give coherence to the whole site, or even to suggest a style or period for the garden. Apart from placing rudimentary box enclosures in front of the handsome eighteenth-century house, Russell Page was unable to do much to improve its immediate setting. But his wealthy anglophile patron was also willing to expand the garden. Page linked the existing features by means of a handsome wooden bridge in white chinoiserie to a steep narrow valley near by, which he developed as a long natural walk. For nearly 400 m ($\frac{1}{4}$ mile) it ambles gently past a score of waterfalls and pools, each section or glade filled with massed plantings – brunneras, astilbes or *Iris sibirica*, for example. The valley is lined with flowering trees and handsome evergreens appropriate to the sub-alpine setting. Though the main ride resembles nothing so much as a fairway on one of Surrey's more exclusive golf-courses, the garden remains a brilliant example of Page's post-Robinsonian woodland style of gardening.

When Russell Page was asked to advise a cousin of Avvocato Agnelli at Villa Silvio Pellico in a fashionable suburb of Turin, he found a handsome orange-ochre house already surrounded by English-style lawns and a nineteenth-century landscape park. Page decided that it lacked firm features, but chose not to link the house to the park by means of a formal garden: he kept the existing setting almost untouched. He did not, however, approve of the kitchen garden, which sloped away from the edge of the lawn towards the boundary: Page levelled the site and substituted a strongly designed garden of water, hedges and parterres. He intended it to echo the architecture of classical Italian gardens while reflecting the sky and the expansive view: it links the house

to the Po valley beyond. By creating a formal garden right on the edge of the park, Page was able to extend the influence of the house and restore the balance between nature and architecture.

Page worked best with knowledgeable and enthusiastic clients. Such was Susana Walton, wife of Sir William, the composer, who lived for many years on Ischia, in a house at Forio called La Mortella, named for the wild myrtle that grows on the hillside. It was a semi-redundant granary when the Waltons bought it, perched above a small steep valley that had been used as a quarry. Great boulders gave it the appearance of a gorge: Russell Page was quick to see the possibilities of landscaping this to create a real rock garden. He made it the central feature.

Page got on well with the Waltons. Susana Walton says that he gave her much good counsel. 'He advised me to make dry stone walls, to hold the earth in place on the hill, and to make them straight, not curvy, so as to avoid pockets; also to free the great boulders of creepers, to show up their dramatic impact; and

Villa Silvio Pellico. Italianate parterres on a hillside above Turin designed by Russell Page in the 1950s for the Marsan family.

La Mortella. Russell Page worked with Sir William and Lady Walton for twenty years to give structure and style to this luxuriant plantsman's garden on Ischia. Note how the spiky plants contrast with the pines behind.

to plant very young trees, which were cheap to buy and would not be blown down by the first gales. It took us seven years to landscape the hill' (*William Walton: Behind the Façade*, 1988). Lorry loads of peat and soil were imported. Hedges of cypress were planted for protection from the sirocco and, when these died, they were replaced by bay trees, native to the island. Lighting and irrigation were brought to every part of the garden, the watering varying from mist to heavy spray, to satisfy the needs of all plants.

Susana Walton became an enthusiastic plantsman, growing plants and sowing seeds from all over the world. Jacarandas, magnolias, Judas trees, chorisias and flowering eucalyptus were some of the early plantings: these were followed by hemerocallis, Japanese anemones, campanulas, hibiscus, lilies, daturas and hebes. When Sir William visited Australia, he sent home some *Dicksonia antarctica*: they became the basis of a flourishing collection of sub-tropical ferns which only survive through constant overhead watering in summer. Page suggested using the beautiful creeping fern *Woodwardia radicans* to form large patches of ground cover. Woodwardia is a very rare native to Ischia, found only in one cleft

high in the volcanic mountains of the interior. The plants of La Mortella, however, were the gift of Viscount Chaplin and of quite different stock.

Ten years after his first designs, Russell Page returned to make the large egg-shaped pool beneath the house. It is dominated by a huge rock in the middle and planted with scarlet water lilies, papyrus plants and the sacred Indian lotus *Nelumbo nucifera*. On the steep banks around it are cacti, succulents and spiky plants: aloes, cordylines, yuccas, puyas, crinums, phormiums, grasses, sedges and a grey-leaved form of *Erythea armata*. The Waltons bought a pair of marble sphinxes to guard the steps from the house to the pool. These did not find favour with Russell Page, but Lady Walton was determined to keep them, having been told by Christabel Aberconway of Bodnant that sphinxes were Egyptian gods who protected gardens. So she planted ivy round them to cover all but their faces. 'They now look like green poodles,' she declared, 'each with only its face and one claw visible.'

Russell Page returned again to La Mortella in 1982 to design an eightieth birthday present for Sir William, a small fountain in an octagonal tank at the top of the valley, linked to a fountain at the lower end by a channelled rivulet in the Persian style. Two tall evergreen *Magnolia grandiflora*, pruned back into narrow cones, terminate the axis. Page declared on his last visit that the garden was becoming 'rather distinguished'. La Mortella exemplifies the best of his work as a modern English garden designer in Italy.

References and Further Reading

I have used Camillo Fiorani's *Giardini d'Italia* (Roma, 1960) as a general guide but the most plant-oriented book on Italian gardens is Marella Agnelli's *Gardens of the Italian Villas* (London, 1987). It includes many of the modern gardens in this and successive chapters, and is particularly useful for the work of Russell Page. Olive Hamilton's *Paradise of Exiles* (London, 1974) is a good account of the English community in Italy. The quotation from Giuliana Artom Treves comes from *The Golden Ring* (London, 1956), Sylvia Sprigge's translation of *Anglofiorentini di cento anni fa* (Firenze, 1953). The quotation from Francis Toye comes from his memoir *For What We Have Received* (London, 1950), itself already a period piece. The Margravine of Anspach's *Memoirs* (1826) are a good read and reveal the vigour of her character, but my knowledge of Villa Rae is based largely on an article in *Napoli Nobilissima*, vol. 25, May–August 1985: '*Villa Rae a Posillipo: Ricordo della Margravia di Ansbach*'. Charles Lacaita's memoir of his father, *An Italian Englishman, Sir James Lacaita* (London, 1933), is more valuable as a source of information about Naples and liberalism than for any mention of gardens. My accounts of Villa Rúfolo and Villa Cimbrone at Ravello are pieced together from many minor sources, including articles on Cimbrone in *Country Life* (23 February 1935) and *Il Giardino Fiorito* (1987), and from the memoirs of Lord Grimthorpe's many visitors

(see, for instance, E. H. and A. Brewster, *Reminiscences and Correspondence*, London, 1934, for details of D. H. Lawrence's misdemeanours at Cimbrone); if a substantial work on these gardens has already been published, it has eluded me. The gardens of Capri are mentioned in James Money's lightweight *Capri: Island of Pleasure* (London, 1986) and in passing in Faith Compton Mackenzie's *More Than I Should* (London, 1940) and *Always Afternoon* (London, 1943), autobiographical portraits of a sad and sick society. The most delightful account of Maniace is Alec Hood's own study *The Duchy of Bronte*, subtitled *A Memorandum Written for His Family in 1924*, which was privately printed in Weston-super-Mare: there is a copy at Cambridge, but none at the British Library. His article in *Country Life* on 17 August 1929 is less useful. Frances Elliott's *Diary of an Idle Woman in Sicily* (London, 1881) is hard going; nor are the novels of such popular writers as Mrs Lynn Linton and F. Marion Crawford the easy read they must once have been. I have found no written account of Florence Trevelyan Cacciola's garden at Taormina, but gratefully acknowledge my debt to David Boswell's account of Casa Cuseni in *Building Design* (11 October 1985), which is a model of analytical exposition. Douglas Sladen's books on Sicily are minor classics: *In Sicily* (London, 1901) and *Sicily: The New Winter Resort* (London, 1905). The Edens' garden in Venice is featured in *Country Life* (21 July 1900) as well as Eden's own book (*Our Garden in Venice*, London, 1903), while Alethea Weil's article on Salce appears in *Country Life* on 26 January 1901. The latest word on Venice is *The Gardens of Venice* by Alessandro Albrizzi and Mary-Jane Pool (New York, 1989). Russell Page's *The Education of a Gardener* (London, 1962; Harmondsworth, 1983) is essential reading for anyone in search of an aesthetic of gardening: brief accounts of the Agnelli gardens have also been published in the International Dendrology Society's *Year Book*, 1990.

Chapter Six

LANDSCAPE STYLE IN ITALY

The Natural and the Gardenesque

'THE GARDENS of the park are stupendous,' declared Goethe when he visited the royal palace, or *reggia*, of Caserta in 1787. He was referring to the newly laid out landscape that is one of the outstanding examples of an English eighteenth-century garden in Europe. So famous has it become that to many Italians '*il giardino inglese*' designates not the English garden in the sense used in the title of this book but specifically the garden conceived, designed and planted by Englishmen for King Ferdinand V of Naples between 1785 and 1800.

The English Garden at Caserta was the brainchild of Sir William Hamilton, the British minister to King Ferdinand, at a time when English influence with the Bourbons of Naples was particularly strong: the King's prime minister was another Englishman, Admiral Sir John Acton. Sir William Hamilton was a man of learning, an antiquarian and scientist as well as a diplomat: it was he who initiated and financed the first systematic excavation of Pompeii. Although he lived in Naples for many years, Hamilton did not like Italian gardens; he considered them 'vulgar', or at any rate old-fashioned, and he thought that the spectacular waterfalls and formal gardens at La Reggia were in the worst possible taste. But Sir William had the ear of Queen Maria Carolina of Naples, the ambitious and innovative daughter of the Empress Maria Theresa of Austria. Her sister, Queen Marie-Antoinette of France, had laid out the Petit Trianon at Versailles, a landscape on the English model. So it was not difficult for Sir William Ham-

ilton to persuade Maria Carolina to fund his project to create an English garden at Caserta, and she immediately appointed him director of the scheme. About 20 ha (50 acres) of land were appropriated by the King, on a site adjoining the great waterfall, and work began in February 1785. Eighty workmen were employed on the actual landscaping while a further five hundred worked on the boundary walls.

The palace at Caserta and its grounds were designed on a massive scale and the park is famous for its extended waterworks. A long formal drive runs from the palace, passes through vast ruined parterres, then splits and continues along each side of a sequence of cascades which fall gently for over 3 km (2 miles) in a straight line down the hillside. At the top is a basin with life-sized marble groups depicting Diana with her maidens and Actaeon surrounded by his hounds: King Ferdinand was a passionate huntsman. These set pieces lie in turn at the foot of the great waterfall, wide and steep, which issues from near the top of the hill and is itself fed by an aqueduct running from a spring on Monte Taburno 32 km (20 miles) away. The vastness of the waterworks, and of the rest of the garden, and indeed of the palace itself, is astonishing.

This was the garden that Sir William Hamilton considered vulgar. His alternative idea was to lay out lawns and plant a landscape as beautiful as any in England, something of which no one at the Neapolitan Court had experience. It would be a botanic garden too, because Sir William had from the beginning enlisted the assistance of Sir Joseph Banks, President of the Royal Society and botanist extraordinary. Banks found a head gardener to supervise the project and sent him out to Naples; Johann Gräfer had worked for the Earl of Coventry at Croome and for

---

The English garden at Caserta. The discovery of this white marble statue of Venus bathing in an artificial creek surrounded by a ruined crypto-portico is the climax of a visit.

The English garden at Caserta. The Gothic-Moorish folly was the first to be built in Italy and seems remarkably English, despite the exotic vegetation.

James Vere at Kensington Gore. He was a competent and industrious man, and the partnership with Sir William Hamilton proved harmonious.

Results came quickly, partly because the site was very fertile and abundant water was available for irrigation from the sources that supplied the cascades in the formal gardens near by. A camphor tree *Cinnamomum camphora* was planted to test whether it could survive outside and flourished to such an extent that it put on 2 m (6 ft) in three months. Hamilton was soon writing to Banks that they would make, in addition to the botanic garden, a *ferme ornée* to experiment with different kinds of forage for domestic animals. This would not only interest the Queen, but also be of public utility. Hamilton hoped that courtiers would then make use of the experiment by repeating it at home on their estates. Unfortunately, however, the idea fell foul of the King, who maintained that Nature had no need of assistance, and this view was immediately adopted by most of the nobles.

The English Garden at Caserta is a classic English landscape set among rolling grassy hills, grand but naturalistic. The background is mainly of evergreen oaks, Portuguese laurels and bay trees, but also has palm trees, which create distinctly unEnglish contrasts. Gräfer was moreover sent botanising, in Sicily, Capri and the hills behind Amalfi, to bring back specimens of the natural flora for cultivation in the garden. Central to the design and spirit of the garden is the use of water. The fountain of Venus first appears as a sheltered combe from which issues a small cascade: you can just make out the white marble figure of Venus bathing on a rocky ledge inside. A path leads into the cave, which then reveals itself to be a fern-lined grotto round a small lake, all surrounded by a ruined crypto-portico. It is a place of the utmost enchantment. Downstream is a much larger lake, surrounded by open parkland: the island in the middle has a ruined temple, the first example of a romantic folly in Italy. All around are the trees sent out by Sir Joseph Banks and planted by Hamilton over two hundred years ago: the tulip tree *Liriodendron tulipifera*, the evergreen *Magnolia grandiflora*, the American persimmon *Diospyros virginiana*, and the original specimen of *Cinnamomum*

Villa Borghese, Rome. An early aerial photograph showing traces of the landscaping by Jacob Moore in 1787–8. The formal gardens are now a wilderness.

camphora that grew so well in its early years and is the ancestor of all the camphor trees now growing in Italy.

King Ferdinand and his obsequious nobles may have scotched Hamilton's plans for a *ferme ornée* but Sir William did have the pleasure of knowing that his English landscape garden was well received, not least by visitors to the Caserta. Among them was Goethe, accompanied by Hackert, who painted Vesuvius from the vantage point of the English Garden. Goethe observed that 'the gardens of the park are ... in perfect harmony with a stretch of country that is all a garden'. A more detailed appreciation was shown by Count della Torre di Rezzonico after he visited the English Garden in the company of Sir William in 1790:

with the greatest pleasure I disported myself for a long time along beautiful paths and artificial wandering ways ... The British custom of gathering together the rarest gifts of Flora and using them to make winding flower-beds, broad slopes, curving hills ... varying in a thousand ways the prospect and the forms ... is much to be preferred to

cold symmetry and the rigid uniformity of the asthmatic Europeans ... For us, everyone sees and understands in the blink of an eye the plan of a vast garden. In English gardens, on the contrary, a little area of terrain is multiplied and extended by frequent comings and goings and with every step changes the magic perspective ... When the garden is finished it will be, thanks to the design, one of the most beautiful in Italy for the variety of its contents and for its views.

(Quoted in Carlo Knight, *Il giardino inglese a Caserta*)

That an Italian could write with such perception only five years after the English Garden was begun is a measure of how successful Hamilton, Banks and Gräfer had been in altering not only the landscape but also the Italians' attitude to landscaping.

At the same time as Hamilton was laying out the English Garden at Caserta, the Scottish painter Jacob Moore (1740–93) was landscaping the Villa Borghese in Rome. It had always been an important garden. John Evelyn remarked in 1644 that it 'abounded with all sorts of the most delicious fruit, and Exotique simples: Fountaines of sundry inventions, Groves &

small Rivulets of water', although by 1765 Tobias Smollett's verdict was less favourable: 'here we see a variety of walks and groves and fountains, a wood of four hundred pines, a paddock with a few meagre deer, a flower-garden, an aviary, a grotto, and a fish-pond; and in spite of all these particulars, it is, in my opinion, a very contemptible garden, when compared to that of Stowe in Buckinghamshire'. Jacob Moore was called upon in 1787 to give Villa Borghese a more natural and picturesque air: Moore had lived in Rome for fifteen years and was the most fashionable landscape painter in the city, although he had no experience of planning gardens. Nevertheless, it was thought quite proper for a painter to turn his hand to garden design: indeed, it gave the project greater cultural status, raising it from craft to art. In a letter to Lord Cowper in March 1788, Moore explained that he had 'made them extend it to double the Size and ... caus'd them to plant Trees in Groups in a Picturesque manner which they were not acquainted with such as weeping willows &c', and added that 'the Prince is highly pleas'd with it, and intends to give a great Entertainment there after Easter'. Unfortunately, the finer features of the garden have been effectively destroyed since it was acquired by the Municipality of Rome as a public park in the middle of the nineteenth century, and it is difficult now to discern Moore's work. Symptomatic is the fate of the balustrade around the 'Casino', which Evelyn called a 'stately Balustre of white marble': it was sold to William Waldorf Astor in 1896 and transported to Cliveden in Buckinghamshire.

Despite the examples of Caserta and Villa Borghese, the landscape movement never took hold in Italy as firmly as in France and northern Europe. Sir William Chambers's *Dissertation on Oriental Gardening* likewise spawned Chinese pavilions and pagodas all over Germany, but failed to move the Italians. It became a common assertion of English visitors by the end of the eighteenth century that the Italians were not interested in gardening because they did not plant landscape gardens. Lady Morgan even wrote in 1819 that they had no *love* of gardening because they did not plant or farm for ornament: 'terraces, balustrades, colonnades, pavilions, Courts, fortifications, towers, temples, and belvederes, abound very generally; but green, fresh, delicious nature, is almost everywhere excluded'. When Italians did try to design in the new style, the results were not always recognised as English landscapes. After Lady Blessington visited Villa Lomellini near Genoa in the company of Lord Byron, she wrote in

her journal that it contained within a small compass all that bad taste could attempt to spoil the gifts of Nature, 'and this incongruous medley of island, four foot square, sundry bridges, rococo hermitages and temples à-la-turque and à-la-chinoise, was − O profanation − called a *jardin à l'anglaise*'.

There were exceptions, of which the most important was Count Ercole Silva, whose study of English gardens, *Dell'arte dei giardini inglesi*, was published in 1813, following a trip to England during which Silva visited Stowe and Blenheim among other famous eighteenth-century landscapes. He even complained that English gardens relied on too limited a range of trees and shrubs and made poor use of flowering plants, a criticism which sounds strange to English ears. It is explained partly by the revelation that Silva was an enthusiastic botanist who sought variety, but also by knowing that the English passion for flowers, taken for granted after about 1830, was not such a national characteristic before the influence of John Loudon. Silva's own estate was at Cinisello in Lombardy. Lady Morgan described it as 'the Leasowes or Stow [*sic*] of the Milanese'. Silva and such other landscape architects as Giuseppe Japelli and Gianbattista Meduna worked mainly in the north of Italy: there was less scope for landscape gardening in the harsher climate of the Two Sicilies, although a *giardino inglese* was opened as a public garden in Palermo in the 1840s.

The English style did not establish itself in Italy during the course of the nineteenth century, despite alterations to such famous gardens as Villa Borghese in Rome and Villa Medicea di Castello in Florence, which was substantially remade in the natural manner. Nevertheless the modified landscapes of Victorian England quickly gained ground after about 1850. These gardens were usually laid out by Italians anxious to follow the latest fashion or to reduce the cost of upkeep. A few were made by Englishmen: one of the most interesting was designed by Frederick Stibbert around his villa north of Florence.

Stibbert was an Anglo-Florentine: his father was a retired lieutenant-colonel in the Coldstream Guards, while his mother was called Giulia Cafaggi, and came from Florence. Frederick was born in 1838, and educated at Harrow and Magdalene College, Cambridge. His father died when he was still a boy, so Stibbert inherited a substantial fortune at the age of twenty-one, although this did not prevent him from joining Garibaldi's extraordinary Trentino campaign of 1866. He then settled down to become

Villa Stibbert, Florence. Trecento Venetian colonnading around an Istrian well-head, both part of the collection of bric-à-brac which Frederick Stibbert employed in his landscape garden. Note the tall banana trees.

a collector of *objets d'art*, buying anything that caught his fancy, from Flemish tapestries to German suits of armour, from Turkish armaments to Chinese costumes. That Stibbert's was an eclectic and capricious taste is clear from the confusion of styles and artefacts still to be found in the house and garden of the Villa Stibbert.

A contemporary description of Villa Stibbert in 1900 confirms this.

Driving up the slopes, the attention is caught every moment by some interesting piece of stonework, disposed with great care and meaning. Here is a little shrine of the Renaissance, there a fine old carved well-head, set against a graceful scrolled iron rail, iron torch-holders project from the walls, and the space round the entrance is covered with shields bearing the devices of half the ancient houses of Tuscany. It is as a museum that Mr Stibbert's residence must be regarded, for the house and garden exist only for the collection.

Actually, that is not entirely true so far as the garden is concerned, for Villa Stibbert is an English garden in the style that developed out of the eighteenth-century classical landscape, with elements of the designs made popular by such later writers as John Loudon. It is the style that we call gardenesque or Victorian, and the Italians describe as late romantic or bourgeois-grandiose.

It has been suggested that Stibbert may have had the advice of Giuseppe Poggi (1811–1901) in making the garden. Poggi was the architect of Florentine neo-classicism, who created monumental public buildings and government offices when Florence became Italy's capital in 1861. He was himself a supporter of the Risorgimento and a friend of the leading Tuscan liberals, whose sons he had known in the field of battle, but it is not certain to what extent he, rather than Stibbert himself, laid out the garden. On stylistic grounds it would appear to be the work of the owner rather than the architect. Only Stibbert could have arranged the Gothic terrace around a Venetian well-head of Istrian marble, enclosed it with reconstructed Gothic trecento colonnading, and planted it in summer with lemon trees and vast banana plants: over-dramatic perhaps, but certainly more English in taste than Italian. At the bottom of the garden Stibbert built a substantial neo-Egyptian temple, its entrance guarded by priests of Osiris, on the edge of a very small lake where steps flanked by couchant lions and sphinxes lead down to the water's edge. A rocky islet, no more than a large boulder but of different geological origin to the stones of the embankment, has a solitary swamp cypress perched precariously right on its summit, with only the croaking bullfrogs for company. This neo-Egyptian temple is thought to be English, and Italian historians draw parallels between it and the temples designed by J. B. Papworth. On the other hand, an avenue lined with busts on plinths, many of them imitations of antique pieces, with ivy at their base and collections of bedding plants along the edge, is a typical element of the Italian garden. More specifically Florentine as opposed to Italian are the terracotta statues, probably the work of Cantagalli; such pieces are commonly used within the structure of a classic Italian garden, for example at the house in Fiesole which used to belong to the sculptor Giovanni Dupré, but Stibbert placed them in a woodland clearing. Byzantine columns, old oil jars, chunks of stalactites and innumerable other curiosities are all disposed around this nineteenth-century gardenesque landscape. The setting presents an intricate network of glades and paths which rise and fall and twist and cross, with places for exploration, points for stopping, and seats for contemplating the view: all uniquely Victorian in character. The plants too were partly chosen to produce different effects according to the season, so that the splendours of the garden were seen to change throughout the year.

Villa Stibbert is difficult to classify. One school of opinion believes that it is the garden of an undisciplined and undiscriminating collector with too much money and too little taste. Thus runs the usual verdict of English critics. A more charitable view, which finds favour with Italian commentators, is that the garden is a fascinating amalgam of different traditions and fashions, welded together by the extraordinary character of Frederick Stibbert and his late-romantic ideas, to create a unique entity which is worth more than its individual components and represents the purest example in Italy of a middle-class Victorian landscape garden.

One thing is certain – Villa Stibbert is a shocking indictment of the Italian inability to manage its artistic heritage. Frederick Stibbert left the house and its collections to the British government, but the bequest was not taken up, and eventually passed to the city of Florence. Under-endowed and undervalued, both house and garden are now in a piteous condition: the grottoes are crumbling, the staircases are dangerous, large areas of the garden are fenced off from visitors, and the best artefacts have long since mysteriously disappeared. The Gothic colonnade where Queen Victoria sketched is no more. It is hard to believe that for many years the British Consul held the official birthday reception in this garden where neglect and decay now hold court. But two legacies of better days remain. First, there is a good collection of mature conifers, planted by Stibbert, which makes clear that his passion for collecting was not confined to architectural bric-à-brac. And, second, there are many photographs of the garden in its heyday which could be used for a comprehensive programme of restoration if the will and money were available. But the trouble with Italy is that money, position, power, privilege and patronage exist only to be enjoyed. There is no tradition of stewardship, public service or benefit; indeed, the concept of 'trusteeship' is unknown to Italian jurisprudence. Small wonder then that there is no altruism attached to the arts in Italy, and that gardens such as those of Villa Stibbert are but shadows of their former glory.

The gardenesque style was especially popular in Sicily, where English influence was strong throughout the nineteenth century: among the famous seventeenth-century gardens replanted *all'inglese* were Bagheria and Mezzomonreale in Palermo. Much was due to the Marsala wine trade dynasties, of whom the richest and most influential by far were the Whitakers. They were the heirs and successors of Benjamin Ingham, who had bought Villa Racalia outside the town of Marsala in 1837. Villa Racalia still belongs to an English descendant of the Whitakers; indeed, there is no other house in Italy that has for so long belonged, and still belongs, to an English family. When Lord Ronald Gower visited it in 1891 he noted the 'pretty shaded pergola walks, terraces and clear fountains', while a few years later Lady Paget was enchanted to discover that the terraced gardens were covered with flowering shrubs

Villa Sofia, Palermo. The ruins of the Moorish conservatory built by Robert Whitaker in 1907.

Palazzo Whitaker in Via Cavour, Palermo, built in the Venetian Gothic style for Joshua and Effie Whitaker and surrounded by a magnificently gardenesque planting of palms, conifers and spiky plants.

even in January. Indeed it was the climate of Sicily as much as any fashion, trading connection or political expediency that made possible the development of gardens in the English style. The western end of the island has a climate which, provided water is available, allows a large variety of tropical and sub-tropical plants to flourish. Not only do plants grow luxuriantly, but they seem also to survive neglect. When Mariella Agnelli observed recently that 'the difficulty of keeping in check the disorder of this explosion of plant life was such that any desire to evoke contrasting emotions had inevitably to give way to a glorification of the energy of nature itself', she might more simply have said that such gardens quickly became jungles. Such a style suits the Sicilian character, too: the writer Douglas Sladen observed in 1905 that a marked feature of Palermitan gardens was that 'wild flowers are nearly always allowed to grow where they please in the most formal gardens, even the Botanic Gardens of Palermo'. Nevertheless

a hybrid style did evolve after the middle of the nineteenth century that took something from the English landscape movement, something from the climate and something from the unique character of Palermo itself. It was not so much a provincial copy of a universal fashion, but an example of the island's well-tried capacity for absorbing foreign cultures, a distinctly Sicilian development of the romantic garden.

The first substantial Whitaker garden in Palermo was Villa Sofia, opposite Ferdinand I's hunting park, La Favorita. It was bought by Joseph Whitaker the Elder in 1850 and was said, fifty years later, to boast 'the choicest palms in Sicily', to the extent that Douglas Sladen observed that they made the house a little dark. The gardens were already well known by then, and open to the public twice a week. Many years later Joseph Whitaker's son, also called Joseph, wrote that at first 'the flower garden ... was limited to the square plot immediately in front of the house, with its *vasca* or fish pond, surrounded by four lofty cypress trees'. But, he explained, 'gardening was my father's hobby, and the laying out of new grounds afforded him intense enjoyment and interest. Every tree and shrub was planted under his personal supervision.' He was forced to add ruefully that 'the fine paper-tree walk, with its large carob tree at one end ... has disappeared, as has also the adjoining long path, with its vine pergola, a favourite haunt of ours when the grapes were ripe'. Now, seventy years after Joseph's account, it is not only the paper tree and the vine pergola which have disappeared; so too has much of the garden itself, which for many years has been occupied by a hospital run by the Italian Red Cross.

Villa Sofia still contains a few mature trees planted by Joseph Whitaker the Elder over a century ago: the finest are Turkey oaks and species of palms, though there is also an avenue of *Yucca elephantipes*, and substantial patches of agapanthus remain from the original herbaceous planting. A Moorish conservatory lies roofless and empty. It was built by Robert Whitaker, one of the younger sons of Joseph Whitaker the Elder, and contained a rill of water which twinkled down a jagged marble slope and through a sunken channel into two octagonal pools surrounded by tiles. The rusty trellis-work of a defunct summer-house, rustic wrought-iron gateways and a waterless pool with a rocky island at one end have also survived. These relics of family life give particular poignancy to the Whitaker coat of arms set above the stable block with its motto *Spes et Fides*, 'Hope and Trust'. Fulco Santostefano della Cerda, Duke of Verdura, a friend of Robert Whitaker's younger daughter, wrote of the very Englishness of the house and garden: 'everything proclaimed firmly the word *Britannia*'. The garden and its trees were one of his most vivid childhood memories, inextricably bound up with the Whitakers. Though the little that remains now resembles the dense jungle of any Sicilian garden, the *vasca* or fish pond is still intact, as are two of the four lofty cypress trees that surrounded it in 1850. Those venerable specimens have seen the Whitakers come and go.

In its day, the greatest of the three Whitaker gardens in Palermo was at Villa Sperlinga, but it too has all but disappeared. It belonged to Joshua Whitaker, another son of Joseph Whitaker the Elder, and was developed independently of his house. This was because Joshua chose to live in a palace in the centre of Palermo, built in imitation Venetian Gothic, with only a small garden densely planted with palm

Villa Malfitano, Palermo (c. 1910). *Joseph Whitaker, a rich English wine exporter, is standing under a fine specimen of the dragon tree* Dracaena drago. *English garden owners in Italy made gardenesque landscapes with exotic trees and shrubs that would never be hardy at home.*

trees, araucarias, nolinas and bananas. Sperlinga, by contrast, occupied an entire block of perhaps 12 ha (30 acres) in the northern suburbs of the town and was made from old groves of oranges and lemons. The name recalls the only castle in the island that did not rise against the Angevins during the Sicilian Vespers of 1282: the English Whitakers thus proclaimed a different allegiance to that of their neighbours. No less than twenty-five gardeners were employed in the garden at Villa Sperlinga and it quickly became one of the sights for English visitors to Palermo. In the 1950s, most of the garden was sold off for building development but about 1 ha (2½ acres) remains as a public park to give a pale impression of what it must have looked like in its heyday. The paths were wide enough for large parties to promenade and included broad avenues of jacarandas and *Chorisia speciosa*, the kapok tree with its distinctive spiky trunks: among the underplantings were massed groups of hibiscus, aloes and

Villa Malfitano, Palermo (c. 1889). The two small girls in the newly planted garden are Norina and Delia, daughters of Joseph Whitaker the Younger ('Pip'). The garden was originally designed to enjoy distant views of the hills, now obscured by apartment blocks and evergreen screen plantings within the garden itself.

strelitzias. The pool, with islands in it, is very like the one at Villa Sofia, save that it still contains water, as well as water lilies and papyrus. The only building left in the garden is an oriental pavilion with conspicuous pink domes, clearly based on San Cataldo and San Giovanni degli Eremiti, the Arab–Norman churches of Palermo. There is no trace of the rose garden for which Villa Sperlinga was once famous, nor of its three tennis-courts, known as Purgatory, Heaven and Hell.

The best example of the gardenesque landscape style in Sicily is Villa Malfitano, laid out in 1889 by Joseph Whitaker the Younger, three years after he built the house. He was helped by his father's head gardener from Villa Sofia, Emil Kunzmann (1835–1908), who was an enthusiastic plantsman. Kunzmann came from Frankfurt, and certain features at Malfitano, including the collections of palms and succulents, belong as much to the German botanic tradition as to the English gardenesque. Mal-

fitano in 1889 was in open countryside at the edge of Palermo: now it is hemmed in by a populous suburb. It is therefore difficult to believe that Malfitano was laid out so that the mountains which ring Palermo would seem to come down to the edges of the garden. Sladen wrote enthusiastically that he could not 'imagine a more delightful garden than Mr Joseph Whitaker's except, perhaps, one or two round Posilippo, which run right down to the sea. For from its broad expanses of smooth English turf spring the choicest palms and yuccas, disposed with admirable taste from the landscape point of view.' Sladen may not have been an expert on gardens, but he knew a good thing when he saw one.

The entrance to Malfitano is through large wrought-iron gates. The carriageway divides immediately past the gate lodge and both arms sweep up to the house through a landscaped park planted with evergreen and shrubs. There are cedars, pines, cypresses, palms

Villa Malfitano, Palermo, in Delia Whitaker's day. The complicated curving paths in the centre and the Victorian use of palms and cycads as elements of a permanent bedding scheme are typical of late-nineteenth-century English taste. Nothing appears to have changed in this garden for one hundred years.

and the relics of a herbaceous underplanting in the form of such plants as *Clivia nobilis*. A large pool, which is still fed from the house's private water supply, enabled the purple gallinule to nest and raise a brood, much to the delight of Joseph Whitaker, a keen ornithologist. The garden is walled, and at first the walls were planted to climbing roses: one early visitor said that these flowered so thickly that the blossoms concealed the walls. As privacy from the encroaching development of Palermo became more important, shelter belts were planted of strong-growing evergreen trees, notably cedars, *Ficus benjamina* and *F. rubiginosa*. At the end of the carriage-way, by the turning circle, stands a spectacular specimen of the evergreen aerial-rooting *F. magnolioides* (*F. macrophylla*), which was said to have a span of 41 m (135 ft) when eighty years old and to be capable of sheltering three thousand people under its branches. This species is popular in the streets and parks of Palermo: handsome avenues were planted at

the Orto Botanico and in the Giardino Garibaldi at about the same time as Joseph Whitaker made his new garden.

The formal garden at Villa Malfitano is unusual. In the shape of a double helix, its paths radiate out slowly from the small central fountain to encourage dawdling among its flowers and scents. Broad steps run up to the house between recumbent lions from Mario Rutelli in Rome, while the central portico is covered in wisteria, *Rosa banksiae* 'Lutea', and the climbing rose 'Maréchal Niel'. A permanent planting was made around the edge of the formal garden: palms, cycads, nolinas, aloes and other nineteenth-century favourites, chosen for their shapes. Joseph Whitaker brought some of the palms from Villa Sofia, including the Canary Island date and *Phoenix reclinata*. He added *Washingtonia filifera*, *Livistona chinensis* and *L. australis*, together with dracaenas, jubaeas, and *Yucca aloifolia*. All the trees and shrubs are set in grass: expansive lawns

Yuccas in the Orto Botanico at Palermo, the source of many of the plants grown in English gardens in Sicily.

provide a green and English setting for their exotic forms.

The condition of the garden at Villa Malfitano today is critical. The detail is slowly disappearing. The kitchen garden with its citrus fruits, loquats and prickly pears is deep in weeds. Some of the paths are entirely surfaced by moss, while others are engulfed by trees. There is a handsome Victorian greenhouse with a curving roof and a hedge of *Salvia involucrata* all along the front, but it needs repair and panes of glass are not replaced when they break. A seedling phillyrea grows up through a gap in the glazing. Near by are the ruins of a small water-garden, whose neat, rock-edged channels are now choked with leaves. Nothing remains of the aquatic plantings save one papyrus descended from the original which Joseph Whitaker brought from Villa Sofia over a hundred years ago. The tufa grotto, with its inset shellwork, is alike overrun with weeds. Seedlings of ash and laurel have reached considerable heights, and are surrounded by wild acanthus and nettles. But a charming mixed border near by, of *Aloe arborescens* and orange trees with a lawn of *Narcissus tazetta* in front, is still colourful and attractive in January. So all is not lost: the garden manages to be both green

and alive in winter, and dark and shady in summer. It also retains a spirit of serenity, walled in and protected from the noise of Palermitan traffic outside. There are just three gardeners now, and they have no contact with English ideas of planting and maintenance. When Joseph Whitaker's daughter Delia died in 1970, there were five gardeners; in her father's day, fourteen. It was then that Joseph's wife Tina Whitaker reigned supreme as queen of Palermo society and a succession of English visitors, from King Edward VII and Queen Alexandra down, came to visit Malfitano during the winter season. There was a viola raised at Malfitano in the 1920s called 'Tina Whitaker'. It was for long recommended by the British Ministry of Agriculture as suitable for the cut-flower trade, but a recent description of it as 'thin and unrefined' would not have pleased the important person after whom it was named.

All Palermo's English gardens contained unusual plants. It is sometimes said that, through their trading connections with America and the British Empire, the Whitakers were able to import novelties from nurserymen and seedsmen around the world. That may be so, but a likelier source would have been the Botanic Garden in Palermo where, according to Douglas Sladen in 1905, 'they will sell specimens of anything'. The Orto Botanico has long had an outstanding collection of exotic plants, displayed in a formal and traditional manner. No less a man than Goethe described it as the most wonderful spot on earth, and visited the garden repeatedly to muse on his quest for the Primal Plant, while the English botanical artist Marianne North exuberantly described it as 'the palm-house at Kew, with the glass lifted off'. Indeed the collections of plants at the Orto Botanico were always more extensive than any others on the island. What distinguishes the Whitaker gardens, and those which they influenced, from contemporary Italian gardens, is the natural landscape disposition which they gave to their plantings, their use of grass as a setting for plants, and their enthusiasm for the plants themselves. In no sense, however, were these gardens intended for botanic research. So one cannot compare the Whitaker villas, with their tennis-courts and thatched cottages for children to play in, to a serious botanic garden like La Mortola. They are closer to the Blandys' garden in Madeira, though Quinta do Palheiro has had the advantage of continuous development over the last hundred years, while only Villa Malfitano is left of the Whitaker gardens, and that has remained substantially unchanged for exactly the same period. One is tempted to point out that the Blandys, like the Whitakers, were wine merchants, whose fortune was founded on Madeira just as the Whitakers' was made in Marsala; but this is merely a coincidence. Whatever the similarities, it is probably best to regard Villa Malfitano not as a garden which is capable of further development, but as a museum piece in need of a good curator.

References and Further Reading

The most complete study of Hamilton's garden at La Reggia is Carlo Knight's *Il giardino inglese a Caserta* (Napoli, 1986). Villa Borghese is well known, but there are two interesting modern articles about it in *Country Life*: by Hugh Honour on 23 November 1961 and by Patricia Andrew on 23 April 1981 ('An English Garden in Rome'). Villa Stibbert is scarcely documented, but I had some assistance from the museum's official guidebook, the introduction to *Il catalogo del Museo Stibbert* (vol. 2) and a broadsheet on the garden also published by the museum. Franco Borsi's *L'architettura dell'Unità d'Italia* (Firenze, 1966) gives the background to Poggi's work but does not mention his landscaping. Raleigh Trevelyan's comprehensive study of the Whitakers in Palermo, *Princes under the Volcano* (London, 1972) is authoritative and fascinating. Lord Ronald Sutherland Gower's *Diaries 1881–1901* (London, 1902), are useful only because he travelled so widely: they reveal the author to be a snob and a poseur. Fulco Santostefano's memoirs, *Estati felici* (Milano, 1977) are delightful and, like Marianne North's autobiography, *Some Further Recollection of a Happy Life* (London, 1893), worthy of a wider audience. The article on Malfitano by Lady O'Neill of the Maine (née Jean Whitaker) in *Country Life* (5 April 1984) is balanced, clear and full of facts. But the spirit of Goethe's *Italienische Reise* ('Italian Journey') runs through much of this chapter, and there is no better book to accompany a visitor to Italy even now.

Chapter Seven

TUSCANY

The Renaissance Ideal

THE ENGLISH connection with Florence is a long one; there has been an English community in the city for at least five hundred years. Bankers and traders were first to take up residence, attracted by the mercantile rule of the Medici. Prince Charles Edward Stuart, the Young Pretender, lived there in exile in the eighteenth century, in a palace whose rooms were furnished with tartan hangings. In the nineteenth century, Florence became 'a paradise of exiles', many of them poets and radicals attracted by the politics of the Risorgimento. '*Ville toute ang-laise,*' it appeared to the Goncourt brothers in 1856, 'for the palaces are the same depressing black as in London town, and everything seems to smile only on the English ... who say of S. Croce "the Westminster Abbey of Tuscany!"' After the House of Savoy moved its capital to Rome in 1870, Florence became a cultural rather than a political centre, whither Englishmen were drawn by its artistic patrimony and the opportunities for living well on a modest income. For Florence was cheap, and sometimes behaviour was tolerated that would not have been acceptable at home. Few of the foreign residents spoke Italian or moved in Florentine society. With one or two exceptions, such as the novelist F. Marion Crawford, it was Italy they loved, not the Italians, and they continued to conduct their lives in the certainty that the English were a superior race. Unsatisfactory younger sons and extravagant minor members of the royal family, including Queen Mary's parents, the Duke and Duchess of Teck, were encouraged to live

in Florence so that they might be less of an embarrassment to their more important relations. In *Portraits of Places* (1883) Henry James rooted the attractions in terms of hard cash:

the villas are innumerable, and if one is a stranger half the talk is about villas. This one has a story; that one has another: they all look as if they had stories. Most of them are offered to rent (many of them for sale) at prices unnaturally low: you may have a tower and a garden, a chapel and an expanse of windows, for five hundred dollars a year.

Florence became, above all, a city of women. Formidable or genteel, artistic or literary, impoverished or extravagant, unconventional or proper, Englishwomen of every variety came to live in Tuscany. There was Vernon Lee (born Violet Paget), an observant writer on Italian gardens, who dressed like a man and was, according to Maurice Baring, the cleverest person he ever met. There was Mrs George Keppel, once the mistress of King Edward VII, who lived at Villa dell'Ombrellino; Iris Cutting remembered her shouting '*Bisogna begonia!*' (the two words pronounced to rhyme with each other) as she prodded her Tuscan gardener with her long parasol and marked the precise spots in the beds where she wished the flowers to be planted. There was Janet Ross, a high-spirited and enchanting girl who was to become an intellectual terrifier and write a classic work on Florentine villas; she lived for many years at Poggio Gherardo where she grew herbs for the vermouth she concocted from a secret recipe of the Medici and sold at the Army & Navy Stores in London. Not least was the even more formidable Walburga, Lady Paget, who restored Villa Bellos-

---

Villa La Pietra, 1989. English residents of Tuscany have tended to reconstruct Renaissance gardens in the Florentine style, rather than gardening in the English manner.

Florence, 16 March 1894. Queen Victoria arrives at the old railway station for a spring holiday.

guardo and laid out a Burne-Jones garden of 'roses, lilies, honeysuckle, and poppies of the most unreal size and colour'.

For many of these residents, and for the visitors who came for a season or two, it was the flowers that mattered. Lady Blessington wrote early in the nineteenth century that the flowers of Florence were considered among the most beautiful of Italy 'and grow so abundantly in the environs that the rarest, or at least those considered the rarest in our colder clime, may here be purchased for a trifle'. Half a century later Florence was the City of Flowers, whose reputation was such that English firms would exhibit at its annual flower show. Antonio Gallenga recalled seeing several species of dracaena on Messrs Veitch of London's stand in the early 1870s. Florence's reputation appears to have been built upon garden flowers, not upon the cut-flower trade. The popular novelist Mrs Lynn Linton wrote, one wet December day, 'No, the winter climate of Florence is not good, and very, very trying ... As for flowers, they do not exist ... neither love nor money can give them to you.' The winter migrants, however, were enraptured by the earliness and profusion of flowering that they found in Italian gardens. Some liked to insist that as a consequence there were no flowers to be seen in summer or autumn. Alfred Austin, who was himself a good gardener and ought to have known better, wrote that

Italy has not its true garden season ... it is brief in its marvellous beauty, like the people themselves ... when the roses come they will come in battalions, the wisteria will run riot over wall and pergola ... the Madonna lilies will astound you by their height, and irises by their profusion. For a month ... one will be embowered in bloom; then suddenly ... have no garden at all ... a short life and a merry one.

Henry and Janet Ross, the leading lights of English intellectual life in Florence a hundred years ago, made an English woodland garden around their castellated villa at Poggio Gherardo and planted it with rare trees and shrubs.

When Queen Victoria stayed at Florence in the spring of 1888 the Royal Horticultural Society of Tuscany presented her with a basket of flowers entirely composed of plants originally native to some part of the Queen's dominions: they included vandas from Burma, rhododendrons from the Himalayas, freesias from Natal and epacris from Australia. The offering was accompanied by these lines:

> Our Flora's bowers, proud to receive
> The visit of Great Britain's Queen,
> With pressing courtesy beg leave,
> As welcome to this Southern scene,
> Within her august hands to lay
> These blooms that thrive where Britons sway.

For most of the Englishmen who lived in Florence during the nineteenth and early twentieth centuries, gardens meant flower gardening in the English manner. A good example of the English Victorian type was made by Henry Ross, husband of the formidable Janet, after he bought Poggio Gherardo in 1889 and planted up the hillside all around the square crenellated fortress villa which had withstood the arms of Hawkwood and his Pisan soldiers. The long steep drive which wound its way up was bordered by hedges of roses, and a visitor in 1912 remarked that 'they tumble in great cascades over the walls above the carriage drive, mixing their pink and white flowers with the yellow Banksia and pale or dark blue irises'. Ross grew the useful and ornamental plants that were so attractive to serious garden owners at the time: his trees included specimens of *Cinnamomum camphora*, which yields camphor wood, the bead tree *Melia azedarach* and *Paulownia tomentosa*, which is sometimes called the foxglove tree. Drifts of the moutan paeony, *Paeonia suffruticosa*, were underplanted by such plantsman's specialities as the Oncocyclus iris *Iris susiana*, hardy nerines including *fothergillii* and the giant *Dahlia imperialis*. He also imported an early-fruiting form of *Diospyros kaki* known as 'Giboushin' from Japan. His most abiding interest was in orchids and he bred a hybrid cypripedium called C. × *rossianum* which frequently carried twin-flowered stems. Janet Ross painted all her husband's orchids: there were over 1,800 of them.

THE CERTAINTY of some English residents that British was Best runs through *In a Tuscan Garden*, the book which Georgina Grahame wrote in 1902 about her villa below Fiesole. She maintained that Italians were 'the most conceited people on the face of the earth' and that 'the bedrock of Tuscan character is suspicion'. As for their gardens, Mrs Grahame doubted that 'it had occurred to anyone to wish to possess ... the Villa d'Este at Tivoli, or that of the Villa Lante near Viterbo', since these were not gardens in the English sense of the word: the well-ordered English garden, beloved of its owners, and cultivated by them and their forefathers for generations, was not to be met with in Italy. What Georgina Grahame liked best was *plants*, and she had in excessive measure the English enthusiasm for quantity, variety, colour and effect. She had no care for what might be appropriate to the site of her garden, one of the few flat pieces of ground in the hills above Florence, nor did she perceive any need to pay homage to the Italian tradition. Indeed, she thought at first that no more unpromising piece of land could be imagined than the conventional Italian garden she acquired, although it did possess 'one great treasure' in the form of a grass walk which ran down to the very end. It was this, she was certain, which gave the garden its peculiarly English look, and she recounted with approval that 'one friend ... used to come and look at it, and aver with a sigh that *that* grass walk was worth the whole of the place put together'.

Georgina Grahame's idea of a garden was 'a succession of beautiful pictures'. She enjoyed the changing seasons and liked to walk around the garden so that features revealed themselves in sequence. She planted in masses and strove to produce such colour effects as white Madonna lilies *Lilium candidum* in front of the collection of red China roses she received from Guillot of Lyons. Roses were her greatest love. To the 'Safrano' and 'Maréchal Niel' that came with the house she added pink Chinas, pale teas, crimson

hybrid perpetuals, mosses and Scotch roses, all backed by pale lines of 'Gloire Lyonnaise' and 'Kaiserin Augusta Viktoria'. The beds were edged with violets and the roses underplanted with narcissi, jonquils and pansies. Georgina Grahame covered the walls of her house with greenery, in the English taste. She collected garden pots, and made arrangements with them, to display carnations, chrysanthemums, geraniums, coleus, arum lilies, cannas and ferns. She concluded that when she looked out on the garden and thought of 'the piece of wasteland of which I took possession fourteen years ago', there was a distinct balance to the good, adding in self-congratulation 'as well there might be'.

No greater contrast to Georgina Grahame can be imagined than the enthusiasm, charm and lucid prose of Joseph Lucas's *Our Villa in Italy*, published in 1913. It displays on every page a love of Italy and a respect for the Italians. When he writes of Leo X, the Medici pope from Florence, that 'the joyousness of life in him runs wild, the gaiety of his disposition is spontaneous and irresistible', the words could be used of Lucas himself. Never was a more blissful hymn of praise to the Tuscan way of life sung by an Englishman. Italian workmen were quick-witted, intelligent and artistic in temperament. His head gardener was 'six foot of good, strong, broad, Tuscan manhood, with a charming cordiality of manner and an honest light in his eye'. And Lucas understood the need to adapt to Italian conditions: 'I should no more think of importing my English gardener into Italy than bringing an English cook with me.'

Lucas's quattrocento villa at Fiesole had belonged to the Palmieri and Frescobaldi families; it was a quiet country property surrounded by vineyards and olives and sunshine, within sight and sound of the Duomo. The garden was simple and formally laid out. Adjoining the upper garden was a *stanzone*, a conservatory, where orange and lemon trees were housed in their pots from November to April. 'The pots are heavy, and need a crowd of men to move them. There are four-men pots, six-, eight-, ten-men pots. We have two venerable lemon trees each over a hundred years old, and they are in fourteen-man pots!' The lower terraces were empty and dilapidated when he bought the villa but, far from hankering after an English garden, Lucas was concerned to restore what he had acquired in the proper Italian style. The leaking pools were repaired, and the fountains made to play again. Rather than cover the walls with creepers, he set to rescue the stone eagles on the pillars of the garden gate from the climbing roses

Joseph Lucas's Edwardian garden in Tuscany was as close to the Tuscan ideal as possible. He wrote with particular enthusiasm of his collection of old lemon pots.

which had nearly strangled them. 'It was beautifully picturesque, but very rough on the eagles. We came to their rescue none too early.'

Joseph Lucas represents the type of Englishman who respects, understands and admires the traditions of the country in which he has chosen to live. Not that Lucas lacked the romantic passion which the northern races have long engendered for Italy. Far from it: he wrote with intense pleasure of the nightingales and fireflies, and of the wild flowers that graced his orchards – narcissi, anemones, irises, tulips and gladioli. But he sought to operate within that country's aesthetic instead of imposing English ideas on foreign materials.

Despite the English predeliction for plants and flowers, Italian gardens have at all times been much admired in England: indeed they dominated English garden-making in the seventeenth century. Even the origins of the landscape movement owe much to the classical landscapes of Italy, while the Italianate style was an essential element of grand garden-making in England after about 1830. So persuasive were Italian gardens that their traditions are more significant than any other in the history of English gardens abroad. The styles of France, Spain and Portugal made little impression on Englishmen creating gardens in those countries in comparison to the influence of the Tuscan style in Italy. Historically sensitive members of the English community in Tuscany seldom chose to maintain or make anything other than an Italian-style garden, although it would probably be embellished with garden plants and gay flowers in the English manner. Iris Origo wrote of members of the English community with their chintz curtains, framed water-colours, silver rose-bowls and library books, a fragrance of home-made scones and freshly brewed tea ('But no Italian will warm the teapot correctly, my dear') that if they had a villa, 'though they scrupulously preserved the clipped box and cypress hedges of the formal Italian garden, they yet also introduced a note of home: a Dorothy Perkins rambling among the vines and the wisteria on the pergola, a herbaceous border on the lower terrace, and comfortable wicker chairs upon the lawns'. Marchesa Origo was a keen observer of the Anglo-Florentine scene, but we shall see that in her own house at La Foce creative tensions between architect and plantsman gave rise to a romantic synthesis of the kind she appeared to eschew.

One villa in Florence enjoyed a particularly long and strong association with England. Villa Palmieri at San Domenico was bought by Earl Cowper in 1765 and remained in English ownership for 150 years. Cowper fell in love with Florence, and the Florentines in return took him to their hearts, for he was a man of such charm and eccentricity that he gave a new phrase to Italian usage – *matto inglese*. Villa Palmieri was sold by his heirs in 1824 to Miss Mary Farhill, and subsequently acquired by the Earl of Crawford and Balcarres in 1873. It was there that Queen Victoria chose to stay in 1888.

The 'three sentinels' at Villa Palmieri at San Domenico, a house owned by English families for 150 years. This garden was restored and expanded by the Earl of Crawford in the 1870s.

The garden started with the advantage of having played an important part in the history of Italian literature, for it was at Villa Palmieri that Boccaccio chose to intern the ten young men and women fleeing from the plague in Florence who amused themselves by telling the stories of the Decameron. His evocation of the garden in 1348, whatever it may owe to fancy, was a potent inspiration for later owners and visitors.

The walkes and allyes were long and spacious, yet directly straighte as an arrow, environed with spreading vines ... In the midst of the Garden was a square plot, after the resemblance of a Meadow, flourishing with high grasse, hearbes, and plants, beside a thousand diversities of flowres, even as if by the Art of painting they had beene there deputed. Round was it circled with very verdant Orenge and Cedar Trees, their branches plentiously stored with fruit both old and new, as also the flowres growing freshly among them, yeelding not onely a rare aspect to the eye, but also a delicate savour to the smell. In the midst of this Meadow, stood a Fountaine of white marble ... and within it ... such abundance of water, and so mounting up towards the Skies, that it was a wonder to behold. For after the high ascent, it fell downe againe into the wombe of the Fountaine, with such a noyse and pleasing murmure, as the streame that glideth from a mill ... The sight of this garden ... so highly pleased the Ladies and Gentlemen, that among other infinite commendations, they spared not to say: if any Paradise remayned on the earth to be seene, it could not possibly be in any other place, but onely was contained within the compasse of this Garden.

It is pleasant to think of Queen Victoria sketching in the garden where all those ribald stories were tossed around five hundred years before.

Ever since Palmiero Palmieri rebuilt the house in 1691, adding such baroque details to the garden as the sweeping double staircase which connects the great terrace to the oval lemon garden below, the Villa Palmieri has suffered from being a cynosure. Each owner and each generation has added to or altered it, and the garden to some extent became a casualty of its own fame. The Crawfords planted rambling roses, creepers and ivy up all the walls, added a wooden pergola, and planted a 'Cactus Walk', in reality a short avenue of agaves. Later, Lady Crawford put in a tennis-court and a swimming-pool. As at other British-owned gardens in Florence, much of the nineteenth-century work was a distinctively English interpretation of a classical Italian model. The box parterre, for example, with its complicated fan-shaped layout of beds, retained its

Villa Gamberaia in about 1920. The garden, restored in the 1890s with water in place of the original parterres, was for long regarded as a cynosure. It is an interesting example of how northerners perceived the Florentine style.

baroque formalism, but was always planted with bright bedding plants in the contemporary English taste. But the parterre itself was laid out by the Earl in the 1870s. Only the oval lemon garden remained unchanged from the time of Palmiero Palmieri.

The other paragon among Tuscan gardens towards the end of the nineteenth century – and indeed in modern times – was Villa Gamberaia at Settignano on the hills above Florence. It was owned by Princess Jeanne Ghika, the sister of Queen Natalia of Serbia; according to her niece Princess Marthe Bibesco, she was rich and beautiful, and hated both men and mankind. The garden was much visited, photographed and praised for its water parterres, although they were actually a modern anachronism; it is also clear that Gamberaia was intensely planted and colourful in an unTuscan way – the bottom of the little sunken grotto garden was, for example, carpeted with tulips and bedding plants. Nevertheless, as David Ottewill has recently pointed out (*The Edwardian Garden*, 1989), Villa Gamberaia

skilfully incorporated a diversity of elements within an awkwardly shaped site, the whole being tied together by axes and vistas ... At Gamberaia, assembled into an area of only 3 acres, was the complete design vocabulary and many important lessons for the Edwardian garden designer: disposition of outdoor rooms, treatment of levels and water, contrast of sunlight and dense shade, simplicity of form, human scale and controlled use of colour.

To this should be added the special relationship between house, garden and landscape which architects and designers discovered and promoted at the start of the twentieth century.

In Tuscany, the origins of that relationship are much older. They can be traced to Alberti's fifteenth-century treatise on architecture, *De re aedificatoria*, and his insistence that buildings should rely more on beauty of design and convenience of disposition than size and ornament. Sir Harold Acton, for instance, believes that in Tuscany, more than anywhere else in Italy, 'buildings seem to grow out of the landscape, as if in sympathy with the hills and local vegetation', while the American novelist Edith Wharton explained that in the Renaissance the architect had three problems to deal with: 'the garden must be adapted to the architectural lines of the house it adjoins; it must be adapted to the requirements of the inmates of the house, in the sense of providing shady walks, sunny bowling-greens, parterres and orchards, all conveniently accessible; and lastly it must be adapted to the natural landscape around it. At no time,' she concluded, 'and in no country has this triple problem been so successfully dealt with as in the treatment of the Italian country house from the beginning of the sixteenth to the end of the eighteenth century.' Edith Wharton clearly felt that the natural harmony which should exist between the house, the garden and the countryside had been lost during the course of the nineteenth century. It was a time when fashionable Italians planted gardenesque landscapes and arboreta; examples that she would have encountered near Florence include the Parco di

Sir George Sitwell, scholar and aesthete, on the terrace at Montegufoni. His Essay on the Making of Gardens *(1909) is a classic work based on years of research in Italy.*

Pratolino at Vaglia, the arboretum at Vallombrosa and the Parco Frescobaldi at Borgo San Lorenzo. Given the Englishman's love of flowers, it is perhaps surprising to find that the return to traditional Italian garden styles at the beginning of the twentieth century was led by Englishmen – notably Arthur Acton and Sir George Sitwell – and that the classic Tuscan gardens they owned were in fact their own creations.

The 1890s and 1900s saw a resurgent interest in the houses and gardens of Renaissance Italy: it was a development of the movement which had begun with the publication in 1878 of the first English edition of Burckhardt's *Civilisation of the Renaissance in Italy*. The most enthusiastic student of Italian gardens was Sir George Sitwell (1860–1943), the owner of the Montegufoni estate in central Tuscany, who published *An Essay on the Making of Gardens* in 1909. Sitwell believed that 'the formal garden in England falls short of the great examples of the Italian Renaissance; it is seldom related as it should be to the surrounding scenery; it is often wanting in repose and nearly always in imagination'. He stressed the importance of relating the garden to the landscape, and the need to include elements of wonder and surprise, harmony and contrast, and to use the element of water which he regarded as 'the principal source of landscape beauty', taking as the three most perfect examples of the Italian style Villa d'Este at Tivoli ('in all the world there is no place so full of poetry'), Villa Lante at Bagnaia ('a paradise of gleaming water, gay flowers and golden light') and the Giardini Giusti at Verona ('nothing could be so beautiful'). Sitwell was a stylist who argued, for instance, that garden-makers of the Italian Renaissance

learned the value of striking contrast; of sudden and thrilling surprise; of close confinement as a prelude to boundless freedom; of scorching sun as a prelude to welcome shade or cooling river; of monotony, even of ugliness, set for a foil to enchanting beauty, as a discord is used in music, as the lowered tone of a landscape brings up fires of sunset or the primrose light of dawn, as a dwarfish figure on a Greek sarcophagus gives grandeur to a frieze of fighting heroes.

Sitwell visited over two hundred gardens in the course of long researches for the book, in which he sought to emulate Bacon's essay 'Of Gardens' (1625). Even his son Osbert, so often untruthful and unfair to Sir George, conceded that 'his knowledge of

Villa La Pietra. The long straight entrance drive from the old Florence–Bologna road. Hedges of the ever-blooming China roses flower beneath the avenue of cypresses.

gardens – Italian in particular – was unrivalled'. The emphasis of his book was on an aesthetic perception of gardens, and their appreciation by the four senses: sight, sound, scent and touch. Sitwell's analyses were perceptive and his analogies effective: he was a persuasive authority and adopted a style of poetic fervour that was admired at the time. Almost every Englishman living in Tuscany came to share his unquestioning belief that if the world were to make good gardens again then 'we must both discover and apply in the changed circumstances of modern life the principles which guided the garden-makers of the Renaissance'.

At the Villa La Pietra on the old road to Bologna out of Florence, Arthur Acton was already practising what Sitwell preached. La Pietra is reached by a straight and stately avenue of cypresses, perhaps half a mile long. Underneath are hedges of a pink form of *Rosa chinensis*, known locally as *la rosa d'ogni mese*, the monthly rose, which flowers from March to November. They give the visitor the first hint that the garden at La Pietra is not entirely Italian. Not that it is English in style either, for the whole garden was designed or reconstructed on seventeenth- and eighteenth-century models. It was made by Arthur Acton in the early years of the twentieth century, and it is preserved in its original spirit by his son, the writer and aesthete Sir Harold Acton. La Pietra is, in effect, an English Edwardian interpretation of a Florentine garden. The original gardens, laid out on a steep hillside, were largely swept away by the fashion for the English landscape movement in the early nineteenth century, so it is fitting that it should have been an Englishman who restored to the garden what he perceived to be pure Tuscan lines. 'My father,' wrote Sir Harold, 'refined upon the traces of the former garden and its retaining walls, with all the creative ingenuity of a cinquecento architect.'

La Pietra was built as a country house in the 1460s by the Sassetti family, banking partners of the Medici, and remodelled by Cardinal Luigi Capponi in the 1650s. The cardinal's hat still surmounts the Capponi coat of arms behind the house. Immediately in front of the house, which is enormous, almost palatial, is a broad gravel terrace. This is edged by a stone balustrade surmounted by statues, which look down to a formal garden set with stone benches and a fountain in the middle, all enclosed by low walls and clipped hedges. The geometrical plots of grass are now hemmed in by tall clipped hedges of box with golden Irish yews (looking uncomfortable here) at some of the corners. These yews are an anachronism, for they were unknown before the nineteenth century, and their yellow leaves are out of place among the greens of a Tuscan garden. A short staircase leads between statues down to the lowest terrace, guarded by a pair of twin columns with a broken pediment. The pool in the middle is enclosed by parterres, planted with pink and blue larkspur in summer. The far side is bounded by a dramatically curving peristyle of Corinthian columns, screened from the valley by a copse of holm oak. A mighty statue of Hercules by Orazio Marinali (1643–1720) stands in the central position. Paths, mainly of gravel, stretch out to the sides: the lines and axes focus on further architectural fragments and splendid sculptures by Marinali, who worked with Palladio to produce pieces for his villas in the Veneto. 'The statues,' wrote Sir Harold, 'collected by my father for many years, deserve a special monograph; there are over a hundred of them, exclusive of what Nollekens calls *bustos* ... in no other private Florentine garden have I seen statues of such individual strength and grace, from the lone Mantuan colossus by Marinali to the Venetian figures which have stepped on to the open-air theatre as for one of Goldoni's comedies.' To some extent the garden at La Pietra was designed to provide a proper background for the collection. To one side of the house is an enclosed orchard or *hortus inclusus*, its baroque walls richly decorated with many-coloured *rocaille* work, the piers alternately topped by busts and finials. Peach trees are trained up these walls, while oranges and lemons in vast terracotta pots line the paths in summer. The restoration of this walled garden was one of Arthur Acton's first undertakings after buying La Pietra in 1902. It gave him the desire to re-create the Tuscan garden, rather than planting a modern reinterpretation of traditional Italian forms.

La Pietra is nevertheless a foreigner's perception of the ideal Italian garden. The series of outdoor rooms, especially the green theatre with its footlights clipped in box and wings cut in yew, are typical of the late Florentine Renaissance, the age when gardens begin to be called baroque. So too are the hedges of box and bay laurel, and the patterned steps of black and white pebbles forming here and there the outline of a Florentine iris. Even the concept of collecting statues from an earlier period of artistic excellence and incorporating them into a garden where they can be appreciated in an appropriate setting recalls the Renaissance fondness for treating antique Roman pieces in the same manner. Georgina Masson, however, explains in her classic work *Italian Gardens* that the extensive use of topiary and the mixing of motifs in the classical style with Venetian garden sculpture have 'given the garden a curiously individual character'. One might add that the use of yellow Irish yews in the garden immediately below the house, the planting of wisteria around the Corinthian peristyle and 'Dorothy Perkins' roses against the staircases, and a pergola draped with Banksian roses, are all representative of the English love of flowers. While they complement the Italian garden, they do not belong to the Tuscan sixteenth century, nor even to the Venetian eighteenth century. Not that La Pietra is a garden of flowers; indeed, the Actons were always quick to assure visitors that the garden had no need of flowers. Rather, it is a unique example of English homage to the Italian Renaissance by the one family whose house, garden and very personality have come to represent to Englishmen and Italians alike all that is best in the Anglo-Florentine connection.

Villa La Pietra. The garden which Arthur Acton made in the 1900s was intended to be as close to the sixteenth-century Tuscan ideal as possible, although many of the details were taken from later periods.

I Tatti: there is a hint of pastiche about this staircase at the end of the long entrance avenue planted by Berenson.

The return to a more formal style of gardening in England after the excesses of the landscape movement was not confined to the Italianate gardens of the mid nineteenth century designed by Sir Charles Barry and William Nesfield. By the end of the century, the Pre-Raphaelite brotherhood and the Arts and Crafts Movement had created a more popular demand for historical authenticity. It was no longer good enough for gardens to be Italianate: they had to be Italian. In England, designers looked back to Tudor times in search of purer and simpler fonts of inspiration. In Florence, *com'era quand'era* became the maxim of the new school, reacting against the fussy luxuriance of such gardens as Villa Palmieri and Villa Gamberaia. It was only to be expected that the large community of artistically sensitive Englishry in Florence would need the services of an architect, garden designer and adviser working on the purest of Tuscan principles. Cecil Pinsent materialised to satisfy this demand, and for nearly forty years was passed from one satisfied client to the next.

Cecil Pinsent was fortunate to receive his first substantial commission from the American art historian Bernard Berenson. It was the sort of lucky break that can set a young man up for life, and did no harm to Berenson's reputation as a talent spotter. Edwin Lutyens had been just twenty-one when Gertrude Jekyll asked him to build her house at Munstead Wood; now Cecil Pinsent at twenty-five, and fresh from England, was commissioned by Berenson to design a garden at I Tatti. This was the villa at Settignano, near Florence, which he had acquired at the time of his marriage to Mary Costelloe, sister of Logan Pearsall Smith, and which was to remain his home until his death in 1959. When Pinsent started work in 1910, Berenson's reputation as an attributor and historian was at its height. I Tatti was not an impressive villa: in the words of Berenson's faithful companion Nicky Mariano, 'an unassuming well-proportioned Tuscan house with a small enclosed lemon garden to the south and groups of old cypresses to both sides'. The lemon garden was a long narrow *hortus inclusus*, bounded on one side by the house and on the other by a large *limonaia*. Pinsent incorporated this lemon house into the garden's design by driving the main axis of the new garden right through its tall arched doorways and down the steep hill beyond. This extension became known as the Green Garden: it was Pinsent's first and most successful attempt to re-create an early Renaissance garden.

Pinsent's biggest problem at I Tatti was the one most common in Tuscany: a steeply sloping site. He solved it in the Italian fashion by terracing the hillside and running short sharp flights of steps between the levels. Right at the top, the gradients were too precipitous for a single central staircase. Pinsent devised a double staircase to negotiate the drop and used its curves to enclose a small pool. On every terrace he planted a symmetrical pair of parterres, each of a different geometric shape, until at the lowest level they were replaced by two lily ponds. The landings on the central staircase were embellished by rectangles of *ciottolato*, the art of making patterns from pebbles of two or more colours. Mary Berenson wrote enthusiastically to her family in England of 'the wonderful patterns we have made for the terraces': in fact they are competent rather than inspired, neatly arranged on each level like a succession of rugs. The box parterres were clipped low and simple, apart from some dumpy green obelisks on either side, which appear more Tudor than Tuscan. High hedges of cypress enclose the whole half acre, stepping down

Some things at I Tatti are not in the best of taste. Berenson placed this sentimental carving on the balustrade above his very correct neo-Tuscan 'Green' Garden.

in broad flat tiers like a giant's staircase. The Green Garden contains no flowers, and the water lilies have gone from the pools.

The descent continues beyond the two pools at the bottom of the Green Garden. Again, the steepness of the site obliged Pinsent to employ a double staircase, at right angles to the main axis, to lead down into the ilex wood at the bottom. The trees are cut to a height of about 8 m (25 ft) so that the view from the top of the Green Garden across the Tuscan hills is kept open. A statue of Flora serves as a focal point at the bottom of the plantation.

Looking back over eighty years, it is clear that neither Berenson nor Pinsent was as innovative or infallible as their friends and clients supposed. Pinsent was perhaps too young and overconfident for such a major commission: indeed Mary Berenson remarked that 'Cecil understands nothing of gardening – or of making gardens – but he is cocksure.' A more mature architect would have been truly bold, imaginative and original. Pinsent absorbed the detail of Renaissance architecture and gardens, but not the substance: the result has the look of a pastiche. He had an imperfect grasp of the principles of fifteenth-century garden design, and so his work at I Tatti appears as a sequence of incidents that fail to coalesce. The clock tower is too small; the urns and curving cornice on the roof of the *limonaia* look spurious; the stone carvings of a puppy and a kitten carrying baskets of fruit overwhelm the statuette of Our Lady below; and the mossy stone encrustations on the lower balustrading are little less than ridiculous. Furthermore, there is a paradox of scale and size at I Tatti. The garden is much larger than it would have been at the time of the Renaissance, yet it resembles a scaled-down model. The effect is unintentional and was probably not even apparent in 1910. It is the product of changing perceptions.

Pinsent's difficulty, as he would undoubtedly have complained, was that Mary Berenson put herself in charge of his work. She was an unenthusiastic convert to the Tuscan ideal. Her own predilections were for flowers, woodlands and natural gardening in the Robinsonian manner. 'It is curiously soothing to go about and see things growing,' she wrote to her children; 'our wire netting is being covered with roses and honeysuckle and wisteria and clematis and bignonia and all sorts of creepers.' She went behind Pinsent's back and consulted Aubrey Waterfield, whose wife was a niece of Janet Ross. Waterfield was an able artist who lived in Italy but had an English interest in plants: Mary subsequently complained when he pressed 'his idea of a wild garden on English lines'. She could not cope with the conflict which, like all the bickering at I Tatti, was entirely of her own making. In November 1910 she wrote, 'I think the garden is awful and I have come to the conclusion that it can only be done by a man who combines what Aubrey has, a knowledge of flowers and plants, and what Cecil has, a knowledge of design and the ability to stake out.' The result was a British compromise. Pinsent made the Green Garden, and Waterfield planted the woodland.

It follows that the other areas of the garden have quite a different character. An enclosed parterre by the house is swagged with wisteria and decorated with piers, altogether more baroque than the austere Green Garden: it is not known who designed it, possibly Berenson himself. He certainly planted the handsome ilex avenue which runs down to a circular pool. This is encased within a tall ironwork cupola, open to the sky: as an essay in geometric perspective the dome recalls Mantegna's ceiling in the wedding chamber of the Palazzo Ducale in Mantua. Nor is there any doubt that the first feature to be planted at I Tatti was Berenson's own design. This was the long avenue of tall cypress trees that connects the house to the gate at the bottom of the estate. Berenson too had to introduce staircases on the steep gradients

at either end: one runs up to a monstrous statue of a giant. The planting of the avenue is tapered to increase the sense of perspective: it is the single most effective composition in the whole garden.

Waterfield planted an open meadow with narcissi, anemones and fritillaries below an avenue of wisteria. This, and the old olive orchard, became Bernard Berenson's own preferred areas for walking. Kenneth Clark went so far as to assert that Berenson 'always disliked' the garden that Pinsent made. Berenson's own writings are ambiguous. Late in life, he claimed that 'though I have travelled all over the world and seen many lovely places, I now feel all the beauty I need is my own garden'. Eric Linklater remembered visiting him shortly after the Second World War. 'You must see my garden,' Berenson said, and showed him the cypress avenue. 'This is the part of it,' he explained, 'that Logan Pearsall Smith admired. He used to say that it was the only civilised arrangement in my garden. But I think the olive grove is more truly civilised.'

It is important to remember that Pinsent, Waterfield, the Berensons and most of their friends were pioneers of historic research and reconstruction. The gardens at I Tatti should be compared to such neo-Elizabethan English gardens as Avebury Manor and Montacute House. All were serious attempts to create an appropriate setting for a period house. Berenson and Pinsent were anxious to do the right thing and be seen to do it. They should not be dismissed as mere aesthetes or poseurs, even if at times they were more responsive to matters of detail than substance. Berenson may not have enjoyed Pinsent's work as much as Waterfield's, but he recognised its superiority.

Cecil Pinsent's long association with Antonio and Iris Origo produced the marvellously harmonious house and garden at La Foce whose development is well recorded in Iris Origo's writings. She was the only child of Lady Sybil Cuffe and her American husband Bayard Cutting, and was brought up in the 'hyper-sophisticated and hyperintellectual' Florentine circles that her mother chose to embrace. Iris Origo was a serious and industrious woman who lived for the things of the intellect but also sought to put her commitment to public service into practice. Making a garden was less important for her than the work of her writing and the struggle to create a model farm at La Foce, the estate near Chianciano which she and her husband Marchese Antonio Origo bought on their engagement in 1923.

La Foce is not in the lush classic heartland of

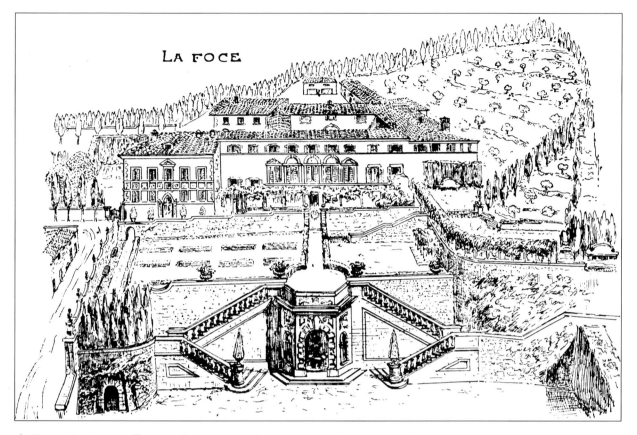

La Foce, Iris Origo's villa near Chianciano, looking rather grander than it really is. This sketch illustrates the problem of levels, and Cecil Pinsent's solutions to it.

Tuscany, but on an arid windswept upland that forms the divide between tributaries of the River Ombrone, which flows west past Grosseto to the sea, and the River Tiber, which runs south towards Rome. 'Long ridges of low, bare clay hills – the *crete senesi* – ran down,' she wrote many years later, 'dividing the landscape into a number of steep dried-up little watersheds. Treeless and shrubless but for some tufts of broom, those corrugated ridges formed a lunar landscape, pale and inhuman.' Antonio and Iris Origo made La Foce their life's work, and built up the estate to nearly 6,000 acres while planting vines and olives, building roads, restoring the woodland, repairing the farms and cottages, putting the arable land into good heart and introducing modern ideas of husbandry.

It was a dry, windy, cold site. Making a garden was not a priority, not least because there was barely enough water to run the household, let alone to irrigate plants. Then Iris Origo's American grandmother gave them the means to lay a water-pipe from a spring some 10 km (6 miles) away, and in 1927

Cecil Pinsent could turn from working on the house to creating the first small garden. It was small, enclosed and Italian: a stone fountain standing on two dolphins with a small lawn around it and flowerbeds edged in box. A pergola of roses and wisteria connects this garden to the house and to the new wing which Pinsent built at the same time. At the opposite corner, a stone seat and table are set deeply into a recessed arbour of laurel. In 1930 came the first extension when Pinsent added a larger walled garden: box hedges around a slightly less formal flower garden, with huge lemon trees in terracotta vases which were put out on stone plinths for the summer months. The grass was edged with spring bulbs and irises, while the retaining walls were covered in climbing roses, honeysuckles and *Trachelospermum jasminoides*, with tree paeonies and pomegranates in front. Pinsent returned in 1938 to design the rose garden, beyond a pergola that winds away from the house above the first two enclosures towards the woodland garden. There is an astounding revelation halfway along the pergola, where a

La Foce. The last part of the garden to be made, in 1939, was in the Tuscan style, with standard evergreen magnolias in grassy parterres and double hedges of box.

break in the shelter screen of evergreens gives a view of the entire Val d'Orcia. It bursts open to expose buzzards cruising in front of the soaring peak of Monte Amiata to the south, the famous *crete senesi* across the valley and a driveway lined with cypresses winding up to a farm on the estate. This was planted by the Origos as an exercise in the picturesque, and is now reproduced on the arty landscape postcards that can be bought from every news-stand in Tuscany. Finally, in 1939, more ground was levelled and a curving line of cypresses planted to conceal a new garden which projects over the steep valley below. Within its irregular outlines are eight wedge-shaped or triangular beds, symmetrically placed and surrounded by double hedges of box; these were directly inspired by such early Renaissance designs as can be seen at Palazzo Piccolomini in nearby Pienza. The effect is rather more baroque than Renaissance, but the huge trees of *Magnolia grandiflora* which occupy the four largest beds have no place in either historical period.

The outline of the gardens at La Foce is classical, based on fifteenth- and sixteenth-century precedents, and executed with an eye for what was appropriate to the site. The design is less rigid than it would have been four hundred years ago, and even appears to some critics to have grown piecemeal, so that it lacks unity both with the house and within itself. Features were adapted to the lie of the land, to follow the contours of a difficult site. The curves of the pergola and some of the walks run with the natural lines of the hillside. A wild garden runs up the olive terraces to an eighteenth-century statue of a negro, bowed under by the fruits of autumn, from which a cypress-lined alley leads down again to the steps of the rose garden. The hillside is planted with Judas trees, flowering quinces, forsythia, pomegranates, shrub roses and natural herbs of the countryside, among them lavender, thyme and rosemary. It is clear that Iris Origo had an English interest in plants. She knew what she wanted to grow and in time she discovered what the climate would allow.

Gradually, by experiment and failure, I learned what

would or would not stand the cold winters and the hot, dry summer winds. I gave up any attempt, in my borders, at growing delphiniums, lupins or phlox, as well as many other herbaceous plants; and I learned, too, to put our lemon trees, plumbago and jasmine under shelter before the winter. But roses flourish in the heavy clay soil, and so do paeonies and lilies, while the dry hillside is where rosemary thrives.

She looked to the wild flowers that grew in the woodlands for violets, crocuses, cyclamen, anemones and colchicums, transplanting them to her garden and adding exotic daffodils and scillas. She found that bluebells from England were impossible to establish and so too, more strangely, were the *Tulipa australis* that grew a few miles away in the fields around San Quírico. There is an English plant-loving exuberance and a profusion in the way in which the plants at La Foce are allowed to spill out over the strong neo-Tuscan lines of the ground plan, and in the drapes of climbers and creepers which cover the balustrades, pergolas, revetments and walls of the garden. Indeed, the front of the villa itself is obscured by two vast old holm oaks clipped to the shape of mushrooms that flank the entrance. Italians believe that trees so close to the house are most unhealthy.

La Foce suffered much in the Second World War, as did many of the English gardens in Italy and on the Riviera. In her diary, which was later published as *War in Val d'Orcia*, Marchesa Origo recorded the sorry extent of the damage to La Foce. There were shell holes and machine-gun trenches on the terraces, the lemon trees were torn from their terracotta pots to die and the estate was sown with landmines left by the retreating Germans. This was nothing in comparison to the damage to farms, houses, woodlands, livestock and farming equipment, nor to the destruction of furniture, pictures, books, china, glass and items of sentimental or personal value. And these in turn were as nothing to the sufferings of the ordinary people during the Allies' slow push up the peninsula. Much of Italy's cultural heritage, damaged or destroyed in the long civil war, has now been restored or rebuilt, and no garden of importance was destroyed beyond repair. Such is the beauty and tranquillity of the gardens at La Foce, or the Villa Hanbury at La Mortola, that it is difficult to realise that men died fighting here in the worst war that Italy has ever known.

Since then, most especially in the 1960s and 1970s, the English have recolonised Tuscany. But whereas the grandparents of the new arrivals would have rented a *palazzo* in the city or a large house in the hills around Florence, most of the latest generation of Anglo-Italians have bought farms or *case coloniche* in the remotest parts of the region. No new gardens of particular merit have yet emerged, the owners enjoying neither the means nor the staff that their forebears had. One immigrant, however, stands out for his commitment to both garden restoration and garden making: Lord Lambton, whose seat at Cetinale is in the part of Italy for which he coined the name 'Chiantishire'. There are actually two gardens at Cetinale. The more important is the grand late-seventeenth-century park laid out by Carlo Fontana for Cardinal Fabio Chigi of Siena, which Lord Lambton has uncovered from the Tuscan wilderness and saved from further decay since buying the estate in 1977; and there is also a new and very English garden which Lambton has added for his own pleasure.

The old approach to Cetinale was by a very long avenue at whose end Cardinal Chigi placed a colossal statue of Hercules. Nowadays it is reached along a dusty road and through the farmyard of the estate *fattoria*. A gate leads straight into the courtyard in front of the house; this courtyard is set with square and rectangular box-edged enclosures, cut along the top with little domes, with large yew shapes surrounded by grass inside. There are lemon trees in new terracotta pots at the corners, and allegorical statues carved to represent Abundance by one of the Mazzuoli. The main axis of the garden runs right through the *piano terreno* of the house, and out again in a long broad avenue on the other side; 'an unusually protracted vista' the American Rose Nichols called it in 1929. Edward Hutton, perhaps the most learned, and certainly the most affectionate Englishman ever to write about Italy, described Cetinale in 1955, after more than fifty years' acquaintance, and concluded:

the most splendid thing here is the park called La Tebaide, to which a long grass path, wide as the house, between high walls, leads to another statued gateway with ivy-clad niches and obelisks and balls. Thence one passes into great *boschi* of ilexes, and thence by a rude flight of steps to Fontana's Romitorio on the highest point hereabout, to be rewarded by a wide and magnificent panorama all over the Sienese *contado*.

Now the walls of the villa and olive orchards above it have been planted with ornamental climbers that are seldom seen in Italy: roses such as 'Mermaid', the

Cetinale. The house and first section of the cypress avenue which leads to the Tebaïde; the English garden is tucked beneath the ramparts.

Whoever you are who approach
That which may seem horrible to you
Is pleasing to myself.
If it appeals to you, remain.
If it bores you, go away.
Each is equally agreeable to me.

The English garden at Cetinale is designed as a series of smallish outdoor rooms, connected by gravel paths and often symmetrically planted. A piece of grass, almost a lawn, at the edge of the swimming-pool has two large bushes of wintersweet *Chimonanthus praecox* in the middle, while the borders around it are to an extent planted as mirror images across a central axis. Further down, a line of four *giardini segreti* is traversed by a central gravel path. Two of these secret gardens are devoted to the cultivation of vegetables, with the little pink polyantha rose 'The Fairy' all along the front. The other two gardens are kept purely for flowers, among the roses the old-fashioned *gallica* 'Cardinal de Richelieu', the modern shrub 'Raubritter', and the cabbage rose *Rosa × centifolia*. The *giardini segreti* are separated by pergolas: one is covered with vines and under-planted with pale roses and Florentine irises, while another is wrapped in pink and white *wichuraiana* ramblers. Roses are not the only shrubs: a rich tangle of lilacs, hibiscus, deutzias and phlomis is under-planted with columbines, pansies, lavender, paeonies and lilies. The colour schemes here are quite original, with the soft pinks and purples of old-fashioned roses placed next to the harsh red of 'Scharlachglut' and the bright orange of the day lilies. These contrasts increase the sense of being in an artless English cottage garden. But Lord Lambton admires ordered disorder: Sissinghurst is his ideal garden.

A pair of loquats *Eriobotrya japonica* flanks the path that leads out of the secret gardens, through a cottage gate, and on to a walk lined with upright rosemary to a sequence of more open enclosures. A rough croquet lawn is fringed with almond trees and olives. An orchard of fruit trees, with everything from medlars to quinces, has climbing and trailing roses set to ramble up the old fruit trees in the conventional English manner. More roses and occasional shrubs such as the purple form of smoke bush *Cotinus coggygria* 'Purpureus' and the under-rated *Buddleia crispa* are dotted around the mown grass, which would be left long and cut for hay in an Italian orchard. To one side is an avenue of young lime trees, which will develop as a feature of the garden in the future, while the retaining walls are

climbing potato *Solanum crispum* and, all the way from Surrey, the blue flowers of *Clematis × jackmanii*. This modern overlay is a by-product of planting a new and intensely English garden underneath the ramparts on the southern side, where the English wife of one of the Chigi (the daughter of Frances Elliott, who wrote *The Diary of an Idle Woman in Sicily*) laid out a flower garden in the early years of the twentieth century.

It is perhaps characteristic of Lord Lambton that he should astonish his English neighbours in County Durham by designing a formal Italian garden at Biddick Hall, and mystify his Italian neighbours in Chiantishire by inserting an English cottage garden into the baroque landscape at Cetinale. There is an apt inscription over the porch at Cetinale which has been there since at least 1802, when James Forsyth noted it. It translates:

covered with wild snapdragons, valerian and capers.

The English garden at Cetinale is Lord Lambton's own creation, though with assistance from the garden designer Claire Ward. The apparent paradox of choosing an English garden for Italy and an Italian garden for England is explained by Lord Lambton's love of order and ordered disorder which are common to both gardens, as are geometry, evergreen hedging and variations in height. But the garden at Cetinale is unusual in one respect: almost all the plants in it are plants that we grow in England. There are no roses from the Italian hybridisers Cazzaniga and Aicardi, nor magnolias from Lake Maggiore, nor ornamental trees from the nurseries of Emilia-Romagna. Walking through the kitchen-garden sections of the *giardini segreti*, with a bank of 'The Fairy' on either side, there is nothing that would look out of place in England. Only in the orchard outside does the Italian landscape begin to assert its personality. Here the roses ramble over almond trees as they would in an old English apple orchard: it should be the best part of Cetinale, an Anglo-Italian hybrid, but it is as yet too young to have developed such a character. The most interesting section remains the *giardini segreti*, which are miniature mid-twentieth-century school-of-Sissinghurst outdoor rooms, the purest example of the style in Italy.

Nevertheless, in a hundred years' time, when the Lambtons have retreated to County Durham and the Chigi rule again as merchant princes in Siena, it will be the splendours of Fontana's baroque Tebaide that dazzle and amuse our descendants, and not the ruins of the twentieth-century English garden, by then a jungle of old French roses and back-to-nature columbines. For the English tenure on Tuscany has left no lasting monument to the English style of gardening. Only the gardens imbued with an Italian spirit seem likely to survive beyond the passing of their English owners, while the others will fade quietly away, without fuss, almost unnoticed – *partendo all'inglese*, as the Italians say.

References and Further Reading

The Golden Ring: The Anglo-Florentines 1847–1862 (London, 1956), by G. Artom Treves, translated by Sylvia Sprigge, is a good introduction to English intellectual circles in Florence in the mid nineteenth century. Several Anglo-Italian gardens appear in Georgina Masson's *Italian Gardens* (London, 1961), an important and influential book, but largely concerned with real Tuscan gardens rather than English reconstructions. Among the more useful older works on Tuscan gardens are Charles Latham's *The Gardens of Italy* (London, 1905), Edith Wharton's *Italian Villas and their Gardens* (New York, 1904), and Harold Donaldson Eberlein's *Villas of Florence and Tuscany* (Philadelphia, 1922). Best of the modern studies is Harold Acton's *Tuscan Villas* (London, 1973), while his autobiography *Memoirs of an Aesthete* (London, 1948) has a good account of La Pietra. Fred Whitsey also wrote perceptively of La Pietra in *Country Life* (30 March 1978). Antonio Gallenga's *Italy Revisited* (London, 1876) – also quoted in Chapter 4 – is rather too dry to be of interest nowadays. The quotation from Alfred Austin comes from *Lamia's Winter-Quarters* (London, 1898). The Rosses' garden at Poggio Gherardo is twice described in *Gardener's Chronicle* (3 December 1898 and 11 May 1912). Janet Ross's autobiography *The Fourth Generation* (London, 1912), also referred to in Chapter 5, deserves to be better known. Joseph Lucas's charming *Our Villa in Italy* ought to be seized on by a talent-spotter and republished, as should Sir George Sitwell's *On the Making of Gardens* (1909). Villa Gamberaia was portrayed in its Edwardian heyday in *Country Life*, 26 May 1906. Cecil Pinsent's career is treated in the *Journal of Garden History*, vol. 3, no. 1, by Erika Neubauer. Patrick Bowe published a short account of his work at I Tatti in *Country Life*, 5 July 1990: Fred Whitsey's article in *Country Life* on 29 March 1979 is unreliable in some of its details. I am grateful to Harvard University for letting me use the letters and papers of Mary Berenson in the library at I Tatti. There are several good biographies and sketches of Bernard Berenson; the best is *Forty Years with Berenson* by the enchanting Nicky Mariano (London, 1966). The quotation from Eric Linklater comes from *The Art of Adventure* (London, 1947). Iris Origo – *War in Val d'Orcia* (London, 1951) and *Images and Shadows* (London, 1970); there is a detailed study of La Foce by Penelope Hobhouse in *Hortus* (Autumn 1987). There is little published about Cetinale, apart from a chapter from Marella Agnelli (see Chapter 5). The quotation from Edward Hutton comes from *Siena and Southern Tuscany* (London, 1955).

Chapter Eight

THE ITALIAN LAKES

The Pleasures of Plantsmanship

THERE HAS been an English colony in the Italian Lakeland region since the early years of the nineteenth century. It was once especially vigorous on Lake Como, where there was an Anglican church at Menaggio, a sure sign of a settled community of expatriate Englishmen. By the early 1900s it was said that Cadenabbia had 'been annexed by the English, with ... tea-parties and gossip, and an intensely British atmosphere of the type savouring of evensong and the parish magazine'. But it was not only the English who fell for the beauty of the region. 'Nothing in the world can compare to the charm of ... the Milanese lakes,' wrote Stendhal as early as 1817.

Lombardy and the Veneto were Austrian provinces after the 1815 Congress of Vienna and the affinity which the German-speaking peoples have for the lakeland region dates from this time. The Villa Carlotta at Cadenabbia was bought by Princess Albrecht of Prussia for her daughter the Duchess of Saxe-Meiningen in 1843, and it was under the influence of the German romantic movement that this great subtropical nineteenth-century woodland garden was made. Even during the eighteenth century, the boats that plied from north to south provided an easy means of travel for the grand tourist as he passed from the alpine splendours of the Helvetic Confederation, an important part of contemporary aesthetic education, to the classical and artistic attractions of Lombardy. Goethe was only one of

---

Villa San Remigio. The Garden of Melancholy, perhaps the most Italian parts of this magnificent Anglo-Italian garden, focuses on Giambattista Marchiori's giant statue of Hercules slaying the Hydra.

thousands of travellers to enter Italy by boat from Riva di Garda; indeed, the popularity of Tennyson's injunction to 'row us out from Desenzano' owed much to the fact that many of his readers were already acquainted with 'sweet Catullus's all-but-island, olive-silvery Sirmio'.

The Italian Lakes were never such a fashionable honey-pot as the Riviera, nor such a cultural lure as Florence and Rome. The attractions of the region were its climate and natural beauty. The painter Edward Lear considered that Lake Varese represented the 'true Italian Ideal or Claude Landscape'. It is true that Queen Caroline of England (1768–1821) owned the Villa d'Este at Cernobbio between 1815 and 1820 – she de-formalised its garden by replacing the Renaissance layout with a landscape park in the English style – but she was not the sort to make anywhere smart. Of more significance was Queen Victoria, who spent a month at Villa Clara in Baveno on Lake Maggiore in the spring of 1879. She busied herself there with painting and garden visits, and wrote in her diary how she was strongly attracted by the 'ever-changing lights on the lovely scenery' and by the beautiful gardens with 'dazzling Camellias' and evergreen trees. Lady Paget, whose husband was British Ambassador to Italy at the time, also admired the 'tall blossoming camellias' of the Villa Clara when summoned from Rome to attend upon the Queen, but she (unusually among English visitors) did not care for the beauty of Lake Maggiore. 'It does not do to see the lakes after having lived long in Italy,' she wrote, for 'there [is] something meretricious in it all after the sober lines of the Tuscan hills and the sombre tones of the *campagna*'. The Italian Lakes were distinctly middle class. Richard Bagot described Villa Clara in 1905 as a

Villa Clara, Baveno, where Queen Victoria stayed. The terrace frames a distant view of the Sasso del Ferro and the Isola dei Pescatori. Painting by Gabriele Carelli, given to the Queen by Princess Beatrice.

'remarkably ugly building, so completely out of character with its surroundings' that it was a 'veritable eyesore in the landscape ... a replica of the Wimbledon or Putney residence of a retired tradesman'. But Queen Victoria liked it, and that was her prerogative.

It should be said that the lakeland region was never wholly Italian: the northern part of Lake Maggiore and most of Lake Lugano have for long been part of the Canton of Ticino, while the tip of Lake Garda was for centuries part of the Hapsburg dominions. The climate, however, is the same in all parts – mild and wet. The Lakes do not suffer the dry cold winds of the Riviera, and gardens along the water's edge are seldom troubled by prolonged periods of cold. Temperatures may fall below freezing during winter nights, but they rise again during the daytime. Rainfall is heavy, and rather more abundant in the growing months of spring and summer than during the winter. Lugano has an annual rainfall of 1.73 m (68 in), which is more than twice the average of London and the Home Counties. The result is a steamy temperateness, highly conducive to idle tourism. English garden owners wonder at the speed

of plant growth and the sheer variety that can be planted: practically nothing will fail in the Italian Lakes that can be grown in England, while much will flourish that does not survive the cool summers and cold winters of northern latitudes. Perhaps the two best-known Italian gardens are Isola Bella and Isola Madre in Lake Maggiore, one a masterpiece of baroque extravagance and the other a model of the English landscape style. English visitors tend to prefer the natural lines and luxuriant growth of Isola Madre. Dorothy Wordsworth went so far as to describe Isola Bella as the 'peak of absurdity, a garden not of flowers but of stone', while Lady Blessington, writing at about the same time, was in tune with many of her fellow countrymen when she concluded that 'Isola Madre has been less dressed by art than Isola Bella, and therefore pleased me more.' Charles Dickens reminded his readers, nevertheless, that 'however fanciful and fantastic the Isola Bella may be, and is, it still is beautiful'.

The English landscape style adapted well to the conditions of the Italian Lakeland. Indeed, some of the sumptuous gardens on the shores of Como and Maggiore would not look out of place in south-west

Above: *Isola Madre, a nineteenth-century landscape garden in Lake Maggiore, replanted in the 1950s by Henry Cocker.*

Above: *Brissago. Mimosa bursts over the embankments of this island garden; mountains and water dominate all the gardens of the Swiss–Italian lakeland region.*
Opposite: *Villa San Remigio at Pallanza. A sideways view along one of the terraces, known as the Garden of Happiness, illustrates the richness and complexity typical of many Anglo-Italian gardens in the Lakes.*

Above: *Vico Morcote. A double-flowered cornus underplanted with wood anemones and other shade-loving flowers in Sir Peter Smithers's plantsman's garden on Lake Lugano.*
Below: *Pink and white forms of* Cornus florida *at Villa Táranto. They flourish in the humid heat of the Italian Lakeland.*

Villa Táranto. It is difficult to understand why Neil McEacharn called this prettily planted enclosure the 'Italian' garden.

Above: *Villa Táranto. The nineteenth-century house is rather detached from the gardens, and is best seen from the modern formal garden beyond the Valletta.*

Opposite: *Neil McEacharn kept this group of old* Trachycarpus fortunei *palms at Villa Táranto and made it a feature of the formal garden.*

Above: *Quinta do Vale*. Rosa brunonii *and white crinums against the pink wall of an outbuilding in this plantsman's garden north of Lisbon.*
Below: *Quinta do Vale*. Azulejos *set into the wall of the house create a feature for the garden.*

Isola Bella. This important baroque garden, tiered up like a galleon in Lake Maggiore, has long been a challenge to English preconceptions of gardens and gardening.

Scotland, Ireland or parts of southern England. The typical villa has a gravel drive leading to the house; the cast-iron gates are emblazoned with its name in gilded lettering upon the railings; loggias, colonnades and bowers all garlanded with wisteria rise above the lakeside; a token formal garden occupies the front of the house; around it, lies an open parkland planted with palms, cedars, magnolias, hedges of camellias, great barrages of rhododendrons, drifts of azaleas in every outrageous colour and a springtime abundance of flowers such as enchanted Queen Victoria. This pattern can be seen clearly at Villa Pallavicino at Stresa and Villa Carlotta at Cadenabbia: it also describes the early-nineteenth-century garden at Villa Melzi near Bellagio, despite its modern overlay of azaleas and rhododendrons introduced from English nurseries in the 1950s by Duke Tommaso Gallarati-Scotti after a tour of duty as Italian Ambassador at the Court of St James. The style developed in the Italian Lakeland owed much to the English and German taste for opulence, and has changed less in the last hundred years than in almost any part of Europe. The Riviera, Sintra, Biarritz and Baden-Baden have all altered almost beyond recognition,

but the Italian Lakes are still pervaded by the spirit of comfort and relaxation that Victorian travellers created there. They exhale orderliness, decency, success and that enjoyment of wealth which characterised so many respectable magnates of the nineteenth century.

Horticulture is still practised on almost an English scale in the Italian Lakes. Flowers, and the pleasure of growing them, are part of the way of life, and there are nurserymen and plantsmen to prove it. In the nineteenth century, the Rovelli nursery at Pallanza on Lake Maggiore advised almost all the great gardens of the region. Supply creates demand: because Rovelli was such an enterprising introducer of exotic plants, there are now more mature specimens of rare and beautiful trees and shrubs to be found in the region than in any other part of Italy. In the mid twentieth century, the garden at Villa Táranto was another potent source of new ideas and plants. When Henry Cocker, who had been director of the garden, set himself up in 1960 as a garden consultant, he reinvigorated many of the best gardens of the Italian Lakes. His commissions included replanting Isola Madre in Lago Maggiore for the

Baroness St Leger, the driving force behind the garden at Isole di Brissago, and inspiration for the Circe theme in James Joyce's Ulysses.

Borromeo family and laying out the gardens of Baron Heinrich von Thyssen's Villa Favorita on the Swiss part of Lake Lugano.

JUST INSIDE the Swiss border, between Locarno and Cernobbio, lie the islands of Brissago, the larger about 5.5 ha (13 acres) and the smaller about 3 ha (7 acres). In 1885 they were bought by a young couple from Kingstown, Co. Dublin, who called themselves the Baron and Baroness St Leger. The St Legers had been living for a while on Lake Maggiore, because the Baroness suffered from a serious lung condition and had been advised by a doctor that the climate of the Italian Lakes might be productive of a cure. This advice proved to be correct, for the Baroness wrote in 1912 that she had never had a relapse of her troubles, and then survived another thirty-six years to reach the age of ninety-two. In 1885 the islands of Brissago were little more than mud-flats, barren and inhospitable, swept by winds, home only to a few miserable oak trees and swarms of poisonous snakes. The ruined convent upon the larger of the two islands

had until recently been a store for the dynamite used to build the St Gotthard railway. The island had not been cultivated for many years; even the landing stage was silted up. Nevertheless the romantic Baroness took what she described as a 'specially unfortunate fancy' to the task of transforming the islands into 'this now delightful spot in the midst of the most gorgeous and beautiful tropical vegetation'.

The St Legers began by making an easy approach to the house, and then built walks and paths around the island. The Baroness explained that these were designed 'with the sole object either of absolute utility or necessity, or with the intention of obtaining a certain vista, or to lead to a certain spot desired to be as handy as possible ... [with] no specially intricate or useless windings'. The Baron was a competent amateur botanist, interested in taxonomy and research; his wife became an energetic garden-maker and searcher after good plants. It was a fruitful combination, though they parted company in 1897. She, full of ideas and energy, without considering the cost, directed everything; he advised and assisted. She supervised the workmen, and threw herself into the study of gardening, entering into long correspondence with William Robinson, then at the height of his influence as editor of *The Garden*. The St Legers imported boatloads of good black soil and manure from the mainland and worked hard at the acclimatisation of exotic plants. They took pleasure from the variety of vegetation that could be persuaded to prosper in this super-temperate corner of the alpine foothills. Some plants proved difficult to establish: the *Eucalyptus viminalis* which Baroness St Leger raised from seed sent from Australia failed to grow until they had been planted no less than ten times. Twenty-two years later, when they were 25 m (80 ft) high, the Baroness observed 'when their bark, which they throw off every year, loosens itself and hangs down in long streaks, one might imagine oneself walking under the lianas of a virgin forest'. They are now vast specimens, prized by the Swiss authorities for being by far the largest in the country. But the Baroness exaggerated the difficulty of establishing her gum trees; eucalyptus are perhaps the least fastidious of exotic trees, flourishing in poor soils where little else will survive. Prince Troubetzkoy at nearby Pallanza was already growing 266 different kinds at the time of Queen Victoria's visit in 1879, and *E. viminalis* is one of the most accommodating of species.

The outstanding features of the garden at Isole di Brissago today are its conifers and palm trees. These creatures of nineteenth-century fashion have now grown into their prime. The palms include the Canary Island palm *Phoenix canariensis*, but the St Legers also grew the true date palm, which has not survived. The Baroness planted a line of the comparatively hardy Chusan palm *Trachycarpus fortunei* to curve along the edge of the embankment on the eastern side of the main island. These are now exceptionally tall trees, their height accentuated by the species' habit of growing thicker towards the top of the trunk and thinner at the base. Each specimen acts as host to a different rambler rose: the chocolate-coloured trunks of these palms are a popular foil for climbing plants in the Italian Lakes. Baron St Leger had a characteristic Victorian interest in economic plants: there are two species of banana at Brissago, *Musa basjoo* and *M. textilis*, and specimens of the papyrus sedge *Cyperus papyrus* and the Japanese paper bush *Edgeworthia chrysantha*.

Much of the garden at Isole di Brissago today is modern, remade by the present owners, the Swiss state. The garden is important to the Swiss authorities because it is the most southerly and temperate in Switzerland and gives students the opportunity to study a range of subtropical trees and shrubs which is unique in the country. The Baroness lived at Isole di Brissago for over forty years, welcoming visitors to the island with increasingly unreliable accounts of how difficult she had found the eucalyptus to establish. In 1927 she sold both islands to a German armaments millionaire, who left the garden untouched until the Swiss took over in 1950. With no garden traditions of their own, the Swiss have created a parody of their island in the sun, adding such features as an Italian-style well-head topped by a complicated wrought-iron confection in the middle of a border dedicated to nurserymen's bulbs. So the visitor has to discriminate between the old and the new, the good and the bad. The essential Englishness of Brissago lies in its wooded exotica, not in the self-conscious aping of the style of Italian public parks. The layout of the garden is also peculiarly English, with its collection of trees planted so thickly that the island seems much larger than it is. Indeed, the

Isole di Brissago. The house built by Baron and Baroness St Leger, demolished in 1928, and surrounded by 'a cunningly devised jungle paradise', according to Frank Budgen.

mound which the St Legers made in the middle consists exclusively of *Trachycarpus fortunei*, and several hundred specimens of this palm have naturalised there to form a dark thick copse, in whose shelter grow aspidistras, shade-loving ferns, and the giant-leaved *Rhododendron grande* from the Himalayas.

It is now time to consider how anyone calling themselves Baron and Baroness St Leger can be considered English, when the usual style of a baron in the United Kingdom is 'Lord'. The truth is that Baron St Leger was neither an English peer nor a nobleman of any other nationality, but an Anglo-Irish adventurer who adopted the title because of some supposed relationship to Viscount Doneraile, whose family surname was St Leger. St Leger was not even the imposter's real surname. He appears to have been called Richard Fleming and, according to his marriage certificate, was the son of an Irish admiral, although no naval officer of such name and rank was gazetted in the Navy Lists of the day. So Richard Fleming remains something of a mystery, despite the Swiss insistence that he played more than an equal part in creating this rich and rare garden. Of his wife there is an even stranger story to tell. James Joyce visited her in 1919 in the company of his inseparable companion, the artist Frank Budgen, who described Brissago as an 'enchanted isle . . . a cunningly devised jungle paradise, holding, among other wonders, a grove of superb Eucalyptus trees'. Joyce's visit resulted in a still more exotic legacy. Before they went, the Baroness gave him a packet of letters and a valise of books on the theme of erotic perversion, with the hope that he might find the contents useful for his writing. As it happens, Joyce knew that, among her neighbours, the Baroness was known as Circe, and it is under that name that she finds herself immortalised in *Ulysses*.

We have seen that the English were by no means the only foreigners to feel an attraction for the Swiss–Italian Lakes: there have at all times over the last two hundred years been substantial colonies of Germans, Austrians, French and other nationalities. Many Italians too from other parts of the peninsula have come to live in the lakeland region. The result has the emergence of a distinctive style of gardening, based largely on the German and English landscape traditions, but with elements taken from the Italian formal tradition. Some of the best-known gardens could well have been made by persons of almost any nationality. There is no stylistic reason, for example, why the gardens of Villa Carlotta on Lake Como

and Isola Madre in Lake Maggiore should not have been made by Englishmen, rather than by a German and an Italian respectively. Villa Carlotta has long been admired by English visitors to the Italian Lakes for its natural landscape and the richness of its plantings. Our Victorian ancestors gasped at the bamboos 10 m (30 ft) high, the banana plants and Indian azaleas, and sighed that they could scarcely be grown in England. It was the same at Villa Melzi, whose hedges of *Lippia citriodora* and *Fuchsia fulgens*, flourishing lagerstroemias and camphor trees they invariably admired and envied. It is scarcely surprising, therefore, that English gardens in the Italian Lakes have tended to a natural style and a wide variety of plants, rather than architectural forms.

There are exceptions. The best formal garden to have been made in northern Italy during the last two hundred years is the one laid out at Villa San Remigio in Pallanza by an Anglo-Italian family. Their name, I Marchesi Silvio e Sophie della Valle di Casanova, could hardly be less English; it looks an awkward fit in the story of English garden-making abroad. But Sophie was wholly English – or, more accurately, Anglo-Irish – and, since her husband Silvio was also her first cousin, it follows that he was half-English too. The grandfather they shared was a British diplomat called Peter Browne. In 1859, he had bought a small estate on the summit of Castagnola, the hill which forms the promontory around which Intra and Pallanza are built. The present house was built right at the top in 1903 and has spectacular views on all sides, from the mountains of the Monte Rosa range beyond the Ossola valley in the west to the peaks of Piz Bernina in the north-east. The land drops away quickly to the south and used to run down to the edge of Lake Maggiore itself. It became the largest landholding in the Pallanza peninsula; Silvio di Casanova's father had bought the property next to Peter Browne's, and eventually the two were combined in the ownership of their grandchildren.

Part of the garden at Villa San Remigio is in the Victorian landscape style. The driveway winds up to the house through clumps of palms, camellias, box hedges, banks covered in bergenias and collections of unusual conifers until it passes through an archway and opens out in front of the house. It is more mansion than house, a palatial pile built in the style of the Neapolitan eighteenth century. A plaque on the edge of the terrace declares: 'This garden was made by us, Silvio and Sophie della Valle di Casanova, where we were united in our childhood. It was born of a dream that we shared in our youth, planned during our adolescence, and carried out when we were married.' They began the garden in 1905: their labour of love became the work of a lifetime.

A stupendous series of terraces forms the backbone of the garden on the western side: views across the lake towards Stresa provide the dramatic backdrop for a theatrical progression down towards the gate lodge. Since the garden was open to the public even in its early days, a wide curving staircase leads up directly from the lodge to the lowest terrace. Great attention was paid to the finish of the retaining walls because they meet the eye as one climbs from one level to the next. Nevertheless, the garden was designed to be viewed from the house. The six terraces call for detailed description: most can be seen from the gravelled one at the top, which is balustraded about with statues of the Four Seasons. Broad steps wreathed in the single yellow form of Banksian rose *Rosa banksiae* 'Lutescens' descend to the second terrace which is laid out as an outdoor gallery. A topiary armchair sits at one end, while along the sides are moulded seats in the shape of

scallops. Both features recur throughout the garden – there must be nearly a hundred of these shell seats. The yew armchair is straight out of the English Arts and Crafts tradition; the scallops are pure Italian rococo. The retaining wall on this terrace has been given a false façade of classical columns and the interstices of this colonnade are planted with closely cropped myrtle: green archways relieved by stage-set pillars. Roses were planted at the bases of these columns, among them the early hybrid China rose 'Gloire des Rosomanes'. Four fountains or stoups have also been built into the wall. Their water trickles from a dramatic mask and drops into a shell-shaped basin. Each piscina is surrounded by a pedimented pair of columns and backed by neo-Roman mosaics: twin dolphins with their tails twisted together, bordered by garlands. There is more than a hint of Anglo-Saxon romanticism about the design, a suggestion of Alma-Tadema's neo-classical paintings. The dolphins, like the shells, form part of the Casanova coat of arms.

The next terrace down – the third – projects high above those below it, which gives it fine views of the

Villa San Remigio. The house and terraces on the western side, seen from the lowest, the Garden of Melancholy.

mountains beyond Domodossola to the north-west. It also forms the roof of the conservatory on the terrace below. The sides of the hill are here planted as a rock garden, with *Iris japonica*, hemerocallis and bergenias flourishing on the slopes. A path at one end offers an alternative way down and leads through a wild garden to a long, high, curving portico, in effect an undercroft to the terrace that surrounds the house. The heavy stone columns are planted with wisteria, the creeping fig *Ficus pumila* and the double white Banksian rose *Rosa banksiae* 'Alba Plena'.

The fourth terrace has a sundial near its centre and is known as the Garden of the Hours. An inscription on the dial reads 'Silvio and Sophie placed this here so that the new light of day might dissolve the shadow of hours past.' Lemon trees in pots and palms surround the timepiece, while the balustrade is marked by four life-sized statues of pagan gods by the prolific Vicentine sculptor Orazio Marinali (1643–1720). The extremities of the terrace are guarded by tall granite obelisks. The dominant feature, however, of the fourth terrace is a large conservatory which encloses part of the rocky hillside. This natural outcrop resembles a grotto, an effect increased by a stream which runs from end to end of the conservatory. A few ferns and begonias flourish in the damp gloom, sole relics of the extensive collection of shade-loving plants which the Casanovas made. A path leads from the terrace into thick woodland at the side and splits into three. The middle track passes through an underground tunnel to a grotto of Pan, so that the spirit of the wild wood is immediately encountered in person as you leave the ordered classicism of the formal terraces. Near by is an enclosed garden in the Renaissance style. It is square and simple, with short straight paths lined by cypresses and cordylines. A stone-set central pool has the shape of the ground plan of a Byzantine church: superimposed circles and squares. On a plaque the inscription begins '*Alta quies liquidique potentia somni . . .*', ('Deep sleep: the power of untroubled slumber . . .'), a curious choice of text even for a *hortus inclusus*. Yet here, as throughout Villa San Remigio, the classical propriety of the design is interrupted by stunning views of Lake Maggiore and the mountains beyond. The English love of a distant prospect takes precedence over historical correctness.

The fifth terrace is perhaps the loveliest, the Garden of Happiness. In the centre a life-sized statue of a near-naked Venus stands on a cushion in a huge pearly shell chariot, hitching up her cloak. She is drawn in triumph by two horses whose hooves have been transmuted into fins. This statue by the Neapolitan sculptor Riccardo Ripamonti gives the terrace, and indeed the whole garden, its prevailing sense of pagan luxuriance. Around the edge, delicate baroque broderies in low-cut box and black and white pebbled *ciottolato* paths in simple geometric patterns have been interplanted with roses and bright seasonal bedding. The retaining wall conceals another greenhouse, perhaps 40 m (130 ft) long, used for overwintering the lemon trees. Four griffons on slender columns stand guard over the sixth and final terrace, the Garden of Melancholy, a green garden, surrounded by dark evergreens: osmanthus, hollies, palms, ferns and aucubas. Stylistically the most restrained, it is also the most faithful to the eighteenth-century Neapolitan rococo. Intricate ironwork encloses simple grass rectangles and box topiary in geometric shapes. The focal point is a mosaic nymphaeum whose giant statue by the Neapolitan sculptor Giambattista Marchiori (1698–1778) represents Hercules slaying the Hydra.

The Casanovas laid out a grander but less exuberant sequence of gardens on the eastern side of Monte Castagnola. A double gateway at right angles to the descent shields them from view. Passing through one of these gates, and turning the corner, reveals a long stone staircase plunging down through clipped yew hedges and drifts of white azaleas. The hillside is wooded, and the planting lights up the cool shade. The steps lead to a vast semicircular wall with statues in niches, bordered by mosaic garlands and pendants. A false colonnade supports a pediment of rococo balustrading. The whole construction is reminiscent of the famous semicircular nymphaeum at Villa Aldobrandini in Rome, which was admired by John Evelyn in 1644 and later inspired the wall of English worthies at Stowe. Here it is known as the Garden of Sighs: below lies the Garden of Memories, where a broad terrace with a large pool is positioned to reflect the mountains around Monte Rosa. The surround is grass, with putti on plinths, great urns and jars, and rambling roses climbing up the slender columns and the balustrade. A tall archway was built beyond to frame a view across the lake before the trees beneath grew up to obscure it: round the foot of the arch is the hexameter: '*Secretum Nemus et Virculta Sonantia Silvis*' ('A lonely forest and thickets that rustle in the woodland'). This is the only consciously English part of the garden at Villa San Remigio: the English Garden. It is in part a landscaped park, with specimen copper beeches and spruces: the other plantings include clumps of the

Villa San Remigio. The Garden of Memories, whose pool reflects the peak of Monte Rosa while, at the other end, an archway frames the view of Lake Maggiore.

evergreen *Magnolia grandiflora*, rhododendrons and *Choisya ternata*. It is also in part an English woodland garden, with winding paths, steps and glades running down to the shores of the lake itself, where drifts of Japanese maples, yellow azaleas, hollies and laurels grow under a mixed canopy of pine, spruce, chestnut and camphor. It is indistinguishable from the woodland gardens of any number of nineteenth-century villas on the shores of the Italian Lakes.

The baroque terraces on the western side of Villa San Remigio were conceived as a tribute to the Casanovas' Italian heritage and may owe something to the splendid sequence of hanging gardens on nearby Isola Bella. But Villa San Remigio is more spacious and calmer, concerned with serenity rather than display, and built for enjoyment, not to amaze. Georgina Masson considered the garden to be the most fascinating interpretation of a formal Italian garden as seen through romantic northern eyes.

The whole garden is imbued with the same feeling: it is a dream world, Italy and the Mediterranean basin as the northerner imagines it, not as it really is. Thus classical

goddesses drive their chariots through pools surrounded by romantic woodland, and lily ponds mirror the reflections of distant snowy peaks. The conception is neither wholly Italian nor wholly northern, but it provides a charming postscript to the history of lakeside gardens in Italy.

The romantic spirit of Villa San Remigio is intensified by its present condition of decay. Little actual damage has been caused by visitors, as the property is seldom open to the public, scarcely remembered and so tucked away as to be relatively safe from vandalism and theft. Nevertheless the balustrading is collapsing down the hillside, steps are crumbling away and the shrubberies are overgrown with brambles. There was once an English woodland garden of rhododendrons and azaleas where the views of the lake are now obscured, and shell-shaped seats can still be found deep in the undergrowth in places carefully chosen for the enjoyment of long prospects which are no more. Gone is the family that spent such creative endeavour upon its making: the house belongs now to the province of Piemonte and is used for government offices. Gone are the gardeners who maintained it as a showpiece: the present staff are few in number and cannot prevent the deterioration of both structure and planting. Gone are the visitors who marvelled at the exuberant woodland, the busy terraces and the breathtaking views: the garden is no longer open to the public. Gone too are the white peacocks that screeched and scratched around the terraces: Villa San Remigio is inhabited only by ghosts.

THE BEST MODERN garden in the lakeland region – arguably the most interesting post-war garden in Europe – is in fact in Switzerland. It was begun as recently as 1970, when Sir Peter and Lady Smithers built a house at Vico Morcote on a steep south-facing slope above the dark waters of Lake Lugano. The site was not a large one, less than half a hectare (1 acre) in all, a disused vineyard bounded by light oak woodland. Now it contains more than ten thousand species and varieties of plants, and a canopy has been created by the exotic trees that Sir Peter himself planted. In this it resembles the nineteenth-century lakeland gardens, except that its framework is made of the hybrid magnolias that have been bred in North America and New Zealand over the last forty years. The palms, eucalyptus and conifers, which are such a feature of the Swiss–Italian Lakes, have been rigorously excluded.

The house is modern, and space within is provided by screens in the Japanese style; on the terrace, pots of dwarf maples offer an undemanding substitute for bonsai. The garden is English in its rejection of all formality, in the refusal to draw on Swiss or Italian horticultural traditions of design and in the primacy given to plants. The winding path that leads up and down the hillside in a narrow circuit, with short side spurs for diversion along the way, is essentially English too, and descends from the Robinsonian idea of a circular woodland walk. But surely never before was such diversity concentrated in so small a compass.

Sir Peter has planted at least one specimen of every available magnolia. There are now over 150 different varieties represented in the collection at Vico Morcote. Smithers makes his own assessment of their comparative worth, and publishes it in the magazine of the Magnolia Society. Vico Morcote is seen as an unofficial international trial ground, and his opinions are beginning to have the authority of gospel truth. Sir Peter considers the best all-rounder 'Star Wars',

a hybrid of *Magnolia campbelli* and *M. quinquepeta* bred by Oz Bloomhardt in New Zealand, but among the many interesting hybrids at Vico Morcote are two forms of *M.* × *brooklynensis*, the green-pink 'Woodsman' and the finer 'Eva Maria' with broader tepals, and the tetraploid form of *M. stellata* known as 'Norman Gould', which makes a stout small tree with hearty, rigid, upright growths, quite unlike other forms of this species. Among the Gresham hybrids he recommends 'Jo McDaniel', an improvement on the habit of 'Lennei', the voluptuous white 'Sayonara', the late-flowering 'Raspberry Ice', and another white called 'Tina Durio'.

Sir Peter Smithers's gardening interests are not confined to magnolias: he is an authority on many genera, some seldom seen in England. The Hannibal hybrids of *Amaryllis belladonna* from California have been growing at Vico Morcote and in Sir Peter's previous gardens for thirty years: names such as 'Pacifica', 'Stormy Sunset' and 'Concord Lass' are unknown at home. Another ravishing group of plants, few of which have ever been imported into England, are the Florida hibiscus hybrids: some have flowers as large as 25 cm (10 in) in diameter, their colours as brilliant as their size is astonishing.

Smithers has been active in popularising tree paeonies, first by importing them directly from Japanese suppliers such as Watanabe, and then by encouraging European nurserymen – notably Rivière of Lyon – to propagate and list them. Vico Morcote has an impressive collection of modern camellia hybrids, including 'Margaret Davis' from Australia and 'Shocking Pink' from the USA, 'Elphinstonia' from England and the Higo hybrids from Japan, alongside natural species such as *Camellia granthamiana* from Hong Kong. For some years Smithers has also been active in breeding new lilies from the plants of *Lilium sulphureum* which he collected in Burma: the hybrids are yellow or orange in colour and grow as high as $2\frac{1}{2}$ m (8 ft). He is also an authority on the breeding of clivias and nerines.

Much time and money were spent on preparing the garden. For the first four years Sir Peter needed a contractor and a full-time gardener but, as the plants grew up, the workload declined proportionately. All is now maintained by the labour of one part-time gardener: no digging, clearing or heavy work has been necessary for many years. The character of the garden has changed, too. Gone are most of the sun-loving plants of the early years, including irises and herbaceous paeonies, while in their place flourish such shady denizens as aroids, hellebores, cyclamen and the many aberrant forms of wood anemone.

'This garden is an ecosystem, in which the plants now do most of the work,' says Sir Peter: he has strong views on the purpose of a garden. He believes that a garden should be a source of pleasure to the owner and his friends, never a burden or an anxiety. It must therefore be designed and planted to give the maximum return for expense and labour, both of which must diminish as the owner himself grows old. The planting should be permanent in character, so that no annuals or bedding plants are used, nor any that require frequent division or other attention. The planting must be dense, so that there is no space for weeds to establish themselves. The plants must provide their own mulch and protection against the elements.

The magnolias and camellias now set fertile seed and litter the ground of Sir Peter's ecosystem with hybrid seedlings. So do the tree paeonies, wisterias and many other shrubs, including the forms of *Daphne bholua* collected by Sir Peter in Nepal. But Vico Morcote contains only the best forms or hybrids. Sir Peter insists that no plant will be added to his collection if there exists anywhere in the world a superior form that he has a reasonable chance of obtaining. He is convinced that all his plants should be made available to other serious gardeners, stock and labour permitting, and that the pleasure of owning a fine plant is not complete until it has been given to friends. One of Sir Peter's great mentors was Sir Frederick Stern of Highdown, whom he describes as 'an ideal . . . the most generous and hospitable of great gardeners'.

Sir Peter's ideas are important, not because he is an apostle for English gardening abroad, but because they articulate the experience he has acquired in an unEnglish climate and make it available to English garden owners at home. His views on the nature and purpose of a garden are freshly expressed and universal in their application: it may be that the lessons of Vico Morcote, particularly the goal of creating self-maintaining gardens, point the way for the future development of gardening. Sir Peter certainly believes so, and maintains that if Neil McEacharn were starting his garden at Pallanza today, he would be applying the same principles at Villa Táranto.

References and Further Reading

Good general books on the Italian Lakes are few: an Edwardian classic is Richard Bagot, *The Italian Lakes* (London, 1905). For further details of Queen Victoria's sojourn at Baveno, see Delia Millar's article in *Country Life*, 26 September 1985. There is a good description of Villa San Remigio in its prime by R. Boccardi in *Emporium* (1913) – '*Il Giardino di San Remigio*'. The best modern account is in *Italian Gardens* by Alex Ramsay and Helena Attlee (London, 1989). For the St Legers' garden I have found Giuseppe Mondada's *Le isole di Brissago nel passato e oggi* (Brissago, 1975) quite invaluable, while Baroness St Leger's own account of the garden at Brissago was published as 'The Vegetation of the Island of St Leger in Lago Maggiore' in *RHSJ*, 1913, pp. 503–14. The Circe story is well told by Frank Budgen in *James Joyce and the Making of 'Ulysses'* (London, 1934) and in Richard Ellmann's *James Joyce* (London, 1982). Peter Smithers's garden is better known abroad than in England; *Arts of Asia* (March 1984) dwells on his paeonies, *Schweizer Familie* (22 March 1989) emphasises the magnolias and the American version of *House and Garden* (July 1986) deals with camellias. The garden has not yet, however, been accorded even so much as an article in *The Garden*.

Chapter Nine

VILLA TÁRANTO

The Garden as a Status Symbol

CAPTAIN Neil Boyd Watson McEacharn was born in 1884, and educated at Eton and Oxford. He served in the King's Own Scottish Borderers during the 1914–18 war, became a member of the Royal Archers, and later a Justice of the Peace and Deputy Lord Lieutenant of Wigtownshire. He was the only child of The Hon. Sir Malcolm McEacharn, whose country seat was a baronial pile called Galloway House, Wigtown. All this suggests that Neil McEacharn was a conventional upper-class Scot. He was not. His father had come from the humblest origins, a poor Scots boy who emigrated to Australia and made a fortune from shipping. In the 1870s he was the first to use refrigerated cargo ships to bring frozen mutton to the European markets. Malcolm McEacharn bought himself a knighthood and was elected briefly to the Australian parliament, which entitled him to be called The Honourable; when he lost his seat at the next election, he sailed back to Scotland and bought himself into the landed gentry of Wigtownshire. He kept his estates in Australia: Neil boasted that they contained a greater acreage than all the cultivable land in Italy. One of Malcolm McEacharn's obituaries called him a 'dapper plutocrat'. His son never felt at ease in Britain, and his behaviour meant that he had to spend much of his time abroad. Though he married twice, Neil was a drunk and a homosexual. Both wives were unconventional choices: the first came from New York, the daughter of one Walter Raphael. The second, whom he married in 1940, was HSH Princess Imma von Erbach-Schönberg.

There were no children from either marriage.

Neil McEacharn inherited his father's energy and meticulous attention to detail but applied them to plant collecting. He used his money to acquire renown as a gardener among botanists and as a botanist among gardeners. Because of his humble background and complicated personality, he was also something of a snob: making the garden at Villa Táranto gave him something he could be proud of, something to show off. There he introduced a custom which pleases and amuses the Italians, one of whom explains that 'in England when the sovereign stays at a country house the occasion is marked by the agreeable gesture to posterity of planting a tree'. So a plantation of specimen trees bearing the names of the important visitors who planted them lies at a convenient distance from the house. Among those commemorated are Princess Margaret of England, Queen Ena of Spain (a relation of Princess Imma) and endless Italian Christian Democrat politicians including the prime minister, Giulio Andreotti. McEacharn's fortune enabled him to act in the grand manner. We should not assume that he was capable of thinking in the same way: he regarded Villa Táranto as a hobby. 'As some men might spend their money on racing stables or other costly sports,' he wrote, 'I have made these gardens my occupation and my adventure.'

When McEacharn bought Villa Táranto in 1930, he was a man in a hurry. Aged forty-six, and not in the best of health, he was full of ambitious schemes. In those days, estate agents as we understand them did not exist in Italy, and he would normally have learnt that an estate of this kind was up for sale only by word of mouth. He was fortunate, however, that the house belonged to the English widow of the

---

The fountain at Villa Táranto has one hundred jets; the water forms an outline of exquisite loveliness.

Capt. Neil McEacharn (1884–1964), standing on the edge of the formal garden at Villa Táranto.

Conte di Sant'Elia, who advertised it for sale in *The Times*. McEacharn moved quickly to buy the property, together with some adjoining land in separate ownership, and gradually over the next few years he built up the estate to its final extent of about 100 acres (40 ha). Its name was Villa La Crocetta, which he promptly changed to Villa Táranto to commemorate a putative relation who had been created Duke of Táranto by Napoleon I. McEacharn claimed that the Marshall was a distant kinsman; but the Italians are generously prepared to think better of a man than he deserves, and the Duke is now commonly believed to have been a lineal ancestor.

Villa Táranto lies between Pallanza and Intra, on a peninsula that projects into Lake Maggiore, and the house is at the far end of the estate, some 400 m ($\frac{1}{4}$ mile) from the lakeside. The land is almost level near the entrance gates but the drive rises sharply towards the house. A steep embankment with a drop of 50 m (150 ft) runs through the middle of the garden. Villa San Remigio is the neighbour on one side, and its owner the Marchesa Sophie della Valle

di Casanova was a good friend of McEacharn: in the wall between their two gardens they made a gate to which each had a key. It may have been from her that McEacharn got the idea of using local granite from the quarry at Fondo Toce, whether as rough-faced ashlar blocks or as flat flakes of ragstone for all the pillars, retaining walls and stonework in his garden. It was essential to embank the steep slopes of the hillside, and McEacharn claimed that the garden contained over 8 km (5 miles) of dry stone walls which ranged from low borders 50 cm (20 in) high to lofty retaining walls of 6 m (20 ft). He believed that the newly cut stone weathered within a year, looking as if it had always been there, but not every visitor to Villa Táranto today would agree: there is a hardness and twinkling freshness to granite that needs many years to weather. Some of the walls of Villa Táranto have never acquired the covering of lichens, mosses, ferns and wild plants which impart the patina of respectable old age to the rocks of a limestone garden: the great curving pergola draped with wisterias looks as new now as it did when built in 1930. In other parts of the garden, however, rhododendrons have seeded themselves between the stones of the walling. The region of Lake Maggiore has a very heavy rainfall, which means that an adequate drainage system was essential. So was the addition of capacious reservoirs and the distribution of underground pipes to irrigate the garden during summer droughts. Water is pumped up directly from the lake to match demand.

So great was McEacharn's energy and so comprehensive his undertaking that the garden of Villa Táranto was considered good enough to be accepted by the Italian state as a public monument when it was offered to them in 1951. This was achieved only twenty years after the first plants began to arrive, and despite McEacharn's absence from Italy for six years because of the Second World War. Such is the measure not only of the vision and resources of Neil McEacharn but also of his ability to realise his ambitions. It may also have helped that McEacharn's assistant, Antonio Cappelletto, was an old friend of Giulio Andreotti, and that the house and garden had been used for political entertaining. By the time McEacharn died in 1964 Villa Táranto showed every promise of developing into the Italian equivalent of the Royal Botanic Gardens at Kew. That the gardens have failed to fulfil this promise is due to the Italians' administrative and horticultural shortcomings rather than to McEacharn's. His wealth and enthusiasm made possible the garden's distinction. His know-

ledge of trees and shrubs, especially of rhododendrons, was extensive. He was a tireless seeker
after plants in nurseries and seed lists; he also collected plants in the wild on his innumerable trips
around Europe and across the seas. He had already
transformed Galloway House by adding a huge collection of exotics: an article on the gardens there in
The Gardeners' Chronicle by Frank Kingdon Ward
in the year McEacharn bought Villa Táranto makes
clear how passionate was his enthusiasm for rare
plants. Already he was growing such rarities as
Cantua buxifolia, *Rosa gigantea* and *Lonicera
hildebrandiana* in Scotland.

As soon as he knew that La Crocetta was his,
McEacharn began to secure plants from the nurseries, private gardens and botanic collections of Great
Britain and Ireland, from France, Germany and
Switzerland, and from America, Japan, Australia and
South Africa too. After the war, the difficulty of
obtaining import permits for plants meant that many
of the accessions came from seed. In this way, government regulations have considerably restricted the
numbers of new horticultural varieties introduced to
Villa Táranto. Luckily McEacharn was a feverish
propagator: almost his favourite part of the garden
was the nursery at the bottom where he constantly
raised new plants from seed. Every year Villa Táranto
issued an *Index Seminum* of seeds collected in the
garden. Fred Whitsey recalls seeing a dozen distinguished visitors sitting round a table on the
veranda busily scraping seeds out of pods with
crested silver knives and forks. McEacharn knew that
the seed list gave status to the garden, but he was
also genuinely pleased to distribute the good things
that he considered himself fortunate to possess.

The success of McEacharn's work at Villa Táranto
owes much to two others. Antonio Cappelletto was
a young lawyer whom McEacharn befriended. He
became his secretary and administrator, dealing with
all the problems of surviving in Italy. The garden
could not have been made or preserved through the
war years without his assistance, though there was
a price to be paid for it. Henry Cocker was the
director for twenty-six years. He had trained at Kew
and spent a year with Sir Cecil and Lady Hanbury
at La Mortola. After he left Villa Táranto he set up
a garden consultancy and was responsible, among
other commissions, for the partial restoration of the
nineteenth-century landscape garden on Isola Madre.
Cocker recalls that McEacharn told him, 'I want you
to make the best garden in Europe. I want to be
consulted at every stage, but I want you to insist on

*Henry Cocker, a doctor's son from London, whom Neil
McEacharn appointed director of Villa Táranto, and to
whom he entrusted much of the garden's design and detail.*

your views prevailing over mine.' Much of the design
and planting of Villa Táranto was in fact Cocker's,
rather than McEacharn's. He started with a staff
of five or six gardeners, supplemented by builders,
plumbers, stonemasons, carpenters, painters and
other tradesmen. At one time more than eighty men
worked on laying out the garden. Shortly after
acquiring the house, McEacharn bought further
pieces of land adjoining Villa Táranto and expanded
the estate to nearly 40 ha (100 acres). Most of the
additions were small agricultural holdings. Cocker's
men demolished the cottages and barns, removed the
boundary walls, dug out the roads and cut down
over 2,000 robinias.

McEacharn had no strong preconceptions about
garden design, although he preferred the Scottish
tradition of woodland gardening in which he had
been reared and did not admire formality. 'The old
Italian gardens completely lack colour,' he declared;
'flowers are not considered a necessary part of the
scheme and green lawns are almost non-existent.'

Villa Táranto. Building the granite ragstone bridge which McEacharn and Cocker conceived in 1930 to connect the house with the formal gardens. The valley was cleared of scrub and landscaped with groups of Cyathea dealbata, *sunk in huge buried pots for the summer.*

Unlike his neighbours at Villa San Remigio, therefore, McEacharn eschewed an Italian layout for Villa Táranto. There would be formal features, reinterpreted in a modern idiom, but few would be essential elements of the design. The gardens were primarily conceived for the display of plants, above all for the amassing of a collection of trees and shrubs such as he had been unable to form in Wigtown. The cultural needs of the individual plants and lie of the land itself determined the design and layout of the gardens. Little attempt was made to harmonise the plantings into agreeable blends and contrasts of colour or shape. Such as exist are largely accidental: for example, the placing of scarlet-leaved *Fothergilla major* and *F. monticola* in front of orange-yellow *Acer rubrum* for autumn effect. In some English gardens, Westonbirt and Sheffield Park for instance, much more attention has been paid to the potential for such combinations. Cocker was particularly keen on herbaceous plants and bulbs. He vowed that there would be flowers in all the borders throughout the year.

Many of the rhododendrons and azaleas from Galloway House were actually lifted and transported to new quarters on the shady north-facing slopes of Villa Táranto, where for a while they amounted to the biggest collection in Italy. He also moved some of the large camellias already growing at Villa Táranto to new positions within the garden, boxing them up and winching them into place. On one occasion he had to cut the main telephone lines to let the trees pass underneath. McEacharn wrote, 'No one on that connection had any telephones for the day. The telephone authorities were inclined to take a poor view of this, but with typical Italian good nature and tolerance they soon forgave me.' With a clear indication of his own priorities he added, 'I am glad to say we did not lose a single plant.'

McEacharn saw himself as a pioneering horticulturist in an ungrateful and barren land: he was convinced that the experiments he made in his garden would save many years of research and trial elsewhere. Rightly or wrongly, he began to detect a new spirit among Italian owners, eager to change and modernise their gardens, and he considered it fair to claim that his garden at Villa Táranto had much to do with the development of this new spirit. He always intended that the gardens should be open to the public, and they were constructed with the corresponding facilities; flushing lavatories were installed at a time when few Italians had them at home.

Brought up in the spirit of natural gardening that prevails in western Scotland, McEacharn began by planting hundreds of birches and conifers with drifts of camellias, rhododendrons and azaleas underneath. So strongly did he feel the need for natural features that he increased the length of the winding valley known as the Valletta to about 155 m (170 yd). With no bulldozers to help, it was a Herculean undertaking which one hundred men laboured for two years to complete. Looking down now from the single span arch that vaults across the chasm 10 m (30 ft) deep, it is difficult to believe that this magnificent feature is almost entirely artificial. Contrary to Cocker's intentions, however, the bridge has the effect of separating the house from the main part of the garden.

The house is a classic nineteenth-century French-style château which sits above a steep valley over-looking the town of Intra to the north-east. The entrance to the house is on the south-west side, while most of the garden lies to the south-east. The house is seen across a magnificent flat lawn of the finest quality sward surrounding a single simple fountain. Beyond are the Valletta and the main gardens. The bridge is the link that staples the two parts of the garden together, but it makes the formal gardens more distant than they should be, an impression which is reinforced by their not being orientated to the main façade of the house. They arise from a swimming-pool, which has lily ponds on either side and is enclosed by a long curving pergola. Through the middle of the formal gardens runs a channel of water falling over musical chimes as it runs: it leads the eye up to a life-sized bronze fisher boy by Vincenzo Gemito (1852–1929), the Neapolitan sculptor who spent most of his life in asylums. McEacharn greatly admired this piece of nineteenth-century charm, which was first shown in Paris in 1878. The beds on either side are used for seasonal bedding: tulips and pansies in spring, begonias and cannas in summer. To one side of the formal garden a clump of hardy palms *Trachycarpus fortunei* is almost the only element to have survived from the garden that

Villa Táranto. The bridge adds drama to the site; its arch is festooned with Caesalpinia sepiaria.

existed before 1930: it has been incorporated to provide lateral tension to the formal garden. On the opposite side, where the pergola opens out, is a large irregularly shaped tank of *Nelumbo nucifera*, the sacred lotus of India: the spectacle of this in flower quickly brought fame to the garden in both horticultural and botanical circles. Beyond the formal garden lies the arboretum, with a heather garden set among collections of lilac, viburnum, cornus and magnolia. At the head of the valley McEacharn planted a bog garden with a wide variety of aquatic and marsh-loving plants: it is watered by a stream fed from reservoirs underneath the conservatory right at the top of the garden. This part of the garden boasts some especially large trees: *Quercus coccinea*, *Q. palustris*, *Liquidambar styraciflua* and a colossal multi-stemmed specimen of *Acer rubrum*, each of such height (30 m, 100 ft) and girth that it is hard to credit that they have all been planted since 1930. The main path climbs up from the heather garden to a classical four-columned *baldacchino* surrounded by

huge specimens of *Magnolia kobus* var. *borealis*. It used to contain a statue of a satyr ravishing a handsome youth, but that was appropriated by the Fine Arts Ministry and locked away for its own safety. It has been replaced by a well-head of indifferent quality. The driveway now winds down for 1 km ($\frac{1}{2}$ mile), through collections of berberis and cotoneaster, magnolias and forsythias, until it arrives at the public entrance. This part of the garden includes an avenue of tall conifers, a valley of tree ferns, an 'Italian' garden and a sinuous dahlia walk to the tall iron-framed greenhouse where the giant water lily *Victoria amazonica* flowers in summer. From this lily house a broad drive leads back through sun-shot plantings of Japanese maples – one has been named *Acer palmatum* 'Capt. McEacharn' – to the double herbaceous border, with which McEacharn intended to educate Italians in English ways. One end of the border closes with an exquisite white marble fountain which has cherubs at its corners and a complicated pattern of water foaming from a hundred jets; the other leads to the modern chapel which is McEacharn's mausoleum. A steep climb through shady woodland underplanted with rhododendrons and azaleas passes through a magnolia glade, past a particularly large specimen of the handkerchief tree *Davidia involucrata*, and back to the house. This tour, which would take at least a couple of hours, gives only a taste of the plantings. Villa Táranto yields up its secrets slowly: there are some 7 km (4 miles) of paths from which, as the guidebook assures us, 'innumerable unexpected evocative vistas open out'.

The policy of the present administrators is to retain the architecture of the gardens, by which they mean the form and mass provided by the trees. They regard Villa Táranto primarily as a museum, a closed collection of trees and shrubs to which new additions cannot be made without disturbing the spirit of the garden. In a country where so much has unfortunately been lost through ignorance and neglect, they perceive it to be their duty to preserve the garden as it was when handed over to the Italian state. The articles which establish the statutes of the Ente Giardini Botanici Villa Táranto 'Cap. Neil McEacharn' specifically set out an obligation to improve

---

This baldacchino appears towards the top of the drive at Villa Táranto. Neil McEacharn used such features, none of intrinsic merit, to relieve the monotony of systematic botanical planting.

as well as maintain the garden. But this does not appear to cover the development or modernisation of its design and collections. McEacharn himself believed that the garden should continue to improve and he itemised some of the details in *A Scotsman's Garden in Italy*, the book he wrote for Country Life in 1954, which is still compulsory reading for any plantsman making a garden in northern Italy. At one point, for example, he explains how he hoped to propagate and plant an avenue of *Prunus campanulata*. The present administrator of the garden seems not to be familiar with the plans of 'Il Capitano' and denies that it was ever intended to plant more than two specimens of this rich red cherry, 'one on the left, and one on the right', despite McEacharn's own account of how he had received eight plants from Kew in 1936 and managed to increase their number to fourteen.

Garden conservation and restoration are concepts that Italians understand: organic change and adaptation are beyond their comprehension. When one explains that the great English gardens, Hidcote and Sissinghurst for example, have continued to expand and develop since the death of their begetters, so that they are constantly updated in accordance with their original spirit and principles, one is met with bewilderment. The present administrator of Villa Táranto considers that such change is an impossibility, or at least undesirable. Yet the Italians have themselves introduced new ideas to Villa Táranto, many of them alien to McEacharn's intentions. The famous glade of dicksonia ferns, that sits so naturally at the bottom of a dark dell, is now interplanted with cordylines and doryanthes. The conservatory hosts a collection of succulent plants that would be better planted out in a suitable garden on the coast. Nevertheless, some of the features that one might suppose to be modern additions for the benefit of unsophisticated visitors date from McEacharn's days. The annual planting of over 80,000 tulips in cheerful bedding schemes was begun by Henry Cocker to fulfil his promise to provide colour all through the year. Sometimes McEacharn apologised to visitors for it. To English eyes, much of the garden now appears dated. The plants themselves look old, and they tend to be old-fashioned varieties or cultivars. Some of the trees and shrubs have been replaced, but the herbaceous underplantings have been neglected and there are few additions to the catalogue of plants. There is simply no tradition of plantsmanship in Italy to sustain the continued growth of the garden and keep it abreast of international developments, so Villa Táranto

The chapel at Villa Táranto. McEacharn saw himself as an apostle of English gardening in Italy. This double herbaceous border and the lawnmower stripes on the mown grass are much admired by Italian visitors.

remains a closed collection, a museum of the mid-twentieth-century style.

But what a collection it is! Few will ever forget the billowing clouds of *Magnolia kobus* var. *borealis* when it is covered in white flowers at the beginning of April, or the numerous paulownias and davidias that dominate the garden in May. Many have travelled to Villa Táranto in June in the hope of seeing the rare *Emmenopterys henryi* in flower as nowhere else in Europe. The collection is outstanding by any standards, and stretches to over 20,000 taxa: McEacharn reckoned that at least 90 per cent of these plants had never been grown in Italy before. The standard of general maintenance is very high, quite on a par with the best of English gardens. Bedding out is conducted in the grand manner, and the display beds are well prepared and kept free of weeds. Grass is mown short, even where it grows thinly in woodland areas. The concept of woodland gardening is unfamiliar to the Italians: trees tend to be grown in clear circles of bare earth cut from the turf. Shrubs that grow too tall are hacked back enthusiastically, apparently without

understanding how proper pruning could improve their structure and performance. In some parts the trees have grown so much that the views and groupings which the garden enjoyed twenty years ago are lost. The clumps of pink and white *Cornus florida* seen against the snow-capped peaks of the Pennine Alps are now obscured by the mass of other plantings: but perhaps McEacharn the unreconstructed plantsman would have accepted the change.

It is a sad fact that Italy lacks the skilled traditions of English horticulture. There are no schools to train young people for a gardening career in private service, and no national network of colleges where the sciences of garden maintenance, plant cultivation and amenity planting may be learnt. Above all, there is not the understanding of the importance of gardens that pervades English society, the common acceptance of gardening as a worthwhile endeavour. Even the Italian perception of the garden is alien to the English way of thinking. The English version of the official guidebook ends with this extravagant self-praise:

In Villa Táranto the visitor will find dreamt landscapes and imagined scenarios glimmering in transparencies of water or hidden in expanses of mysterious blooms, sacred to Egyptian mythology. From the romantic Valletta to the carpet of Erikas, from the hot-houses to the Azalea, Rhododendron and Camellia avenues, from the rare lilies to the myriad hues of spring blooms, against the background of the Italian garden or in the mellow glow of autumn, Villa Táranto rewards the visitor with endless scenes of changing beauty and deep inner poetry.

Nevertheless, the Italians have found Villa Táranto very useful as a teaching facility: hordes of schoolchildren visit it. As a tourist attraction it is the biggest jewel in the crown of the Italian Lakeland, one of the two gardens (the other is La Mortola) of which almost every Italian has heard. Neil McEacharn is honoured by the Italian government as a symbol of Anglo-Italian friendship and they have recently placed a bust of him in the heather garden, a position chosen to honour his Scottish origins. Naturally, his memory is revered too by all associated with the administration of the gardens. He gave them something that was quite new to Italy, a garden that the Italians never fully understood, still do not understand and perhaps can never understand.

In making his garden, McEacharn combined the urge to collect with the desire to cut a figure, and an obsessive need to astound and to achieve. It enabled him to secure the social position put at risk by his modest origins and his unconventional behaviour. Yet he carried his delusions not only to the grave, but beyond. In March 1964, Neil Boyd Watson McEacharn made his last will and testament according to English law. He declared that he made no provision for his surviving sister or his nephews and nieces as they were already well provided for. Instead, he left extensive personal bequests of cash to his Italian friends, including £4,000 to Giulio Andreotti, £1,000 to each of his children and no less than £40,000 to his wife Livia Andreotti. Their mutual friend Antonio Cappelletto was to have a life interest in the residue. The total in legacies alone came to £120,000, a considerable fortune, but when McEacharn died six weeks later, the net value of his estate was only £5,650. There is no accounting for the disparity between his presumed and actual wealth. Such was the man who made Villa Táranto.

References and Further Reading

Villa Táranto is poorly documented. McEacharn's own book *The Villa Táranto, A Scotsman's Garden in Italy* (London, 1954) remains the prime written source for information about the garden, but it contains many inaccuracies and slights of emphasis that I have tried to correct. McEacharn also published a *Catalogue of the Plants in the Garden of the Villa Táranto* (1963). Although often described in magazines and newspapers (e.g. by Fred Whitsey in *Country Life* on 24 April 1975), no subsequent account of the garden has added greatly to our understanding of the man and his work. I have consulted a large number of people who knew McEacharn, some of whom are acknowledged in the Preface. Nancy-Mary Goodall wrote of Henry Cocker in *The Garden* in August 1990. He is writing his autobiography and this will be published in Italy soon. The article on Galloway House appears in *The Gardener's Chronicle*, 5 July 1930.

Chapter Ten

PORTUGAL

Beckford and Byron, Madeira and Port

THE GREAT GARDENS of Portugal are quite distinct. With their tanks of still water, luxuriantly grown trees and – above all – their blue and white tiles known as *azulejos*, there is nothing like them anywhere else in the world. Yet the Portuguese style has never been taken up and exported: it plays no part in garden history, but remains an isolated development which has led to nothing else. There are no Portuguese gardens in Italy, Spain or France. The converse is not true, for there are many Italian, Spanish and French gardens in Portugal: and there are German, English and American gardens too.

Portugal is best considered as an island. Surrounded by the sea on two sides, and cut off from the Spanish mainland by historic divisions, its culture, its influence and its wealth have all tended to come from overseas. The English connection with Portugal is a long one. Portugal is England's oldest ally, and that alliance dates from the marriage in 1387 of Philippa of Lancaster, the daughter of John of Gaunt, to João I, the founder of the Braganza dynasty of Portuguese kings. The union between the two crowns was reinforced by the marriage of Charles II of England to Catherine of Braganza in 1663, not long after the re-emergence of an independent monarchy from the years when Portugal was absorbed into the Spanish dominions. It led to the opening up of Portuguese markets to English traders and manufacturers: gradually English colonies grew up around their 'fac-

tories' or trading stations. The men who prospered were manufacturers, negotiators, importers and exporters: practical businessman, not spendthrift aristocrats, for Portugal has never been a fashionable playground for the international glitterati. The type of Englishman who went to Portugal may be gauged by such expressions as *hora inglesa* meaning the exact time of day, and *semana inglesa* for a five-day week. Wine, cotton, cork: these three staples in the course of the eighteenth and nineteenth centuries became the preserves of English merchants who grew rich on the proceeds. When Sir William Dalrymple was in Oporto as a young man he 'feasted most voluptuously with the Consul and the Factory'. He added that 'the only thing that I disliked amongst them was their supercilious treatment of the Portuguese, from whom they derived their wealth and opulence'. The rich foreign merchants protected by the Marquês de Pombal were very much more international in their tastes than the old Portuguese aristocracy. By the end of the eighteenth century the port-wine merchants were so graced with wealth and taste that a member of the Harris family commissioned Humphry Repton himself to design a garden on his estate at Gondomar. Nothing remains of it except the irrigation system.

One of the richest British merchants in Portugal was Gerard de Vîsme, whose name was of Huguenot origin: his fortune was founded on a monopoly of the brazilwood trade granted by Pombal. When William Hickey stayed with him at Bemfica in 1782, he noted that 'the establishment was in every respect princely ... the grounds laid out with particular taste, having in them all the rarest plants of the European world and some even from Asia and America'. In fact the garden was laid out in the landscape style with temples, obelisks, and statues: it was built at a time when Portuguese designers were still preoccupied with baroque forms. William Beckford wrote that de Vîsme's garden at Bemfica eclipsed all others. There were magnolias, geraniums, date palms and bananas, all covered in flowers and fruit, and large collections of *cereus* and *mesembryanthemum*. Mme Junot, the wife of Napoleon I's General and at that time Duchesse d'Abrantès, remembered how

on entering the *quinta* I was struck by the sweetness of the perfumes that surrounded me. It was magic! I stopped and raised my head. I was in a long alley planted with magnolias whose white flowers caressed my hair! Between the magnolias were planted daturas, brooms, daphnes ... a profusion of perfumes to give heavenly joy to anyone who loved flowers as I did.

Portuguese gardens are distinguished by their *azulejos*, part of the tradition of tiling that came out of the Renaissance to provide decoration for churches, houses, gardens and public buildings, and established a uniquely Portuguese style that still flourishes today. *Azulejos* are an essential part of Portuguese gardens, and their use reached its high point in the middle of the eighteenth century at the Palácio de Fronteira in Lisbon. Its walls and staircases are entirely lined with huge blue and white tiled tableaux, including twelve life-sized portraits of the Heroes of the Lusiads, renowned for avenging a party of Portuguese noblewomen who had been insulted and dishonoured by some Englishmen. The Portuguese kings championed the use of *azulejos*: tiles are an important feature of the gardens of the palace at Queluz in the hills above Lisbon, where a stream runs through a long tiled tank in which the Portuguese royal family used to bathe in summer, and at the royal palaces of Pena at Sintra and Bussaco near Coimbra. Modern Portuguese gardens still make extensive use of both traditional and contemporary *azulejo* designs, with scenes from Portuguese history and folklore as popular as ever.

Almost as characteristic as *azulejos* in Portuguese gardens is the richness of their vegetation. Portugal has a super-temperate climate with some rain in most parts of the country throughout the year. The average annual rainfall in Oporto exceeds 1,150 mm (45 in) while Coimbra receives 940 mm (37 in) a year. Even Evora, the windy capital of the Alentejo province, enjoys an annual rainfall of nearly 635 mm (25 in), which is more than Greenwich with 585 mm (23 in) and Cambridge with 545 mm (21½ in). The result of

this humidity – at least in the northern and coastal parts of the country – is a remarkable luxuriance common to the natural vegetation of the countryside and the exotic plants grown in gardens.

Cork oaks *Quercus suber* dominate the Lusitanian woodland, their hoary lichen-draped upper limbs contrasting with their trunks stripped smooth of bark. Among exotic introductions, nowhere in Europe is so suitable for Australian plants, and mimosas fill the hedges and hillsides, to the extent that they have become a danger to the natural flora, while eucalyptus forests are the most intensely planted and managed in the world. Such is the combination of climate and soil that an annual growth of 3 m (10 ft) can be expected for some gum species. Gardens, particularly woodland gardens, are full of exotic evergreen members of the laurel family, several brought back from the subtropical colonies of Portugal. There are also areas where the Mexican orange blossom bush *Choisya ternata* and the Australian *Pittosporum tobira* have naturalised and become an integral part of the undergrowth. Tulip trees and magnolias grow luxuriantly, and there are avenues of bamboos 20 m (65 ft) high, varieties that would only grow to a quarter of that height in the cool climates of England and New England. Portugal has fine conifers, too. The cypresses in the forest at Bussaco, elderly specimens of a form of *Cupressus lusitanica*, are thought to have been planted in the sixteenth century from the original introduction of seed to Europe from America: handsome and venerable now, they are still in a vigorous condition. Above all, Portugal is the land of the camellia. Camellias have been grown in Portuguese gardens for over three hundred years, and there are vast tree-like specimens in the gardens of Oporto and the Minho. From the *sasanquas* in September to the *japonicas* in April, the winter gardens of Portugal are governed by camellias. Sometimes the plants are clipped into neat hedges, within which the flowers seem to glow, but usually they are found as tall trunky shrubs stretching up to 5 m (16 ft), 7 m or even 10 m in height. Camellias set seed in great quantity, and good varieties have been bred and selected by Portuguese gardeners over several centuries, largely in isolation from the camellia-breeding activities of other countries, notably the traditions of Japan, Belgium and Italy. As a result, Portuguese camellias remain a separate and distinctive tribe within the whole range of camellia forms and varieties: 'Dr Baltasar de Melo', 'Saudade de Martins Branco' and 'Don Carlos Fernando' are three of the best known.

The cultivation of camellias became a sophisticated hobby among rich Portuguese during the course of the nineteenth century, just as rhododendrons were to be in the British Isles a little later: camellias were bred, grown, exhibited, discussed and judged with all the enthusiasm of Victorian England for roses.

Monserrate is high in the granite mountains of Sintra, a spiky massif of densely forested gloom. The Serra de Sintra rises steeply from the edge of the Atlantic Ocean and draws down thick mists and heavy rain.

As long ago as 1760, when Dr Johnson's friend, the Italian Giuseppe Baretti, visited Sintra, he noted that 'many English have pretty country houses there'. It is an intensely romantic landscape, whose dark woods and huge boulders impressed English visitors as a manifestation of the Sublime and found their way into poetic imagery. The preoccupation with awesome Nature, that alternative aesthetic which was firmly established as an acceptable minority taste

by the end of the eighteenth century, found its wildest expression at Sintra. The village was 'too good for the Portuguese' according to Robert Southey in 1796. Byron declared that it was the most delightful in Europe: it contained 'beauties of every description, natural and artificial. Palaces and gardens rising in the midst of rocks, cataracts, and precipices.' No doubt he had Monserrate in mind. Byron's description of the landscape in *Childe Harold* is better than any guidebook's:

> The horrid crags, by toppling convent crown'd
> The cork-trees hoar that clothe the shaggy steep,
> The mountain-moss by scorching skies imbrown'd,
> The sunken glen, whose sunless shrubs must weep,
> The tender azure of the unruffled deep,
> The orange tints that gild the greenest bough,
> The torrents that from cliff to valley leap,
> The vine on high, the willow branch below,
> Mix'd in one mighty scene, with varied beauty glow.

Gerard de Visme's empty Gothic castle at Monserrate, derelict in the years before Francis Cook bought it in 1856, with few visible traces of William Beckford's garden.

Monserrate, in the Sintra hills, in 1929. Part of a woodland valley lushly planted by Sir Francis Cook with many different palms in the latter half of the previous century.

The gardens at Monserrate are among the greatest in Portugal, and perhaps second only to La Mortola as an example of an English garden abroad. The house was built in 1789 by Gerard de Vîsme of Bemfica, who immediately reconstructed it in substantially the shape that we see it today, but in the Gothic style: Monserrate was in fact the earliest example of Gothic revival architecture in Portugal. De Vîsme was described by a Portuguese contemporary as 'one of the most solid merchants ... characterised by his known probity and by a particular genius for agriculture'. No doubt he was responsible for the intricate Moorish system of irrigation that connects the park to springs higher up the hillside and enables water to be channelled to all parts of the garden: the rich green lawn in front of the house would not be possible without it. Ill health obliged him to retire to England shortly after he acquired Monserrate. Portuguese law at that time restricted the owner's right of alienation, so Gerard de Vîsme's tenure on Monserrate was only leasehold, and in 1794 he sublet it to William Beckford of

Fonthill, 'England's wealthiest son' and the author of *Vathek*, on whose creative imagination it made a great impression. Beckford wrote of Sintra:

the mossy fragments of rock, grotesque pollards, and rustic bridges you meet with at every step, recall Savoy and Switzerland to the imagination; but the exotic cast of the vegetation, the vivid green of the citron, the golden fruitage of the orange, the blossoming myrtle, and the rich fragrance of a turf, embroidered with the brightest-coloured and most aromatic flowers, allow me, without a violent stretch of fancy to believe myself in the garden of the Hesperides.

The Gothic revival in England owes much to Monserrate. Beckford remained a sub-tenant for nearly fifteen years, and visited Portugal several times during that period, spending the whole of 1794 at Monserrate when the Prince Regent of Portugal held court at Sintra.

Monserrate is important in the history of English gardens because Beckford experimented there with some of the ideas he was later to incorporate into his fantasy at Fonthill Abbey in Wiltshire. He built a ruined chapel, Gothic and castellated, on a ledge across the valley. Actually, it was rebuilt from the ruins of a real chapel destroyed in the earthquake of 1755 and moved to its present position for greater effect: it dominates the view of the forest from the house. Montserrate also has a cromlech, not unlike the stone folly Beckford built at Fonthill. Most important of his improvements, however, was the rocky cascade where a stream bursts out over a great cataract and then races down a dark ravine, breaking and turning over boulders in a succession of different movements. This cool and shady glen is now known as *o Vale dos Feitos*, thanks to the great number and variety of ferns that have been planted on either side. It has no parallel at Fonthill.

The estate was acquired by Francis Cook in 1856, and he remodelled the château with the assistance of the English architect James Knowles. Those alterations produced the building that we see today, with three Renaissance turrets in place of the Gothic pinnacles. The external appearance was magically transformed from a neo-Gothic extravaganza into a neo-Moorish fantasy, with Romanesque capitals and Ruskinesque spandrels to give variety to the detail, while the central dome was based on Brunelleschi's design for the cathedral in Florence. The inner structure of the building remained unaltered, and indeed the main lines of the site are still those that Beckford

Sir Francis Cook, and his formidable American second wife, by the oriental gateway at Monserrate in the 1890s.

and Byron so admired. Francis Cook was a textile merchant, sent by his father in 1841 to establish their business in Lisbon. There he met and promptly married Emily Lucas, the daughter of an English manufacturer long established at Lisbon. The firm prospered, and Cook accumulated great wealth: when he died in 1901, his personal estate alone was valued at £1,500,000.

Francis Cook was a man of great energy and enthusiasm. After acquiring Monserrate, he bought several neighbouring properties, quickly expanding his landholding until a large part of the Serra was effectively an English fiefdom. In the manner of rich Victorian merchants and manufacturers, he employed scores of workers to restore the house and create and maintain the garden, while his estate was managed in accordance with enlightened benefaction. Workers and their families were provided with medical care, and in 1874 he opened primary schools at the neighbouring village of Galamares and Colares for the children of his workers, then numbering about three hundred. So impressive was his wealth, and the use to which he put it, that the King invested him with the title of Viscount Monserrate (Visconde de Monserrate) to last, according to Portuguese tradition, for the duration of two lives. Thus Francis Cook, who was also given an English baronetcy in 1886, was succeeded by his son Sir Frederick Cook as the second Visconde de Monserrate on his death in 1901, but there the double-life peerage ended and the 3rd Baronet Sir Herbert Cook did not inherit the title on his father's death in 1920.

Francis Cook set about ornamenting the woods and parkland round his house with a collection of exotic trees and shrubs culled from all corners of the temperate world. In his taste for opulence, his desire to make a collection and his enthusiasm for botanic display, Francis Cook was the quintessential

Monserrate's Gothic marble staircase descends from the drive to the Great Tank. It was designed by Sir Herbert Cook and constructed by the estate workmen.

wardia radicans hang over the rocky edge and quiver in the spray that spits from the torrent beneath. Overhead are tree ferns – species of cyathea and dicksonia. Large groups of pteris, davallia, asplenium, blechnum and other ferns fill the spaces underneath the towering trunks, sheltered by vast cork oaks and beautiful specimens of the strawberry tree *Arbutus unedo*.

Many of the ferns at Monserrate have naturalised themselves and grow epiphytically on the trunks of trees: *Davallia canariensis* is one. Here the cork oaks are not stripped for their bark, but allowed to grow rugged, fissured and thick with moss and lichens. The dense, damp jungle calls to mind the great woodland gardens of Cornwall: cool, shady and sheltered. The similarity is not merely the product of a similar soil and climate: many of the great Cornish gardens were also laid out in the middle of the nineteenth century by rich merchants turned landowners who chose to make botanic collections. The garden at Monserrate would not look out of place in one of the steep rocky valleys that run down to the Falmouth estuary.

The pride of Monserrate is its collection of conifers. The finest specimens, planted by Francis Cook, include the Norfolk Island pine *Araucaria excelsa*, said to measure 50 m (160 ft) and be the tallest in Europe; it is furnished with lower branches down almost to ground level. The garden also boasts *A. bidwillii*, *A. cunninghamii* and *A. cookii*. On the lawn beneath the house are fine specimens of *Cryptomeria japonica* 'Lobbii', and such firs as *Abies nordmanniana* and *A. webbiana*. Cedars, pines, spruces, cypresses, Kauri pines, swamp cypresses and all manner of conifers grow in great abundance throughout the garden. Iron-clad species that flourish in Britain, *Thuja plicata*, for example, rub shoulders with such subtropical exotica as the Canary Island pine *Pinus canariensis*, hopelessly tender in England.

The Lusitanian climate is particularly suited to the growth of Australasian plants, and indeed eucalyptus plantations have quite transformed the natural landscape of Portugal. *Eucalyptus globulus* has grown to 50 m at Monserrate: its huge trunks, grey and smooth, are most impressive. Self-sown seedlings of eucalyptus, acacias and pittosporums are an ecological nuisance and have entirely changed the character of the undergrowth during the recent years of neglect. Banksias, grevilleas, eugenias and calliandras are among southern hemisphere genera that thrive at Monserrate, as do such unusual plants as *Theophrasta imperialis* and *Stenocarpus cunninghamii*, whose curious proteaceous red and

nineteenth-century English capitalist. His ambitions were put into effect by an able head gardener, Francis Burt, to whom should be given, as indeed it was at the time, the credit for acquiring all the rare trees and shrubs that make Monserrate important and for arranging them with some degree of artistic skill. Throughout the century, botanists and collectors were employed by the great scientific institutes and seed houses of England and Scotland to collect new plants that might be grown, admired and studied at home. The forms of exotic conifers, evergreen trees and shrubs and ferns appealed especially strongly to the Victorians' decorative sense: even today, these are the principal elements of design at Monserrate.

Francis Cook was above all a collector. His house in England was furnished with everything from intricately carved teak tables to the throne of the Doge of Venice, and his personal collection of paintings was one of the best ever amassed by an Englishman. His garden at Monserrate became an international repository for plants received from such botanic gardens as Lisbon, Rio de Janeiro and Kew. It was he who planted the ferns on either side of Beckford's cascade where the great glossy fronds of *Wood-*

yellow flowers open in midwinter. Any account of Monserrate runs the risk of degenerating into a list of rare trees and shrubs. Yuccas, agaves, furcraeas, cycads and palms are all represented by scores of species and varieties: so are rhododendrons, camellias and hydrangeas. Some herbaceous under-plantings have naturalised too: there are great drifts of the ginger lily *Hedychium gardnerianum*, arum lilies and Japanese anemones.

The stately park at Monserrate is surrounded by woodland, but opens out below the house, which is set at the top of a steep spur and balustraded around with Gothic stonework. One side looks across to the Sintra hills and the other over the plains to distant Mafra. The lawns in the park cover about 8 ha (20 acres) and make an elegant setting for some of the trees already noted, as well as the giant specimen of metrosideros at the edge of the house, which covers itself in scarlet flowers in summer; its aerial roots and the dense shade underneath give it the appearance of covering a very great area. The lawns run down to a lake at the bottom where black swans nest, but among the architectural features around the house itself are a stone pergola, the 'Roman causeway' (actually rather Gothic in design), a Moghul gateway looted from Delhi after the Indian Mutiny and a terrace where a rectangular Great Tank and Gothic staircase were later worked into the hillside to achieve a more formal effect.

The garden was substantially replanted in the early 1920s when Sir Herbert Cook inherited the estate. Not only was it brought up to date with new trees and shrubs such as hybrid rhododendrons unknown in his grandfather's day, but Sir Herbert Cook also changed the garden's emphasis by planting for hor-ticultural effect rather than botanic purpose. In this respect, Monserrate resembles the great garden at La Mortola, where in the 1920s a younger generation of owners remodelled and updated a botanic collection by giving it a horticultural overlay. Indeed, Sir Herbert Cook went so far as to head-hunt the Han-bury's head gardener Walter Oates and bring him to Monserrate to oversee the changes. Oates was a great plantsman, and from 1921 to 1929, when Sir Herbert decided to put the estate up for sale, the garden at Monserrate basked in a renaissance of horticultural activity. There is still a 1920s rose garden below the house planted with English varieties that were popular at the time. Sir Herbert Cook married a wife with good horticultural connections. Mary was the daughter of the 2nd Viscount Bridport, and therefore the niece of The Hon. Alec Hood of Maniace, while

Monserrate (c. 1905). The great cascade built by William Beckford in the 1790s, which was later planted up as the Valley of Ferns.

her maternal uncle the Earl of Ilchester planted the subtropical gardens at Abbotsbury.

The family's fortunes declined: no doubt Sir Herbert felt the strain of employing seventy-two gar-deners at Monserrate, which he and his family visited for only two months of the year. In 1947 Sir Francis, the fourth baronet, eventually succeeded in selling the whole estate – farms, gardens, houses and fur-niture. The purchaser was a speculator, who dis-posed of the contents at a profit and then resold the rest to the Portuguese state in 1949. The palace was left empty and desolate, and so it remains forty years on.

The garden at Monserrate was to some extent influenced by the great park at Pena Palace, some 200 ha (500 acres) of dense ornamental parkland beneath the old convent at the top of the Sintra hills. It was laid out in the 1840s around the summer residence of the King Consort Ferdinand of Coburg, under the direction of Graf von Eschwege. Between the clusters of rocks, pools and artificial streams were planted camellias, rhododendrons, azaleas, native cork oaks and Lusitanian laurels, and such exotic conifers as thujas, cryptomerias and cypresses from

Bussaco. 'This park is the most wonderful thing I have seen in the world,' wrote Richard Strauss, 'this is the veritable Garden of Klingsor and, above it, is the castle of the Holy Grail.' Pena Park belongs more closely to the German romantic tradition and, although Monserrate is often likened to it, for example in the two collections of tree ferns, most of the inspiration for the gardens at Monserrate came from English precedents. Its expanse of lawn and park around the house is unmistakably English. The use of garden ornaments to link the house to the wilder landscape comes directly from the nineteenth-century return to formality in English garden design. Above all, the passion for collecting trees and shrubs and all the horticultural goodies that were becoming available as the world opened up its booty to botanists and plant collectors was typical of the tastes and fashions of mid-nineteenth-century England. Nevertheless, Portuguese historians are fond of pointing out the similarities between Pena and Monserrate, and playing up the rivalries between them. It was said, for example, that a visitor had sought permission to visit both gardens, and been granted admission to Pena Palace by the King, but refused entrance to Monserrate by Sir Francis Cook. By the time of Sir Frederick's tenure the two gardens were equal in renown, and when Edward VII stayed at Pena with Carlos I the two kings came down to Monserrate and each planted a specimen of the silver tree *Leucadendron argenteum* to commemorate their visit. Being a short-lived species, those trees have now gone, but many of the exotic specimens planted by the Cooks are just coming into their prime and, despite the neglect of Monserrate since the Portuguese forestry commission took over in 1949, the structure and all the elements of design are as strong and vigorous as ever. Fortunately the garden is being restored with assistance from the Royal Botanic Gardens at London in Ontario, under the guidance of their English director and an English landscape architect. So it still enjoys the essential quality of English horticultural skills working with exotic materials in a Portuguese context. When Walter Oates wrote of Monserrate in *The Gardener's Chronicle* in 1929, he described at great length the richness and variety of its plants and concluded 'it is a great achievement and vies with only one other garden of the same kind that I know – La

Madeira. An inland valley showing the typical steep terracing, with peaks covered in tropical laurel forest.

Mortola'. That remains as true now as it was then.

AS A STATION for victualling, and later for coaling the British merchantmen on their way to South Africa and the Far East, the island of Madeira has a long connection with England. In 1809, the British consul was Henry Veitch, a member of the Devon family which established the most important nineteenth-century nursery in Britain. His house on the edge of the Curral, an extinct volcano about 16 km (10 miles) out of Funchal, has a garden whose vast camellia trees were planted by Veitch nearly two hundred years ago. The great gardens of Madeira are concentrated around Funchal and, because of the strong trading ties with England, many have an English connection. Towards the end of the nineteenth century, Madeira became a fashionable winter resort, and English residents planted English gardens complete with croquet lawns and tennis-courts. One of the fascinations of the island for visitors, then as now, was the range of exotic plants that can be grown. Victorian guidebooks often mention the camphor tree, *Ficus elastica*, jacarandas, pawpaws and the screw pine *Pandanus veitchii*. Famous specimens of the dragon tree *Dracaena drago* grew at Quinta do Til near Funchal and The Mount, 550 m (1,800 ft) above the town. Quinta do Til was laid out by a British wine merchant at the beginning of the nineteenth century and planted on a large scale. He intended to build a palatial residence to match the garden, but bad times put an end to his plans. A tank in the grounds had a morbid attraction for Victorian visitors: the only son of George Canning, the prime minister, a naval captain, was drowned while bathing in it.

'The island of Madeira,' declared William Robinson in his rascally, prejudiced but important book *The English Flower Garden*, 'is very instructive in the variety of its gardens; every one I remember was distinct, and this was owing to the owners being free to do as the ground invited them, instead of following any fixed idea as to style, or leaving it to men who are ready with similar plans for all sorts of positions. In France, England, or Germany, this could never happen.' Sir Charles Thomas-Stanford, writing in *Leaves from a Madeira Garden* in 1909, agreed with Robinson that 'of the best and most characteristic of Madeira gardens it may be said that they have grown rather than been made. Those which have been consciously created are perhaps the least successful.' He then explained how the *quintas* around the town

were originally farms or modest country houses surrounded by farmland. The garden would consist of
a small plot in front of the house, often secured by
retaining walls. Between it and the agricultural land
was a kitchen garden, and the first extension of the
garden proper annexed a piece of the kitchen garden
for the cultivation of flowers. This involved building
steps and laying out paths, so that a new feature was
created in the garden. There were generally fresh
fields waiting to be conquered, and so the process
went on 'as the ground invites us' until a considerable
garden was created. Such gardens, of which there are
many, were for the most part made by Englishmen,
and there is no doubt that the biggest and best was
the one which belongs to the Blandy family, Quinta
do Palheiro.

The Blandys had, and still have, extensive interests
in the wines and hotels of Madeira. Their house at
Quinta do Palheiro was built in 1891 by George
Summers Clark, the architect of Reid's hotel in
Funchal, after John Blandy bought the estate in 1885.
It had belonged since the beginning of the nineteenth
century to the Condes de Carvalhal, who were

Quinta do Palheiro, Madeira. The Blandys' house in 1962,
with the formal sunken garden in the foreground.

responsible for some fine formal features including
two huge avenues of oriental plane trees; but the
main elements of the present garden are entirely the
creation of the Blandy family. Quinta do Palheiro is
about 550 m (1,800 ft) up to the east of Funchal and,
at 320 ha (800 acres), the estate is the largest on the
island: its 12 ha (30 acres) of gardens are also the
most extensive. Much of the precipitation on
Madeira occurs in winter and, because the whole
island is volcanic in origin, it is important to conserve
water during the rainy season: this is then released
through a system of canals known as *levadas* during
the drier summer months. Established plants do not
have to be watered, but lawns, borders and anything
newly planted must be irrigated constantly. This
involves considerable time and effort. 'Fortunately,'
declared Mildred Blandy in 1955, 'labour is cheap
and plentiful.'

The garden is surrounded by thick woodland
which is mainly of such pines as *Pinus pinaster* and *P.
canariensis*, but interplanted with more ornamental
conifers including *Cryptomeria japonica* 'Elegans'
and *Cedrus atlantica* 'Glauca'. Camellias seed themselves abundantly, so that the original *japonica* cultivars introduced from Belgium and mainland
Portugal at the end of the nineteenth century are now
greatly outnumbered by their seedling offspring.
It has been estimated that there are over 10,000
camellias at Quinta do Palheiro, including a long
line, which is in effect an overgrown hedge up to
10 m (30 ft) high and nearly a kilometre ($\frac{1}{2}$ mile) long,
in every colour, shape and variation imaginable,
along one side of the driveway leading down to the
house. Good varieties are grafted on seedlings of
Camellia sasanqua, which is the most prolific of
seeders.

Climatically, Madeira lies on the margin between
the temperate and the subtropical, and the possibilities this suggests are reflected in the garden at
Quinta do Palheiro. Plants come from all over the
world: there are notable specimens of *Leucadendron
argenteum* from South Africa, and many proteas,
including *cynaroides*, whose common name is the
King Protea but whose Latin tag indicates a resemblance to artichokes; there are large numbers of
magnolias, often forming tall trees, and of their
relations the michelias, although as often as not the
underplantings are of more tropical origin, such
as gardenias or bauhinias. The garden can also
boast a splendid collection of South African bulbs:
agapanthus set as clumps in grass in the gardenesque style, nerines and amaryllis, and large areas

Quinta do Palheiro, Madeira. The sunken garden, a mass of South African bulbs in winter, with topiary skittles of muehlenbeckia.

where freesias, sparaxis, ixias, lachenalias and cyrtanthus have naturalised.

Madeira is often referred to as the gardener's paradise, but a number of plants that we grow in northern latitudes do not gain admission to this particular abode of the blessed because they are unable to adjust to the climate: these include gentians, lily of the valley, paeonies and lupins. There are compensations, however. At Quinta do Palheiro, many orchids are grown outside, mainly terrestial varieties such as the endemic *Dactylorhiza foliosa* and drifts of bletias, although cymbidiums too are plunged in the soil as an underplanting for shrub borders. The garden has a good representation of native plants, including *Aeonium arboreum* and other species and forms of the giant houseleeks, and the incomparable shrubby foxglove *Isoplexis sceptrum*. Rare plants from other north Atlantic islands include the pink or white *Campanula vidalii* from the Azores and the endangered *Lotus berthelotii* from Tenerife.

The design of Quinta do Palheiro is a late Victorian period piece. Beneath the house is a rectangular formal garden, with Italian cypresses at its corners and small octagonal pools in the centre. Above it are two symmetrically placed palms, and skittle-shaped pairs of clipped muehlenbeckia march up towards them. The surrounding banks are planted with variegated yuccas and other succulents, each in a circle of earth cut out of the grass. It is like an old photograph of a turn-of-the-century Edwardian garden: nothing has changed for a hundred years. The same is true of the rest of the garden. The trees planted around the house in the 1890s are the standard no-fuss mixed half dozen late Victorian standbys – redwood, cedar, evergreen magnolia, ginkgo, monkey puzzle and tulip tree. The lawns are intersected by herbaceous borders, and pergolas trained with roses and clematis. In front of the house is a sunken garden, originally laid out formally and planted with short growing conifers: now they are healthy specimens as much as 6 m (20 ft) high. One of the most charming features is a circular knot or topiary garden of low box hedging, cut into shape by the Portuguese gardeners with broody hens at the corners. Beyond this, a long lily pond contrasts with areas of bog garden, lake and stream. In the part known as the Inferno, a deep ravine in the mountainside with a steamy stream at the bottom forms a natural hothouse for the dense lush growth of tree ferns *Monstera deliciosa* and ginger lilies 3 m tall. But perhaps the most extraordinary part of Quinta do Palheiro is the Jardim da Senhora, or Lady's Garden, where a serpentine path of emerald grass edged with crimson iresine leads through a border of herbaceous plants and foliage shrubs in a style that was fashionable – though not always considered in the best of taste – one hundred years ago.

Quinta do Palheiro remains therefore an excellent example of an English newly-rich garden from late Victorian times. It is unusual for its size and the number of plants it contains, although its design and plantings are typical of its period. Unlike so many English gardens, it was not modernised between the two world wars by efforts to combine or contrast colours and forms in the Robinson–Jekyll manner; nor has it been reduced in size but intensified in effect

Quinta dos Girassóis, Maia, near Oporto, in 1949. In the foreground, the site of the future garden is ploughed by oxen.

Quinta dos Girassóis, Maia. The same view a year later; beyond the newly planted hedge is the rose garden.

by the use of garden 'rooms', the fate of many English gardens after the Second World War had dealt a blow to landed incomes. There are fewer gardeners than before, even on the island where labour is still 'cheap and plentiful', and the standard of maintenance is not as high as formerly, but Quinta do Palheiro remains a garden of delight and, apart from the Portuguese topiary, wholly English in concept and execution.

THREE GOOD examples of modern English gardens in Portugal are Quinta dos Girassóis at Maia, north of Oporto, Quinta de Penaferrim near Sintra and Quinta do Vale near Loures. All were designed, planted and maintained by their owners or by gardeners under their direct supervision. Gone is the desire to garden on a grand scale, the urge to stamp the owners' designs on a wider landscape and the need to impress society with the wealth that makes such things possible. Gardening in the second half of the twentieth century has meant a personal involvement and become a major interest, almost an occupation, for many members of the English upper and middle classes; and this has been no less the case for Englishmen living abroad. The owners of these three gardens involved themselves in every decision

affecting the design and planting, the periodic reorganisation of borders and other features, and above all the acquisition of new plants. Moreover they worked in the garden themselves, alongside their staff.

John and Valerie Delaforce bought Quinta dos Girassóis in 1949. Both were members of the English colony at Oporto associated with the wine trade, a commercial oligarchy sometimes known as the 'portocracy'. Their garden is the most carefully designed of the three, consciously laid out in the modern English style as a series of garden rooms, each with a different feature or planting to contrast with the others. In short, it is a garden of the Hidcote school. Quinta dos Girassóis was entirely the Delaforces' own creation in that they had no advice from famous garden designers or plantsmen as they laid it out and planted it. It is also the most English of gardens in Portugal, which is all the more surprising since both Delaforces have lived in Oporto for most of their lives – indeed, Valerie only knew England as a schoolgirl and during the war – and since the garden was made in a horticultural vacuum with no one nearby to offer help or advice.

The garden is, or was originally, about 1.5 ha (4 acres) in size. Half was woodland, and the rest formed a rough triangle with the house halfway along the longest side. There was a high granite wall the whole way round and, just inside it, a pergola of granite posts for the vines that made *vinho verde*. The retention of these covered walks around the perimeter exemplifies the English taste for incorporating utilitarian features with strong ornamental potential into the fabric of a garden. The Delaforces began their planting by turning over the soil with a primitive plough drawn by a yoke of oxen. Then hedges were planted to form the 'rooms' of the garden. These were mostly of escallonia, which thrives in northern Portugal, but included some informal hedges of hydrangeas which produce intensely blue flowers in the acid soil.

The Delaforces planted up a formal rose garden, divided into four by granite paving, at first filled with many different types; they found, however, that 'Papa Meilland' was by far the most successful modern rose and grew more of that and less of other varieties as the years went by. The herbaceous borders have such English garden plants as delphiniums, scabious, *Campanula persicifolia* and day lilies, but mixed with others that we would never consider reliably hardy in England including *Salvia uliginosa*, *Watsonia beatricis* and yellow arum lilies. Indeed, the Delaforces have found that many of the ingredients of an English herbaceous border – lupins, paeonies, hostas and meconopsis, for example – are unable to cope with the heat of late summer, and do not flourish in northern Portugal. They have had greater success with a border composed entirely of white-flowered and silver-leaved plants, where white varieties of agapanthus, lavender, verbena, dahlia and penstemon are mixed with silver-foliaged *Cineraria maritima* and *Artemisia arborescens*, and backed by taller white-flowering shrubs, *Romneya coulteri*, *Hydrangea paniculata* and 'Iceberg' roses. There are also special beds of irises; a corner thickly planted with evergreen azaleas; fruit trees underplanted with orange tritonias; a rose pergola; and some very fine camellias, including a splendid pink semi-double *japonica* hybrid that ought to be introduced into cultivation in England – as 'Delaforces's Seedling', perhaps.

At the far corner of Quinta dos Girassóis is a path laid with millstones brought by ox cart in the early days from a disused watermill nearby. Now lined with clumps of the bird of paradise flower *Strelitzia reginae*, it leads through a wrought-iron gate to the entrance of the woodland garden. The wood is dominated by eucalyptus, liquidambar, *Magnolia grandiflora* and cork oaks – one magnificent specimen is

thought to be 250 years old – and planted with azaleas, rhododendrons, oleanders and camellias, while the herbaceous underplanting incorporates great drifts of *Amaryllis belladonna*, agapanthus and montbretia. The small town of Maia has, however, grown since the Delaforces first bought Quinta dos Girassóis, and the garden has been considerably reduced in size as a result of a series of compulsory purchases for road-widening and housing schemes. Indeed, the woodland has been appropriated for a public park and the Delaforces are confined to a triangular half hectare immediately around the house. Nevertheless it is the finest part of the garden and the purest example of the Hidcote style in Portugal. Wherever he stands, the visitor is conscious of the pull of the design, urging him to explore further, while the plants detain him and slow down his progress – the classic creative tension of a good, modern, English garden.

English enthusiasts making a garden in Portugal have tended to ignore the Portuguese traditions and plant their gardens in an English style. There is nothing comparable to the deliberate reconstruction of Italian styles which Englishmen living in Italy have frequently affected. None of them uses *azulejos*, tanks of water or any other essentially Portuguese feature. If, however, an English family acquires an old property in Portugal with an established garden in the Portuguese style, it is unlikely to change substantially under English ownership: the good design or plantings of a Portuguese garden are respected. Quinta da Meio on the northern side of the Douro estuary at Oporto belonged to the Tait family for about a hundred years from 1881. Perhaps because William Tait and his daughters Muriel and Dorothy were all keen gardeners, and noted as plantsmen and botanists, they retained many of the original features of the garden. As a result, it now contains some of the largest camellia bushes in Portugal, and a tulip tree so huge that it was claimed to be the tallest in Europe and declared a National Monument by the Portuguese forestry commission. There have also been instances of Englishmen spending their lives and fortunes repairing a decrepit property and restoring both house and garden to their former magnificence. Such was the labour of love which Peter Pitt-Milward performed at the Paço de Gloria, a delicious baroque manor-house in the Lima valley in Minho, between 1935 and 1976. The house and garden are maintained in the same spirit by its present owner, the Hon. Colin Clark.

Quinta de Penaferrim in the Sintra hills was a small

English-run hotel when Richard and Mary Thomas bought the estate in 1955 and decided to turn it into a private house. The garden consisted of 5 ha (12 acres) of pine and eucalyptus woodland, with a parterre in front of the house in the shape of a Union Jack. The Thomases were plantsmen, and wanted to make a garden of interesting plants; the limiting factor was their discovery that, apart from one tiny patch, the soil was not the acid granitic earth of the Serra de Sintra, but alkaline limestone: the rhododendrons and camellias that were such a feature of the *quintas* of Sintra were beyond their power to grow. And they had to adapt to Portuguese conditions, to learn how to garden on a heavy clay soil where they could not rely on the frost to break down the clods.

The parterre was replaced by a lawn of Kikuyu grass. A wooden pergola was erected and is now covered by a scarlet passion flower. Shelter belts were planted of the umbrella pine *Pinus pinea* and mimosa *Acacia melanoxylon*, the species whose pale primrose

flowers are almost the last to bloom. Then the Thomases added internal hedges of such unusual material as *Nandina domestica* and a large semicircular rose garden with a trellis at the centre point covered by weeping poplars *Populus tremuloides* 'Pendula'. If the design sounds all rather formal, that is not in fact the case; the structural features are such as are commonly found in a natural English garden at home.

The planting is utterly English. The borders contain familiar columbines and foxgloves, but mixed with subjects too tender for England: watsonias, arum lilies, clivias, and shrubby echiums from the Canary Islands. Even these are used as herbaceous plants would be in an English border, planted for their colour, bulk, effect and contribution to the overall scheme. English plantsmanship is much in evidence at Quinta de Penaferrim. There are plants from Australia, including species of hakea, callistemon, banksia and grevillea; the tall, yellow-bracted *Cornus capitata* and Banksian roses from

Quinta de Penaferrim. Clumps of strelitzia line the sides of the pool and contrast with the shapes of the many exotic trees and shrubs in this plantsman's garden, evidence of how much will flourish in the warm wet climate of the Sintra Hills.

subtropical parts of China; a grove of Judas trees growing out of the lawn as we would grow Japanese cherries, and varying in colour from palest pink to purple; and vast clumps of the sumptuous Madeiran endemic *Geranium maderense*. Most of these plants have been grown from seed: there are very few hybrids or horticultural selections among them. The Thomases, in common with other garden owners in Portugal, attach great importance to the Royal Horticultural Society's seed list as one of the few benefits, apart from the *Journal*, that members who live abroad can enjoy.

Quinta de Penaferrim and the other post-war private gardens made by Englishmen in Portugal illustrate how well English gardening takes to a warm, wet climate. Gardening in Portugal requires less adaptation, less unlearning of English practices and less learning of another nation's gardening techniques than in any other country in Europe. In addition, the climate of Portugal and Galicia encourages a much greater choice of plants, especially trees and shrubs. It is true that alpine plants are all but impossible to grow, particularly those that come from high altitudes or are endemic to northern regions, but a wider range of plants can be grown between Lisbon and Corunna than anywhere else in Europe except perhaps the Italian Lakes. None of these three English gardens makes any concession to the Portuguese tradition and that is what makes them so interesting. Their inspiration is entirely English, and so they represent very pure examples of the English garden abroad.

As everywhere, most English gardens in Portugal are ephemeral and die with their makers. Residents in the north of the country speak wistfully of the gardens, now lost, of such well-known members of the English colony at Oporto as Patrick Guimarãens. Occasionally a garden is taken over by another enthusiast for the art, and flourishes again under the new régime. Such is Quinta do Vale near Loures. It is still a comparatively young garden, having been begun by Mrs Mary Graham in 1962 and then restored and greatly improved by Nicholas and Marie Kaye since they bought it in 1984, after answering an advertisement in *The Garden* which read:

PLANTSMAN'S GARDEN, PORTUGAL. For Sale, 12 miles easy access to Lisbon: 2.5 acres 'young garden', open views, own water, wealth varied trees, shrubs, climbers etc. from 5 continents. PLUS unusually beautiful 5 bed/4 bath/18th c. style house.

Quinta do Vale is a modern house, built in the traditional Portuguese style using reclaimed materials, on a 1 ha (2½ acre) plot exactly 100 metres square, cut out of gentle sloping farmland. The nearby town of Loures is not fashionable, indeed it is distinctly unsmart. Quinta do Vale was a windy, featureless site, with nothing to use as a theme for a garden. Mrs Graham enclosed it, mainly for security, with high walls on three sides, and a high fence on the fourth, but further shelter against the wind was imperative, and this was provided by belts of cupressus, eucalyptus and *Myoporum tenuifolium*, just inside the perimeter. Not surprisingly, Mrs Graham planted her garden in an intensely introspective way, with nothing to suggest that the world outside existed. Narrow paths, small clearings, and dense shrubberies were the elements of design, her only concession to formality a lily pond in the small lawn which runs around two sides of the house. Around the edge of the grass are mixed borders in the English style: the first impression is that the whole planting would not look out of place in the Home Counties, until it is discovered that pelargoniums have threaded themselves up to the top of two-metre bushes of abelia, and that the creeper that threatens to engulf the veranda is *Thunbergia grandiflora*, a native of Burma.

Mary Graham lived in Portugal for many years before building Quinta do Vale in her widowhood. She was an avid plantsman but a collector of plants rather than a botanist. Among her English gardening friends were Lord Aldenham and Molly, Duchess of Montrose, and so she exchanged plants with Briggens and Brodick Castle. Hilliers was the principal English supplier for Quinta do Vale, while the main Portuguese nursery was the Oporto firm of Moreira e Silva, one of whose directors later visited the garden to see what other interesting plants it contained which he might propagate. Plants came too, by one means or another, from botanic gardens and exchanges with other garden owners. When a keen English gardener pays a social visit to another in Portugal, a root or small plant will often be given and received. The generosity of garden owners is as great among Englishmen abroad as at home – indeed greater, because new plants are often hard to find in local nurseries. As at Quinta de Penaferrim, however,

Quinta do Vale, a plantsman's garden near Loures. The English-style lawn is a triumph of cultivation in this climate.

the majority of the plants at Quinta do Vale were grown from seed, which is the most convenient way of importing propagating material into a country that lacks a well-developed horticultural industry. Mary Graham obtained seeds from the Royal Horticultural Society, the Botanical Society of South Africa, botanic gardens in Australia, Calcutta and Singapore, and friends in New Zealand, South America, Rhodesia and Washington. The main limitation at Quinta do Vale was the heavy limy soil, unsuitable for many genera from Australia and the Far East, and for all acid-loving plants – so no camellias.

Shelter was not the only necessity for making the garden at Quinta do Vale; water, too, was vital. Mrs Graham sank a borehole so deep that she struck an underground tributary of the Tagus, giving her unlimited supplies of water and allowing her to install a system of standpipes to irrigate all parts of the garden when necessary. The result is an oasis of exotic plants flourishing in the dry plains north of Lisbon. The garden now has fine specimens of *Robinia × ambigua* 'Decaisneana', *Bombax mala-*

baricum and *Acacia horrida*; massed plantings of *Iris florentina* and its forms; and a bed of white crinums above a bed of *Narcissus papyraceus*, backed by *Rosa brunonii*. Along the driveway is a hedge of the climbing rose 'Golden Showers' in front of a handsome planting of *Wigandia urens*, while the chauffeur's flat and entrance gate is festooned in white wisteria. Roses such as 'Ramona' and *banksiae* 'Lutea' grow against the house; elsewhere thrives a bed of 'Margaret Merrill', two large thickets of 'Constance Spry' growing on its own roots, and a vast mound of a form of 'Cécile Brunner' known locally as 'Santa Teresina'.

The garden at Quinta do Vale reverted a little immediately before the Kayes bought it in 1984. They have given it considerably more structure by edging and resurfacing paths and adding a second pool and a white-painted arbour. The garden has been restored, renewed and modernised, so that its past achievements and its future development are both secure – all through an advertisement in *The Garden*.

Among the difficulties that English residents in Portugal face is that of finding competent gardeners:

Quinta do Vale. The lily pond, lawn and thickly planted borders in this photograph are as English as imaginable; only the line of eucalyptus trees beyond reveals that the garden cannot be in Britain.

school, of ornamental and amenity horticulture simply do not exist. It is not a new problem. Nearly a century ago, Sir Charles Thomas-Stanford wrote that 'the absence of any garden knowledge among the working people here is indeed a trial ... it would of course be easy to bring over an English gardener, but there is the difficulty of the language to be considered; and Englishmen of that class too frequently develop an abnormal thirst in this climate when left to themselves' (*Leaves from a Madeira Garden*). Nowadays it is usually possible to find men with experience of market gardening, and women to help with the weeding. Many Portuguese have some experience of the basic techniques of planting, watering, manuring and pruning, and the general level of horticultural expertise is higher than in Spain. They are expert at pruning and clipping hedges and they understand the need for spraying: roses and fruit trees are usually sprayed at the same time that the vines are treated with Bordeaux mixture. Portuguese gardeners have a passion for tidiness and in particular for sweeping leaves off paths and raking the gravel underneath: they find the English practice of mulching with leafmould rather puzzling. Traditions and practices differ. A correspondent of *The Gardener's Chronicle* noticed in 1903 'that the Portuguese gardeners never use a spade, but make use of a gigantic square hoe instead, and a large wooden implement shaped like a mattock and fork combined, with three prongs. Both the hoe and the fork are of a much larger size than the fork and spade used in this country.' Portuguese gardeners still dig in the old medieval way, using a mattock working towards the digger, while the English have long adopted the Dutch method of digging with a fork away from the body.

Propagation is another problem. The Portuguese understand layering and grafting, but have very little experience of taking cuttings. And English residents in Portugal find that there are shortages of the garden materials and chemicals that we take for granted, including systemic herbicides and hormone rooting compounds. But at least there is a strong tradition of ornamental gardening among the Portuguese, so that many English people who live in Portugal are happy to leave everything to their gardeners and accept the Portuguese style of gardening with its clipped box hedges, camellias and roses. (No such tradition exists in southern Spain, and English settlers there are forced to make gardens of their own, which tend therefore to be English in style.) Nevertheless, the best gardens made by Englishmen in Portugal are purely English in inspiration, design and content.

References and Further Reading

I recommend Marcus Binney's *Country Manors of Portugal* (Woodbridge, 1988) as an agreeable introduction to houses and gardens in Portugal, but the most comprehensive study of Portuguese gardens is *Jardins em Portugal* by Helder Carita and Homem Cardoso (Lisboa, 1986). An older work, Ilídio Alves de Araújo's *Arte Paisagista e Arte dos Jardins em Portugal* (Lisboa, 1962) still contains some useful material. As well as Mme Junot's memoirs, Byron's letters and Beckford's Journals, all well known, I recommend Robert Southey's *Journals of a Residence in Portugal 1800–1801* (Oxford, 1960) to the general reader. Better still are William Dalrymple's youthful explorations: *Travels through Spain and Portugal, 1774* (London, 1777). The most complete account of Monserrate that I have found is Francisco Costa's *História da Quinta e Palácio de Monserrate* (Sintra, 1985) but there are also articles in *The Gardener's Chronicle* on 26 September and 3 October 1885 and 3 August 1929 and by Clive Dewey in *Country Life*, 1 November 1990. The work of Cook's architect is explored in *James Knowles: Victorian Editor and Architect* by Priscilla Metcalf (Oxford, 1980). The garden at Quinta do Palheiro was written up for *RHSJ* by Mildred Blandy in September 1955 and by Patrick Synge in December 1978. The story of the English community in Oporto is best told by Sarah Bradford in *The Story of Port* (3rd edition, London, 1983) and John Delaforce's *The Factory House at Oporto* (2nd edition, London, 1983). The Taits' garden in Oporto is briefly described by Paul Miles in *RHSJ*, January 1977. I have been greatly helped by a manuscript account of Quinta do Vale by Mrs Graham's daughter Isla Shuttleworth, with additional notes by Nicholas Kaye, and by Valerie Delaforce's unpublished account of Quinta dos Girassóis, 'An English Garden in the North of Portugal'.

Chapter Eleven

SPAIN

Costas and Casticismo

T HE ENGLISH obsession for Spain is a recent phenomenon. Spain was so seldom included in the Grand Tours made by rich young men during the eighteenth century that Dr Johnson was able to conclude in 1761 that 'no country is less known to the rest of Europe'. During the nineteenth century, Englishmen would not take a house in Madrid or Seville for a year or so, as they might in Florence or Rome. 'There is no country in Europe so little known and yet so worth visiting,' wrote the physician Dr Madden in 1864. Travel in Spain was bedevilled by bad roads and the country's reputation for harbouring brigands. Anglo-Spanish relations were further hampered by the natural reserve of both peoples, and the deep historic suspicions that the English had for the Spanish. Spain was the country of the Inquisition and *autos-da-fé* and, with Spanish foreign policy preoccupied with its American colonies and at odds with the expansion of English interests, a natural hostility developed between the two great maritime nations.

As a result the English communities in Spain were seldom substantial. When Sir William Dalrymple visited Seville in 1774 he reported that 'the English *factory* consists of the Consul and three members', although he did add that they were 'remarkably civil and attentive to strangers', as well they might be, for there were few English visitors at the time. Most of the English and Irish families in Spain were recusant Catholics who had fled the penal laws at home. The leading banker in Seville at the end of the eighteenth

century was one James Wiseman, whose son Thomas became the first Cardinal Archbishop of Westminster (1802–65), while the most successful banking family in Madrid in the middle of the nineteenth century was the O'Sheas, though even they spent the summer months at a villa in Biarritz.

It is difficult to generalise about Spanish gardens, so great are the contrasts of climate and nature which go to shape them. The moss-covered *azulejos* of Galicia are stylistically far removed from the plane-tree avenues of New Castile and the Moorish patios of Andalusia. A few elements are constant: trees and evergreens, shade and geometric form, and the use of water, trickling or still. Spain somehow remained largely impervious to the fashions of other countries. Spanish Renaissance gardens were not inventive in the Italian way, the mannerist gardens of seventeenth-century France were seldom seen south of the Pyrenees and the English landscape style which ravaged much of Europe in the latter part of the eighteenth century made little impression on the Spanish countryside. Early in the nineteenth century, domestic interest was awakened in the gardens of pre-Conquest Andalusia, and as Spanish historians began to claim that their Moorish heritage was both unique and of the highest merit, a few garden designers began very tentatively to reinterpret that tradition in contemporary terms.

By 1924, the American Rose Nichols was claiming that 'modern Spanish gardens are essentially idiomatic', and concluding that 'the Spanish enjoy experimenting with fresh ideas and are never hampered by their respect of tradition'. It is difficult to share her conclusion. It is only very recently that Spain has enjoyed an explosion of creative gardening. For many centuries it remained aloof, distinct and

---

The Convent, Gibraltar. The planting in the Governor's garden is English in spirit; many of the plants actually came from England.

proud of its *casticismo*. When Spanish artists became more susceptible to foreign influences at the beginning of the twentieth century, it was to France rather than England that its garden designers turned for inspiration. The Frenchman J.-C. N. Forestier was the architect chosen for the Parque María Luisa, made for the Hispanic-American exhibition of 1929 in Seville, the Parque de Montjuich in Barcelona and such private gardens as the Casa del Rey Moro at Ronda and the Palacio de Liría at Madrid.

Sir William Dalrymple was a soldier, and had no particular interest in gardens, but knew enough when he went to the Royal Palace in Seville to realise that 'the gardens belonging to it are laid out in a very ancient taste ... there are some pieces of water in them, which served the Moors for baths'. Even the royal gardens of Aranjuez failed to measure up to Dalrymple's gaze: 'there are in some parts of the gardens, parterres, where puerile devices are formed in myrtle borders, such as fleur de lis, initial letters of names & etc. They are just now in the same state as when first made; a true taste for gardening has not reached this country.' Dalrymple concluded that 'the coolness of the running river, and the refreshing shade of the umbrageous elms are the only beauties to recommend them; the eye constantly confined within the narrow bounds of the hedges, gives the idea of restraint; and the sameness produced by the straight lines of the alleys is disagreeable, and, after a short time, tires'.

When Lady Holland visited the gardens of the Alcázar at Granada a generation later in 1803 she was delighted to discover that the gardens were preserved in the Moorish style: 'one part is precisely as at the conquest [with] clipped hedges of myrtle and devises cut from them'. Lady Holland herself was quite outspoken in her likes and dislikes, for she declared that 'the English taste for simplicity and nature, which places a house in the midst of a grazing field where the sheep din *ba ba* all day long, has ... driven me into the opposite extreme, and made me prefer to the *nature* of a grass field and round clump the *built* gardens of two centuries back'. At first English interest in Moorish gardens was chiefly historical or academic, but it was increased by the popularity of the works of the American novelist Washington Irving, who wrote *The Conquest of Granada* and *Legends of the Alhambra* while he was living within the walls of the Moorish fortress at Granada during the 1820s and 1830s. The potency of the Arab history inflames another description, Hans Christian Andersen's account of his travels in Spain, translated into English in 1864. He wrote that the

Generalife attracted me more frequently than the Alhambra itself. Here the air was perfumed with roses, reminding one of the poetry of ancient times; the clear waters rushed along, murmuring and foaming as of yore; the primaeval cypresses ... stood rearing their fresh branches in the air that I was breathing. Here I lived so entirely in the past, that it would scarcely have surprised me if forms from the days of the Moors, in rustling damask, and dazzling brocades, had glided past me.

By the late 1880s, the romance of the pre-Conquest gardens had developed to such an extent that Moorish gardens and garden buildings began to spring up as far away as the Riviera.

DESPITE ITS remoteness, Britain had a toehold on the Iberian peninsula. Gibraltar became a British possession in 1715 and during the course of the eighteenth and nineteenth centuries took on the air of a provincial garrison town. Richard Ford never cared for it, and referred to the Rock in 1845 as 'this sink of Moslem, Jewish and Roman Catholic profligacy'. He had, however, nothing but praise for the Alameda created by the Governor-General Sir George Don in 1814–16, 'formerly a burning desert and a cloacal nuisance until converted ... into a garden of sweets and delight'. The Alameda, or Esplanade, was an early experiment in public amenity, laid out for promenading and planted for pleasure. 'Thus Flora is wedded to Mars, and the wrinkled front of a fortress smoothed with roses,' declared Ford.

The statues on the Alameda of the Duke of Wellington and General Elliott are 'mean and tasteless' pronounced the classic nineteenth-century traveller's bible, *O'Shea's Guide to Spain and Portugal*, while the man of letters H. D. Traill observed that 'the mysterious curse pronounced upon English statuary appears to follow it even beyond the seas'. Augustus Hare (*Wanderings in Spain*, 1873), however, was greatly taken by the Alameda gardens, where 'castoroil plants, daturas and daphnes ... attain the dignity of timber, while geraniums and heliotropes many years old, are so large as to destroy all the sense of floral proportions which has hitherto existed in your mind. It is a curious characteristic,' he concluded, 'and typical of Gibraltar, that the mouth of a cannon is frequently found protruding from a thicket of flowers.' Nowadays the Alameda is woefully neglected by the Gibraltarian authorities, although it still has some splendid trees, notably *Melaleuca stapheloides*, several *Dracaena drago* and the only specimen of cork oak *Quercus suber* in the colony. The most enjoyable features are an intricate nine-teenth-century formal garden and a pebble-faced grotto round a pool with papyrus plants, again in a sorry state of repair. They are hybrids between the English Italianate and Spanish Moorish traditions; in England, they would long ago have been repaired with grants from English Heritage.

The government houses, The Convent, The Mount, and Ince's Farm, all have respectable gardens but their fortunes have waxed and waned as new governors, admirals and chief administrators came and went. Richard Ford was fond of The Convent and recalled in 1845 that 'the garden, so nicely laid out by Lady Don, used to be delicious. Scotch horticulture under an Andalucian climate can wheedle everything out of Flora and Pomona.' The Convent can still boast a celebrated dragon tree *Dracaena drago* and a venerable specimen of the carob *Ceratonia siliqua*, whose widespreading lower limbs supported by props are actually used as a bandstand. Of necessity The Convent's garden has to reflect the position of the Governor and be suitable for official functions. Garden parties and receptions are held on lawns of drought-resistant grass, while political confidences can be exchanged during a walk along the borders thickly planted with long-flowering shrubs, daturas and hibiscus. Some of the plants came from England, including varieties of lilies and pinks.

From time to time during the course of the nine-teenth century, an English merchant, banker or consular official would make a garden that attracted the notice of travellers. Such creations are usually transient, their reputations passing, so that they flare briefly in contemporary accounts and then disappear back into obscurity: they have their day and cease to be. One was the house and garden near Murcia that the 2nd Lord Howden (1799–1873) made when minister plenipotentiary at Madrid in the 1850s. Among the date palms and roses – Chinas, tea roses and Banksians – he mixed English hollyhocks, delphiniums, poppies and lilies together with exotic passion flowers and climbing bignonias. One visitor was puzzled to find that Howden grew many plants in a greenhouse that should have been completely hardy outside. He considered it a measure of the winter climate rather than the minister's Englishness.

Very few gardens made by Englishmen in Spain

Finca de la Concepción, near Málaga. The importance of irrigation in Andalusia is emphasised by water pouring from Venus' ewer.

have survived into longevity. In 1889, Thomas Livermore, the British Consul in Málaga, who had married a Spanish wife, bought an estate of 80 ha (200 acres) just outside the city, in the valley which leads towards Antequera. Within twenty years the garden that he made at Finca de la Concepción was widely mentioned in guidebooks as one of the sights of Málaga. His grand manor-house was built halfway up the side of the valley, and round it he planted a magnificent jungle of palms and tropical species where his contemporaries in England would have chosen conifers and North American trees. The garden has since matured into one of the finest examples of a late nineteenth-century English landscape in Europe. Superficially it bears little resemblance to the park surrounding an English country house, because Livermore decided not to risk a grass lawn; but his instinct to make a collection and the disposition of the trees to create contrasts of form are both very English traits. Certainly no contemporary Spanish garden displays such a combination of botanic virtuosity and sensitivity to ornamental effect: and La Concepción is perhaps closest in spirit to the garden begun in the same year by Joseph Whitaker the Younger at Villa Malfitano in Palermo.

The house must once have enjoyed big and distant views, but it was always intended that the trees should obscure the outside landscape. Indeed, the driveway winds slowly up to the front of the house by an avenue of oriental planes as large as any in Kashmir. From the small carriage circle a broad stone staircase leads to a round tank on the terrace below, reminiscent of the famous circular pool at Hidcote. It is hedged around by *Duranta erecta*, while the basin itself sports red and yellow water lilies. In the centre a baby triton clasps a fish which spouts water in a small fountain. The pool is surrounded by unusually tall clumps of cycads, three *Cycas revoluta* and two of the rarer *C. circinalis*.

The most arresting feature at La Concepción is a wrought-iron arcade at the side of the house, perhaps 50 m long and 15 m wide, which Livermore covered with wisterias and ivy. It was meant as an outdoor room for summer entertainment, particularly the receptions and dances that were part of his consular duties. Its sides are lined with shade-loving ferns and pots of butias, clivias and sansevierias. At one end a small waterfall runs into a basin surrounded by *Monstera deliciosa*, which has also naturalised at the bottom of the garden on either side of a stream. Grottoes, cascades and pools where black swans nest are an important element of the garden. The use of water is very Spanish, specifically Moorish, while the constant sound of the water is a reminder that such luxuriance is made possible in this climate only by its presence. Livermore was also a collector of antiquities, which were easily come by in his day, and busts and inscriptions from the Roman excavations at Málaga and Cartama are displayed around a small model of the Pantheon, somewhat crudely executed, with no bases to the columns.

It is the trees that make the garden at La Concepción, and the thickness of their planting. Apart from the plane trees, almost all are evergreens. They include *Grevillea robusta* from Australia; the dragon tree *Dracaena drago* from the Canary Islands; the semi-evergreen persimmon *Diospyros kaki* from China; *Roystonea regia* from Florida and the Antilles, whose seeds contain an edible oil; vast aerial rooting figs; the grey-leaved palm *Erythea armata* from California; and the bird of paradise *Strelitzia augusta* from South Africa. Lists make for boring reading, but this selection shows how international were the sources from which Thomas Livermore drew his collection. The underplanting is a rich assemblage of clivias, strelitzias, hedychiums, belamcandas and such evergreen shrubs as *Pittosporum tobira*. The undergrowth is thick and green, even in summer. Where the jungle begins to thin out and merge with the thin natural pine wood on the edge of the estate, an avenue of palms leads to the very end of a long steep spur and a circular temple topped by a tiled cupola which overlooks the valley down to Málaga.

One of Livermore's daughters, Isabel, married the Duke of Heredia and herself had a good garden at La Finca de San José. The Heredia shipping interests allowed Isabel to import new species from all over the world, and some found their way back to her parents' garden at La Concepción. The Livermores were not alone in their enthusiasm for collecting a multitude of exotic plants. The Prussian Consul too had created a garden, La Consula, which was said to equal La Concepción in the variety and richness of its planting. Clearly, international rivalries were not confined to the struggle for world supremacy.

Livermore himself turned his enthusiasms to the national interest. In 1890, he wrote to the editor of *The Gardener's Chronicle* that the climate of the Málaga region was particularly suited to the growing of such useful plants as lemon-scented geraniums, heliotropes and gardenias, and he suggested that a British enterprise might be started in Andalusia to match the perfume industries of Grasse. He also pointed out that rosemary, thyme and *Lavandula stoechas* grew wild upon the hills and that eucalyptus had been successfully introduced for many years, growing with marvellous rapidity wherever it could obtain moisture.

By the end of the nineteenth century, the growth in British trade and naval power had extended the influence of the Gibraltar community into the adjoining part of mainland Spain, the Campo de Gibraltar, where the most prominent family was the Larios. During that century the Larios had become one of the richest landowning families of southern Spain: almost all the coastline between Algeciras and Málaga once belonged to them. There were five Larios brothers and, despite their name, they were only one quarter Spanish by blood, the remaining three quarters being Gibraltarian or English. They were related to landowning families in Scotland and Ireland, and had been educated at Beaumont, so that in their upbringing they were almost completely

English. Their tastes were formed in the shooting-boxes, hunting seats and fishing lodges of late Victorian and Edwardian society and their brilliance as all-round sportsmen brought them renown at a time when such prowess was more highly regarded than ever before or since.

In 1901, the Larios employed Selden Wornum (1847–1910) to build them a house near San Roque to be called Guardacorte. Wornum had already built the Palacio de Miramar (1889–93) at San Sebastián as a royal residence for the Queen Regent of Spain. Guardacorte is mullioned and transomed like a West Country manor-house. Some of its gables are timbered in the Elizabethan style, while others have the outlines of eighteenth-century Andalusian baroque. It reeks of prosperity. The garden the Larios made there is remarkable for the wide apron of grass which they set around the house in emulation of an English lawn, surrounded by trees, including a large pecan *Carya illinoinensis* and a weeping white mulberry *Morus alba* 'Pendula'. The house is approached by a long avenue of the Canary Island palm *Phoenix canariensis*, underplanted with *Polygala myrtifolia*. Ernesto Larios planted several lines of eucalyptus:

Guardacorte has no fewer than sixty-eight species of gum tree, many of them the first introductions into Spain. Among the best are a large specimen of the rare *Eucalyptus camaldulensis*, and a spectacular lemon-scented *E. citriodora*.

After their father died, Guardacorte was inherited by Carlos Larios, but occupied by his brother Pablo, the Marqués de Marzales, who continued to live there after the estate was sold to the 4th Marquess of Bute in the early 1920s. Bute's daughter, Lady Mary Walker, became a noted plantswoman, responsible for the introduction of many exotic plants into cultivation in Spain. Through an English agent in Gibraltar she brought *Greyia sutherlandii* from South Africa and a wide range of new bougainvillea hybrids for her garden at nearby La Solana, now an hotel. Bute's granddaughter, Lady Fiona Lowsley-Williams, lives at Guardacorte now.

In 1904, Ernesto Larios married Emily Wilson (née Carver), the daughter of a Gibraltar cotton merchant and the widow of an English master of foxhounds. Emily Larios was reluctant to live at Guardacorte with all her brothers- and sisters-in-law – she wanted a house of her own – so in 1905 Ernesto built Monte

Guardacorte. Selden Wornum's Elizabethan manor-house, built for the Anglo-Spanish Larios family in 1901, is set in woodland and surrounded by lawns, closer in spirit to the West Country than the Costa del Sol.

de la Torre up in the cork forests within sight of Algeciras. Like Guardacorte, the house is a curious example of English colonial architecture. The contractors had been responsible for the Reina Christina Hotel at Algeciras and the Reina Victoria Hotel at Ronda. They had also built the local railway line that leads to Bobadillo and it has been said that Monte de la Torre and the two hotels were all based on the designs of the railway stations which the company built along the line.

The house at Monte de la Torre is surrounded by extensive flat lawns, as it would be in England. With half-closed eyes you can picture it as a senior army officer's house, built in the colonial style, at Sandhurst or Bisley. Its green swards are most unusual for Spain. Ernesto Larios sought the advice of C. Starke & Co, nurserymen in Cape Town, for suitable grasses to plant. Starke recommended Kikuyu grass and Rhodes grass as the best of the native South African species. They also supplied native trees,

A fine specimen of Nolina recurvata *at Monte de la Torre, one of many good specimen trees and shrubs at this Edwardian garden near Algeciras.*

notably *Leucadendron argenteum* and *Sterculia populnea*, and bulbs and corms of Cape species of watsonias, babianas and dieramas. Almost a hundred years later, freesias in every colour of the rainbow have naturalised throughout the garden.

Emily Larios planted a double border of roses outside the house. It ran across the lawn and down to a large formal garden immediately above the ha-ha. The roses did not flourish. Even in the Campo de Gibraltar, where the annual rainfall of 750 mm (30 in) compares favourably with most of eastern England, water for irrigation can be scarce. In 1905 the household was a large one and the supply was small: not until relatively recently did Monte de la Torre have plenty of water. It took Emily some years to discover which plants would thrive in the Andalusian climate; the evergreen *Magnolia grandiflora* was a particular success, as were the yellow *Buddleia madagascariensis* and purple *Iochroma violacea*.

Emily's formal garden is about 80 × 25 m (88 × 28 yd), with a path through the middle. Each half is divided into triangles of various sizes by paths that run in from the corners towards circular beds in the centre. Some of these segments were given an edging of semicircular green glazed tiles, the same as were used on the roof of the house. The central beds have evergreen magnolias, underplanted with *Iris unguicularis*, cannas and clumps of agapanthus, but there are also Canary Island palms, big bushes of *Camellia japonica*, citrus fruits and loquats. Part of the retaining wall of the formal garden supports wisteria along its length, and there is a hedge of winter jasmine.

The extensive lawns are punctuated by island beds and specimen trees. The tall New Zealand pine *Araucaria excelsa* immediately outside the house usually has an untidy stork's nest on top. A strange elephant-like member of the lily family *Nolina recurvata* grows on the edge of the drive – members of the family call it 'The Growth'. Around the edge of the lawns, and in the shrubberies cut from them, are banks of *Hibiscus rosa-sinensis* 4 m (13 ft) high, innumerable mimosas (*Acacia* spp.), palm trees and old roses. *Albizia lophantha* has naturalised among the cork oaks, and a tall clump of *Strelitzia alba* lies deep in the woodland, a measure of how everything has grown since Emily and Ernesto Larios first cut their garden out of the forest.

The estate now belongs to Ernesto and Emily Larios's grandson Quentin Agnew, but the design and planting at Monte de la Torre have changed

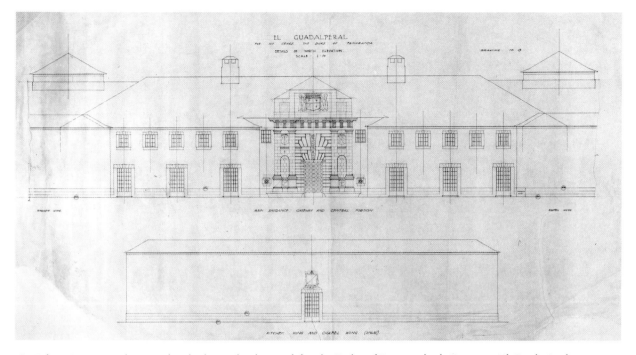

Sir Edwin Lutyens's drawing for the house he designed for the Duke of Peñaranda de Duero at El Gordo in the province of Toledo. The simple garden he planted still survives.

little. It remains an Edwardian garden with a contemporary selection of trees growing in and around a lawn similar to many gardens that were being made all over Europe at that time. It may not be original in design, but it is the most perfect surviving example of a *belle époque* garden in Spain. The cast-iron garden seats in gothic vine-leaf patterns are still painted the same dark green that was so popular a hundred years ago for outdoor furniture.

SIR EDWARD LUTYENS was a friend of the Duke of Alba, a Spanish grandee descended from James II of England. 'Alba is a Grandee of Spain thirteen times over ...' he explained to his wife; 'he could sit in thirteen seats in the Senate if he had as many sit-upons.' This friendship led in 1915 to a commission from Alba's younger brother, the Duke of Peñaranda de Duero, to design a house and garden on his estate at El Gordo above the river Tagus near Toledo. Lutyens warmed to Peñaranda: 'a charming person – thirty-three – very young and simple in the nice way, full of fun and life,' he told Lady Emily, when he visited central Spain that autumn.

Toledo is an inhospitable province of Spain, racked by searing heat in summer and cold dry winds in winter: the historic heart of New Castile was

never a land of milk and honey. The designs Lutyens produced for the house are all the more interesting since Spanish Renaissance architecture and decoration had influenced his own style as a young architect. He had been impressed, too, by the gardens he saw at El Escorial: 'very pleasant, thick-cut box hedges in knots, stone-niched walls, and gravel'. These are the classic ingredients of the austere Castilian style. Lutyens's original designs are now in the RIBA collection in London. They show that the house, arranged around an arcaded courtyard, was typically Spanish in style, with plastered walls, granite stone dressings and a tiled roof. On the south side, a series of terraces and staircases was intended to drop down to a landing-stage on the River Tagus, while to the west there was to be a walled water garden stretching away from the library and sitting-room. Lutyens's drawings incorporated his characteristic continuous walls which extend from the house into the garden and indeed into the retaining walls, breached only by arched openings, shuttered windows, and occasional concentrations of classical detail. In the event, the original design was abandoned and an even grander building commenced on a site two miles away, but left in the lurch by the start of the Spanish Civil War. There survives only a comparatively small house, full of such typical

Lutyens details as red-brick niches and surrounds to the windows and doors. Below it is a sunken garden, still well maintained, a simple parterre planted with trees and shrubs. The brick-edged pool in the centre is shaped in a Renaissance outline. Much of the inspiration for El Gordo must have come from the box hedges, knots, niched walls and gravel paths of El Escorial.

Perhaps the garden at the Escorial, by its very simplicity, was not the most suitable model. Dalrymple, writing in 1774, noted that it lacked 'any garden in the least suitable to such a building'. What he found was 'a terrace on the south side, with a fish pond, and some small parterres of flowers', and that was all. His disappointment has been shared by many critics, before and since. Had Lutyens based El Gordo on the baroque magnificence of Aranjuez or La Granja, his creative imagination could have given the Duke of Peñaranda something much more impressive.

NO ENGLISH family has owned estates in Spain for as long as the Dukes of Wellington, who were also Dukes of Ciudad Rodrigo and Grandees of Spain. Nevertheless, until comparatively recently, members of the Iron Duke's family seldom visited their Spanish properties, presented to the General in 1812 after his victory over the French at Salamanca. There was, however, always a resident agent on the property, the first a Spanish officer who had accompanied the Duke during the Peninsular campaign. Thereafter, the other agents were usually English and it is to one such, Colonel The Hon. Montague Mostyn (1838–1904), that we owe the origins of the garden at the Wellingtons' only remaining estate in Spain, Molino del Rey near Granada.

Mostyn started working for the 3rd Duke in about 1895. Molino del Rey had only a small residence at that time, built about forty years previously. When the 3rd Duke died in 1900, he was succeeded by his brother, who wished to visit his Spanish property. There was nowhere large enough for him to stay, so the 4th Duke told his agent to add a bigger house to the existing farmhouse. Mostyn built it in the style of a Riviera villa, not in keeping with the architectural traditions of either England or Spain. In order to stabilise the house, very deep foundations were dug, as Andalusia is in an earthquake zone and small tremors are common. The earth from these excavations was piled up in front of the house and levelled out towards a high retaining wall. So began the

garden. Col. and Mrs Mostyn planted a grove of Judas trees, conspicuous from a great distance when they flower in March and April.

Col. Mostyn was succeeded as agent by his son Jack (1870–1939), who remained at Molino del Rey until his death. Jack married a Mrs Hannah Cohen in 1921 and she laid out a formal rectangular garden in the Spanish style, filled with santolina, lavender and rosemary, and hedged with cypress cut to a height of no more than 60 cm (2 ft). Many of her ideas came from the Moorish gardens of Granada, which had been somewhat unhistorically restored during the course of the nineteenth century. Hannah Mostyn filled the parterres with tree paeonies and drifts of pale blue irises interplanted with the Madonna lily Lilium candidum: the intention was that the iris and the lily should flower simultaneously. She also planted clumps of arum lilies in the fishponds, where their flowers were reflected in the still water and glowed in the evening sun. Her rose garden was edged by a circle of lavender: roses grown as standards, seldom seen in Spain, were a particular success. In order to irrigate the garden properly, small channels of brick were built around every bed; each could be flooded in turn. Only through copious watering in summer was it possible to make and keep a flower garden in the hot dry climate of inland Andalusia, but the result was a combination of Hispano-Moorish design and English planting which is unique among English gardens in Spain. Beneath the gardens the almond orchards of the Vale of Granada stretch almost to the horizon. High in the sky rises the great whaleback of the Sierra Nevada, snowcapped for most of the year.

Major and Mrs Eudo Tonson-Rye further developed the garden at Molino del Rey when he was agent for Gerald, the 7th Duke, between 1955 and 1965. Mrs Tonson-Rye restored and replanted much of it and added such exotic trees as mimosas and Schinus molle. Gerald Wellington was himself an architect, and had at one time been Surveyor of the King's Works of Art. He felt that the garden should be more traditionally Spanish. He made a patio in one corner with a fount of trickling water – spouting jets belong to the Italian tradition – and tried, unsuccessfully, to establish maidenhair ferns on the pedestal, as seen in the more sheltered gardens of Seville. He also planted arbours of the double yellow Banksian rose and evergreen honeysuckle. The plants came from a market garden in Granada, for at that time nurseries were almost unknown in the south of Spain. Gerald Wellington's ideas on the

Right: *Finca la Concepción, near Málaga. A collection of palms and other exotic trees merges into stands of native pines in this splendid Victorian garden.*

Below: Banksia spinulosa *at La Saleta in Galicia, where Robert and Margaret Gimson have assembled the largest collection of South African and Australian plants in Europe.*

Opposite: *Russell Page laid out this garden at Cala Ratjada in Majorca to accommodate his patron's collection of sculptures; it epitomises his ability to subordinate English horticultural instincts to more dominant themes. The sculpture, by Alfaro, is called 'Linea al Vent'.*

Above: *Puerto de Cortes, 1988. Vernon Maxwell's neat rose beds and lush green lawns are the peak of English horticultural endeavour on the Costa del Sol.*

Below: *The patio garden made by Diana Brinton-Lee in the 1950s at El Almendral, crowded with pots of flowering plants.*

Opposite: *One of the grottos at Bagatelle, which was probably built by Thomas Blaikie for the Comte d'Artois in the 1780s.*
Above: *The orangery at Bagatelle was built by Lord Hertford in the 1840s.*
Below: Clères. *The formal garden in front of the restored castle designed and planted by garden historian Avray Tipping in the 1920s.*

Giverny: the French style of planting. The mixing of colours and the repetition of groupings are essential features of Monet's style and distinguish it from the English ideas on planting developed by Gertrude Jekyll.

Above: *Ninfa. A gateway into the garden, heavy with rambler roses.*
Overleaf: *Ninfa. The main river is crossed by several small bridges of simple design.*

El Palacio, Jerez de la Frontera. A corner of Christopher Sandeman's garden, known for its floral displays as well as the small experimental garden of plants which he called 'El Jardincito Japonés'.

sort of style that would be appropriate for his Spanish property differed from those of Mrs Tonson-Rye. She was more interested in plants: she grew 'Paul's Scarlet Rambler' rose against the grey pillars of the patio, geraniums in pots along the edge of the veranda, and an unusually pale blue morning glory up the side of the house near the front door. She also contemplated sowing a grass lawn which, if successful, would have been a considerable feat of cultivation.

THE WRITER and explorer Christopher Sandeman lived at Jerez de la Frontera during the 1920s in a house whose small Japanese garden had been designed by Charles Garnier (1825–98), the architect of the Paris Opera House. Sandeman called it 'El Jardincito Japonés', but said that the name was misleading because it offended against every canon of Japanese art and suggested only a bowing acquaintance with things Japanese. It was in the middle of

a much larger garden, nearly 4 ha (10 acres) in all. Sandeman was an immensely able and enthusiastic plantsman in his own right, importing plants from North Africa and the Cape as well as from England, to discover what plants would adapt to conditions in Andalusia. Later in life he moved to Grasse where his gardening friends included Lady (Winifred) Fortescue and Elizabeth von Arnim, 'who once had a German garden'. Later still, he mounted a series of botanical expeditions to Peru on behalf of the herbaria at Kew and Oxford.

Mediterranean and South African bulbs flourished in his garden at Jerez. As well as freesias and sparaxis, which can become pestilential weeds in Mediterranean conditions, Sandeman claimed particular success with *Tulipa saxatilis*, *Iris unguicularis*, turban ranunculi, Madonna lilies and Caen anemones, all endemic to Greece or Turkey. Irises did particularly well: he grew *Iris reticulata* and *I. susiana*, as well as *albicans*, the yellow form of *chamaeiris*, and selected forms of *I. alata*, which is native to the limestone hills of Andalusia. Sandeman knew that it was particularly important to find trees and shrubs that would tolerate the Andalusian climate, where summer temperatures can exceed 50°C (120°F) and the summer drought lasts between four and seven months. He used to quote a local proverb, '*Agua por San Juan, No da el vino y quite el pan*', which means that rain on midsummer day spoils the grain harvest and comes too late to help the vines. Sandeman was successful with several pelargoniums, *Malvastrum capensis* and *Erianthemum pulchellum* among small shrubs, and the monthly China rose and *Melianthus major* among taller ones.

Another good plantsman's garden was begun between the wars at San Roque in the Campo de Gibraltar when Lt. Col. J. C. Brinton acquired the estate of El Almendral in 1933. He and his daughter Diana Brinton-Lee made a large collection of plants halfway up a limestone outcrop high above the olive and almond orchards. Like Sandeman, one of their interests was bulbs. The parterres in front of the house were reworked with brick paths and densely planted with tulips, alliums, hedychiums and a wide range of South African monocotyledons. Freesias have naturalised all over the garden and down the hillside below. The formal garden was enclosed by iron railings held in place by short whitewashed pillars; the central section is arched with iron hoops for climbers to give shade to an outdoor dining-room. Sweet-scented daturas line the sides. The patio at the centre of the house was crowded with pots of every shape and style, and filled with an English selection of plants. On one of the patio's columns a form of *Jasminum polyanthum* with unusually dark crimson calyces climbed up to the first floor, while an enormous wisteria took leave of the house, scrambled over the roof, and festooned the fruit trees beyond. The orange trees left by the original owners were underplanted with herbaceous plants in the English horticultural taste: pelargoniums and montbretias were allowed to spread right to the base of the trees, and were not cleared away as they would have been in a Spanish garden. Mrs Brinton-Lee was a botanist, and made a special collection of the Dipsacaceae of Andalusia. Another botanical curiosity is the fine specimen, unique in southern Spain, of the leguminous Mexican tree *Prosopis juliflora*, whose rarity is perhaps explained by its formidable thorns.

At the same time as Brinton and Sandeman were making plantsmen's gardens in Andalusia, a very young English couple were planning an entirely different type of garden at Cap Roig on the Costa Brava. Nicholas and Dorothy Woevodsky bought 40 ha (100 acres) of barren headland around a ruined castle in 1926; they were to live there for fifty years, by which time they could boast that the castle had been restored with architectural imagination to resemble the famous Castillo de Poblet, the coastline transformed into a nature reserve and a substantial garden made among the pine woods. The whole operation was an essay in idealism, their enterprise a lifetime's commitment comparable to the work of Antonio and Iris Origo at La Foce in Tuscany.

A series of terraces and formal gardens was cut out of the woodland at Cap Roig. The first had a garden of four compartments near the house, with squares of *Cupressus sempervirens*, clumps of the pastel blue *Echium fastuosum*, and white arum lilies. Below it the Woevodskys designed a formal scheme of beds edged with variegated griselinia and filled with busy lizzies: the semicircular pool in the middle was planted with tufts of *Cyperus involucratus*. One of the lower terraces was known as 'The Cloister Walk' because it progressed through arches of local stone: plants of *Pittosporum tobira* clipped as standards grew between the arches in round beds underplanted with coleus. The Woevodskys called another terrace, nearly 300 m (320 yd) long, the Geranium Walk. The raised bed on the higher side was filled with many different pelargoniums and edged with all the ivy-leaved types, which trailed down the retaining wall, while the varieties on the seaward side were trained up wire pyramids in vast terracotta pots. The Woevodskys particularly enjoyed making colour features in the garden: Corporals' Walk, for example, was planted with yellow mimosas mixed with pale *Agave attenuata* and underscored by drifts of blue crassulas, while another was lined with broad drifts of *Atriplex halimus* and *Feijoa sellowiana*.

Cap Roig was an extraordinary garden, in its heyday quite unlike any other. It was unusual for its size: in no other Mediterranean garden was such a large area turned into a woodland garden in the English manner. It was remarkable for the vivid colours of the underplanting: few would seek to brighten up a nature reserve by cramming so many contrasts into the composition. The results were little short of spectacular and call to mind the brightly

---

Castillo Cap Roig. A cloistered shady corner of this garden, designed and planted on a vast scale by the English Woevodskys between 1925 and 1975.

Dorothy Woevodsky with Neron, her Great Dane, in the garden she made at Cap Roig, 1968.

coloured rhododendron gardens of southern England – the Valley Gardens of Windsor Great Park, perhaps, or Exbury House. It was exceptional too because many of the effects were obtained with seasonal bedding, which is expensive in equipment, materials and labour. Perhaps the garden it most resembled was Alice de Rothschild's Villa Victoria at Grasse, although that prodigy is known only as a historical memory while Cap Roig still exists, albeit on a reduced scale.

The garden of the Marquesa de Casa Valdés near Guadalajara in central Spain is interesting because it was made in the English style in the 1950s by an intellectual anglophile Spaniard. The Marquesa published the definitive modern study of Spanish gardens, *Los Jardines de España*, in 1973, but in her own garden chose to combine the traditional Spanish elements of water, evergreens and strong lines with an English diversity of plants and an artistic manner in their planting. Most of the plants and many of the garden ornaments came from England. Names such as *Viburnum × bodnantense* were unknown in Spain until the Marquesa introduced them in the mid twentieth century. She was also one of the first Spaniards to make a collection of old shrub roses. You can usually date a rose garden from the roses planted in it: 'Variegata di Bologna', 'Mme Pierre Oger' and the hybrid musks associate the Marquesa's with the early days of the Graham Stuart Thomas movement.

At Cala Ratjada in the 1960s, near the rocky eastern end of the island of Majorca, Russell Page designed a garden to hold Bartolomeo March's collection of sculpture. The hillside was terraced and planted with Moorish arches of clipped cypress, beds of agapanthus and standard specimens of *Magnolia grandiflora*. These frame the view of the house from the entrance gate, but the drive winds up the terraces, criss-crossing the avenues: the perspectives at Cala Ratjada are not for the motor car, only for the eye. Page used the natural woodland of Aleppo pine and its *garrigue* as a background for some of the larger pieces in March's collection. Even the flowers and exotic species are only a setting for the display of art. In a glade cut out of a grove of venerable olive trees, March and Page placed a collection of abstract works by such masters as Barbara Hepworth and Francisco Barón. His treatment of the site exemplifies two of Page's talents, a willingness to work to the specific brief of his patron, and an ability to subordinate his horticultural instincts to the principles of good design.

English plantsmen have long recognised that the north-west coast of Spain has the climate for growing the widest possible variety of plants. Galicia is still a remote and romantic part of Spain, associated in the imagination with medieval pilgrimages to Santiago de Compostela. Visitors tell of the baroque splendours of Pazo d'Oca, where *Camellia reticulata* grows to 10 m (33 ft), and of the annual Camellia Show in Vigo, Pontevedra or Vilagarcía, the social equivalent to the Chelsea Flower Show, attended by the King and Queen of Spain. Frost is unknown in much of Galicia, where rainfall can exceed 2 m (66 in) a year and the fertility is proverbial in Spain. The countryside around the Rias Bajas is parcelled into small landholdings given to vines, maize, cabbages and dairying; 2 ha (5 acres) will support a modest family.

Very few British nationals live in Galicia and, despite its reputation among English plantsmen, only one has ever chosen to move there specifically to garden in a frost-free climate. When Robert Gimson bought La Saleta near Mosteiro in 1969 he was fortunate in this area of smallholdings to find a house with as much as 5.5 ha (14 acres) of land. After a few years, he and his wife decided to build a second house in a better position a hundred metres to the side, with long views down to the south-east and across the valley beyond Mosteiro.

Galicia itself is a massif of granite and the stone is used for every form of construction. La Saleta is an eighteenth-century manor-house with a coat of arms carved on the granite wall of the roof end and a granite belfry on top. There are granite outcrops in every part of the garden. The formal garden and rectangular pool in front of the house have granite edgings. The stone is used in the retaining walls of the terraces, for the kerbs which edge some of the paths and for the rough-cut posts of the pergola of vines which runs round one of the boundaries and yields the sharp stony wine called Albariño. One of the boundary fences is made, in traditional Galician fashion, of narrow upright slabs of granite hammered into the soil.

La Saleta is almost entirely surrounded by pine woods interplanted with tall eucalyptus which give protection from the prevailing westerlies. Many of the exotics planted by Robert Gimson were evergreen, notably from the Australian members of the Myrtaceae, and the camellias, in which he had a particular interest. Even in the depths of winter there is a greenness to the garden which is reflected in the woodland around. The design of the garden is informal, with little attempt to group plants for their ornamental associations. Some of the paths are broad and straight, while others follow a more natural contour. La Saleta is a plantsman's garden, so the cultural requirements of plants come first, and advantage has been taken of variations in aspect to increase the range of what is grown. One of the terraces has been topped with shingle to provide sharp drainage to plants which cannot tolerate the wet winters of north-west Spain. Gimson's collection of Australian and South African natives is formidable. Innumerable species of callistemon, protea, hakea, leptospermum, grevillea and banksia are the result of the extensive correspondence which Robert Gimson maintained with botanic gardens in South Africa, New Zealand and Australia. Among the rarer plants are *Pomaderris lanigera*, *Mirbelia oxylobioides* (a legume from eastern Australia) and *Azara petiolaris*. Gimson turned a small copse of oaks and pines into a woodland garden that would look at home on the Surrey hills or among the ericaceous collections of northern Sussex. Some of the large-leaved species of the Grande section of *Rhododendron* flourish here alongside the mossy paths. Camellias flower from October to April, while autumn colour is given by

The Marquesa de Casa Valdés's garden in Guadalajara province. The borders near the house, and in the formal gardens framed by English-style lawns, are thickly planted in the Jekyll manner. Note how the irises provide contrasts of form and how thickly everything is planted.

acers, liquidambars and *Franklinia alatamaha*, a large shrub from Georgia in the USA which is now extinct in the wild. Not everything has flourished: bedding roses – hybrid teas and floribundas – need richer soil and have not been a success, unlike the less demanding shrub roses. There are large and healthy bushes of 'Fantin Latour', 'Schneezwerg', 'Mme Hardy' and 'Roseraie de l'Haÿ'. Many plants have begun to naturalise: leptospermums, camellias and acers form extensive colonies of seedlings every year.

THE INTENSE development of the Costa de Sol since 1960 parallels the palmy heyday of the Riviera nearly a century earlier. The scale would surprise even the author of *Mediterranean Winter Resorts*, who suggested in the 1908 edition of his handbook that 'if some capitalist were enterprising enough to build a large hotel ... there is every probability that Málaga would, in time, become a popular health resort'. He predicted that 'the exceeding beauty of the country, the lovely climate, and the interesting associations connected with this part of Spain, would probably draw away many winter *habitués* of the Riviera resorts'. If only he could see the hotels, villas, apartment blocks, golf-courses and time-shares that now blight this coast. An extensive landscape industry services these modern developments where quantity is more important than quality, and low cost, easy maintenance and value for money determine the layout, design and planting of gardens. Most of the effects rely on such well-tried staples as *Hibiscus rosa-sinensis*, bougainvilleas, arctotis and *Pyrostegia venusta*. These no-fuss stand-bys cascade from Moorish arches and spill over Andalusian patios, where their lurid brilliance is intensified by white-painted walls. Whatever the season, the tropical flowers of the Costa del Sol are a tumult of easy colour.

All along the Spanish coastline from Huelva to Gerona there is scarcely a kilometre nowadays without an expatriate Briton who is making a garden. Most are elderly or retired, and have gardened for themselves in England, perhaps with a little help with the vegetables or the hedges: now they must discover how to garden in Spain. Their ideas on what a garden should look like are already formed, so their immediate and greatest problem is to adapt their knowledge to Spanish conditions, while their next difficulty is a lack of information about what is possible in their new environment. Fortunately English gardening clubs exist in several parts of Spain, themselves a sign of the extent of the British community. New members discover that they can grow jonquils, quinces and hybrid musk roses but not trumpet daffodils, pear trees or roses bred for northern Europe. They learn that the Spaniards associate cypresses with cemeteries, olive trees with General Franco, and daturas with a superstition that they induce blindness.

The Club Jardinería de la Costa del Sol publishes *A Simple Guide to Gardening on the Costa del Sol* to help enthusiastic amateurs to avoid 'learning the hard way, by trial and error'. It went into its eighth edition in 1989. Its author, Vernon Maxwell, lived between Benahavis and the coast for twenty years prior to his return to England in 1990, and steadfastly encouraged newcomers to try to enjoy gardening on the Costa del Sol, which he considered 'a Gardener's Paradise'. It may enjoy 'a most equable climate', but it is unfortunately not true that there are 'few plants that will not flourish': you will not find a snowdrop, gentian, field geranium or English oak, for instance, on any of the coasts of southern or eastern Spain. Maxwell nevertheless gives a practical list of the trees, shrubs and climbers that do succeed in the deep south, especially if irrigated, and tackles such problems as pests, diseases and the Spanish names for plants and garden equipment. Further sections which deal with the herb garden ('this is a department in which Cook takes a keen interest'), lawn maintenance ('whether the garden is large or small, a trim, well kept lawn is the making of it') and compost ('every garden should try to produce as much as possible') show just how British his approach was.

New British residents tend to conclude that Spain is a barren land in want of all the good things that characterise the English garden – spacious lawns, variety of planting and colourful flowers – and then set to practising English gardening in a very unEnglish climate. Whether this is because the Spanish tradition is not perceived as sufficiently distinct, or whether it is explained by the different social backgrounds of Costa residents from the nineteenth-century Riviera colonists who embraced French and Italian styles, one might have expected more cognisance to be taken of the Spanish fondness for running water and evergreen shade, or their use of neo-classical detail, or even of the utterly original designs of Antonio Gaudí around Barcelona. Only occasionally does one encounter a patio garden designed and planted in honour of one of the Moorish gardens of Andalusia: Group Captain Bill Wells's garden at Casa del Moro above Marbella, for example, includes a courtyard shaded by orange trees planted around a small pool that was inspired by the gardens of the Alhambra and the Patio de los Naranjos in Seville. The absence of the local tradition is particularly perplexing given the eclecticism of the most gifted garden designer on the Costa del Sol. Gerald Huggan has used Moorish and Persian elements, as well as classical colonnades, baroque balustrading and English plantings, in the gardens of Al Khaldiah which he made for an Arab sheik in Marbella. Its extravagance calls to mind the gardens of the Riviera a hundred years before. Huggan's own garden at Benahavis, however, springs the paradox again. It lies on the pine-wood banks of a broad shallow river which ripples through rocks and boulders like a Scottish salmon water. Grass, mixed borders and the largest hybrid musk roses in Andalusia come together in a fluid design that looks fresh from a book on English country gardens.

Vernon Maxwell's own garden was the paradigm of the enthusiast's English garden on the Costa del Sol. The house was called Puerto de Cortes, a modern building with a low red roof, white-painted walls and a long arcaded loggia all along the front. It was surrounded by sweeping lawns which flowed between island beds, and the grass was quite the finest on the Costa del Sol. Part of a lawn to the side of the house was levelled for croquet, that most exclusive of English summer recreations, which can be enjoyed in every month of the year on a well-irrigated sward in southern Spain. Maxwell made boundary hedges of clipped cypress, and internal divisions of trimmed bougainvilleas, which he also trained as short standards or to grow across the beds and down the small retaining walls as ground cover. His mixed borders of shrubs, roses and herbaceous plants held the classic ingredients of the modern English style. Maxwell was not a dedicated plantsman, but he liked plants that grew well and responded to his attentions. Most of his trees were planted around the edges of the 1.5 ha (4 acre) plot.

Gerald Huggan is the leading horticulturalist and garden designer on the Costa del Sol. This example of his work at Al Khaldiah, in Marbella, incorporates English, Arabic and Andalusian motifs.

Jacarandas, eucalyptus, *Tipuana tipu*, *Calodendrum capense* and the tiger's claw *Erythrina lysistemon* were among his more successful plantings, together with grevilleas, callistemons, bauhinias and poinsettias, and the climbing blue *Thunbergia grandiflora*. English expatriates demand a greater variety of plants than has traditionally been available for Spanish gardens. In 1960 there was not one garden centre along the whole coast of Andalusia. Nurseries have sprung up in response to demand and horticulturists from Australia, California, East Africa and the Cape have all tried their luck in the new market. Vernon Maxwell grew two trees of the rare *Acacia xanthophloeia* from a nurseryman who brought his stock from his earlier nursery in Kenya.

Amongst the many generalists, two specialists stand out. Bill Wells moved to Marbella in the 1960s after farming in Suffolk, and developed an interest in exotic fruits, much as Arpad Plesch had on the Riviera some years before. Lychees, pawpaws, kiwis, loquats, avocados and nuts – pecans from Illinois and macadamias from Queensland – have all proved more amenable to cultivation than the Spanish hor-

ticultural experts predicted. Wells's greatest success has been mangoes, now developed as a commercial crop in the south of Spain wholly as a result of his experiments, which alerted the Andalusian Ministry of Agriculture to their potential. Trials have compared varieties for vigour, season and size: 'Julia' from Trinidad, 'Hayden' from Florida, 'Sandershah' from India, 'Abundoso' from Cuba, 'Sabre' from South Africa and 'Glynn' from California. The better forms have now been propagated in such quantities that there are large plantations of mangoes in the sheltered valleys north of Málaga, with some holdings containing 10,000 or 12,000 trees, all planted in the last few years. Perhaps Group Captain Wells is closer in spirit to Daniel and Thomas Hanbury than to Arpad Plesch.

Mrs Geoffrey Allen of Los Barrios is honoured as an expert on the rich native flora of Andalusia. Her tireless explorations through the countryside for thirty years and more have yielded several plants new to science, and many selections of horticultural value. These include albino forms of four Andalusian natives: the blue periwinkle *Vinca difformis*, the soft pink *Phlomis purpurea*, the rare western form of purple *Rhododendron ponticum* known as *baeticum*, and the crinkly flowered *Cistus albidus*, which, despite its name, is normally purple pink. She has also acquired and distributed among knowledgeable garden owners such rarities as a cross between the native *Phlomis purpurea* and the Jerusalem sage *P. fruticosa*, and the strange result of the intergeneric union of *Narcissus viridiflorus* and *Tapeinanthus humilis*, both pretty but none-too-common autumn flowering bulbs. Such garden owners as Mrs Allen are exceptional, but even the most ardent nationalists, determined to make an ideal English garden, have to adapt to Spanish realities. Most of their gardens, however, are likely to prove completely ephemeral, as were the nineteenth-century gardens of the Riviera. The best look to be made in such enclaves as Marbella, Puerto de Banús and Sotogrande, where money can buy splendid layouts, rich architectural detail and fully mature trees transported Alice de Rothschild style from the olive orchards and palm forests of poorer, rural Spain. But it is too early to say which, if any, will survive to be included in, say, a book such as this in one hundred years' time.

References and Further Reading

The best modern work on the gardens of Spain is *Los jardines de España* by the Marquesa de Casa Valdés (Madrid, 1973), now available in an English translation. The earliest comprehensive study in English was *Spanish Gardens: Their History, Types and Features* by Constance Villiers-Stuart (London, 1929): its descriptions and judgements are still sound. Two classics for the general reader are *Hand-Book for Travellers in Spain* (London, 1845) by Richard Ford, still one of the most perceptive and quite the most amusing of commentators, and Augustus Hare's *Wanderings in Spain* (London, 1873). Quotations from Sir William Dalrymple are again from *Travels through Spain and Portugal, 1774* (London, 1777). The description of Lord Howden's garden is based on J. H. Bennet's *Winter and Spring on the Shores of the Mediterranean* (1873). The story of El Gordo is told in 'Lutyens and Spain' by Gavin Stamp and Margaret Richardson, published in the Barcelona-based periodical *Quaderns* in December 1982. The Duke of Wellington's estates in Spain are described in *Country Life*, 4 and 11 September 1980 by J. N. P. Watson; in writing of the garden at Molino del Rey I have been greatly helped by Major Eudo Tonson-Rye and his daughter Rohays Everard-Thomas. Much of my information about such gardens as La Concepción and El Almendral comes from visiting them and talking to people who know them well, especially Quentin Agnew and Betty Allen. There are descriptions of Monte de la Torre and Guardacorte in the 1989 *Year Book* of the International Dendrology Society, and they have also appeared in *Country Life*. There is much too about the Larios family in *Hounds are Home: The History of the Royal Calpe Hunt* by Gordon Fergusson (London, 1979). I know of Christopher Sandeman's garden only from an article in *Gardener's Chronicle* on 23 May 1925 and from the little that he revealed of himself in his published correspondence (see, for example, *Private and Confidential: Letters to Gertrude Konstam*, London, 1935). The Marquesa de Casa Valdés's own garden was written up for *Country Life*, 17 June 1982 by Tony Venison, who has also written two useful articles about gardens and gardening on the Costa del Sol for the same magazine (16 June 1983 and 23 May 1985). Paul Miles's article in *Country Life*, 9 January 1975, is the only account I know of Castillo Cap Roig, although I visited the garden myself while the Woevodskys were still there. Robert Gimson's garden in Galicia is little known to the English horticultural press and is only briefly described in the obituaries which followed his untimely death in 1988. *A Simple Guide to Gardening on the Costa del Sol* by Vernon Maxwell is a local bestseller. The eighth edition was published in 1989.

Chapter Twelve

FRANCE

Le Style Anglais *and* le Jardin Français

THE ENGLISH landscape movement spread quickly in the mid eighteenth century and was taken up in France before it became popular in Germany, the country where it reached its greatest development outside England. Landscaping was at first a fashion among members of the Court during the last years of the *ancien régime* and so it is around Paris that the best examples of *le style anglais* are to be found. Among the earliest are Ermenonville and Monceau. The Marquis de Girardin began transforming Ermenonville in 1764. Although he regarded his improvements as no more than embellishments to the natural landscape, 'designed to heighten the effects of existing natural situations rather than to create new and purely artificial ones', the changes represent a clear break with the traditional style of Le Nôtre. Girardin's own treatise on landscaping, *De la composition des paysages*, was enormously influential after its publication in 1777. Girardin employed a Scottish head gardener named Murray, assisted by a band of Scots gardeners, to create the rich lawns for which Ermenonville became known. At the same time several Englishmen worked in the Paris region as head gardeners or landscape advisers: a Mr Brown was inspector of the King's gardens at Versailles.

Monceau was begun in 1773 for Philippe Égalité, then Duc de Chartres, sometimes described as an ardent anglophile and sometimes as an anglomaniac. His landscaper Louis Carrogis (1717–1806), known

as Carmontelle, was a pupil of the English landscaper Thomas Whateley. Indeed Carmontelle asserted that Whateley's observations on gardening, which were published in Paris in 1771, inspired him to create Monceau as *'un pays d'illusion'*. It was a small garden, all contained within a restricted compass which, although influenced by English precedents, was rather more of a theatrical conceit than anything in England. It was probably this garden that C. L. L. Hirschfeld had in mind when he observed that the French

in their blind imitation of the English taste ... not only repeat its faults but also add new ones of their own. All that a large park can contain is crowded into an area of no more than half an acre ... new trees, Chinese kiosks, extravagant architecture, buildings, ruins, bridges, and so on; the feeling for simple and natural things appears to have been lost completely.

(*Theorie der Gartenkunst*, 1779)

Historians, French ones in particular, have claimed that Rousseau's *La Nouvelle Héloïse*, published in 1759, was more important to the development of natural landscape gardening in France than any English influence. Hippolyte Taine asserted that it was Rousseau who compelled the French to discover the landscapes beyond their windows and to stroll in nature where previously they had 'only walked between tortured yews'. Rousseau undoubtedly precipitated a growing appreciation of wild countryside, but raw nature was not much admired in the garden. Instead, a picturesque adaptation became fashionable, which derived from the lost gardens described in classical literature as well from the landscapes of such painters as Poussin, Lorrain and Watteau,

---

Ferrières. This statue of the dying Penthesileia, Queen of the Amazons, supported by Achilles, is prominently displayed in the park which Joseph Paxton designed for James de Rothschild.

Ermenonville. A bridge on the edge of the Elysian landscape begun by Girardin in 1764, where Jean-Jacques Rousseau was buried.

themselves inspired by the writings of the ancients. There also grew up an element of dramatic manipulation in the French landscape tradition. William Howard Adams explains that 'real trees became stage props, and artificial lakes became rivers. Unexpected tensions were produced through the juxtaposition of disparate elements.' The French garden was something apart from both the house and the wider landscape. British commentators railed against the vogue for creating an over-theatrical English-style landscape on a small area near the house, detached from the traditional French garden and the farms and woodlands outside. Moreover, French landowners never adopted the new farming methods of the English agrarian revolution, so that even at the end of the nineteenth century the American Henry James could note that 'it is a peasant's landscape not, as in England, a landlord's'.

Thomas Blaikie (1750–1838) was the most successful Briton to establish himself in France as a landscape gardener. He spent almost his entire career on the continent, and made his name working for members of the royal family before the Revolution.

He was employed on improving Parc Monceau for Philippe Égalité, by now Duc d'Orléans, trying in particular to link the house to the garden and to fix it in the wider landscape. He also worked for the young Comte d'Artois, later Charles X, at Bagatelle, the house built in 1777 as the result of a wager with Queen Marie-Antoinette. Artois was able to expand the garden surrounding his château to about 16 ha (40 acres), which was enough for Blaikie's satisfaction, and employed a staff of between twenty and sixty gardeners according to the season. He produced undulating surfaces where before all had been flat, and he laid out winding paths with mazes, summerhouses and grottoes. Part was designed *à la chinoise* as a willow-pattern garden, with little bridges, brooks and Chinese pavilions. Water was drawn up from the Seine but, perhaps because money ran short, the artificial river which was to pass through the garden and surround several islets stopped short halfway: one of these islands, prematurely and gloomily named Île des Tombeaux, remained high and dry.

The architect of the house, François-Joseph

Belanger (1744–1818), also had a hand in designing the garden at Bagatelle. Belanger had studied in England and visited Stourhead and Stowe, but he did not always agree with Blaikie, who was an unashamed devotee of Capability Brown. Blaikie would insist, for example, upon large open spaces of grass, isolated clumps of trees and the use of individual specimen trees as focal points. He was interested in introducing exotic trees into the landscape, an English enthusiasm (although Blaikie was actually a Scot) which did not catch on in France until well into the nineteenth century. Blaikie also collaborated with Belanger at the nearby Folies de Saint-James, an extravagant, eccentric project where water was raised by steam pump (as at Bagatelle) to form a large artificial lake, and a vast artificial rock cave was filled with an entire Doric portico on the water's edge. Belanger's very different approach to landscaping is summarised by the concluding words of a lecture on garden design he gave some years later: 'Choisir un site salubre, productif et agréable, enrichir son voisinage de tous les différents aspects que peut conquérir la vie pratique ... y réserver des repos, élever des autels à Flore, à Cérès, à Pomone, à la Céleste Amitié, tel doit être le but qui conduit

l'homme sensible à se créer un jardin.' The intellectual confusion this suggests was scorned by the practical Scotsman: Blaikie noted in his diary that the French 'look upon a house and a garden as two objects that do not correspond with the other'. When he proposed removing the 3 m (10 ft) wall that surrounded Bagatelle 'to give an open elegance to the house, and join the Gardens', he encountered considerable opposition.

In 1835 Bagatelle was acquired by the Marquess of Hertford, one of the richest men of his day with an estimated annual income in the 1860s of £250,000. He spent much of his fortune in the pursuit of fine arts. It was said that he could only be outbid in the sales rooms of Paris by the presence of Baron James de Rothschild. Hertford was able to expand the area of the garden to 24 ha (60 acres): among his improvements are the handsome orangery and classical parterres at Bagatelle. J. C. N. Forestier observed that both Hertford and his son Sir Richard Wallace had a 'goût passionné' for Bagatelle and its surroundings. In fact they formalised and Frenchified it, destroying many of the chinois details, rockeries and mock mausoleums and replacing them with aviaries, belvederes and clipped hedges. Hertford also introduced

This part of the garden at Bagatelle was designed for the Comte d'Artois by Thomas Blaikie in the 1780s.

into the park a number of marble vases and statues from Vaux. It was said that two of his friends wished to fight a duel in the park: Hertford refused permission on the grounds that, although he was indifferent to any injury they might cause to each other, he was fearful that their wild shooting might damage his statues.

The interpretation which French garden designers made of the English landscape style became ever more extravagant after the restoration of the monarchy in 1815. Achille Duchêne, who laid out the new water terraces and parterres at Blenheim in the 1920s, wrote in *Les Jardins de l'avenir* (Paris, 1935) of the mid nineteenth century as '*l'époque d'abondance cossue*' when French gardens were a decadent parody of nature, characterised by

vallonnements de pelouses exagérées, fausses petites-rivières à fond de ciment, ponts rustiques, grottes en similirocher, arbres rares d'importation mis en valeur sur des éminences de terre, abus des oppositions de négundos blancs avec des *Prunus pissardii*, corbeilles de fleurs, rondes ou ovales, surhaussées comme des surtouts de table,

abondance des mosaïcultures, kiosques en série d'exposition, abris, bancs, le tout affligé, le plus souvent, d'une totale absence de bon goût.

There were, however, exceptions to the general rule that French designers learnt nothing and forgot nothing in the nineteenth century. One fresh influence was Alphonse Karr's *Voyage autour de mon jardin*, which was exceptionally popular in France and indeed across the Channel after the first translation into English in 1854. Karr's book is part meditation and part exposition – charming, discursive and original. He taught the French to find a sense of wonder in all the living things within a garden. When he moved to St-Raphaël in 1864 he wrote to a friend back in Paris, 'Come and plant your walking-stick in my garden. When you awake next morning you will find it sprouting with roses.' Karr was a precursor of another colossus, Édouard André, an intellectual anglophile, almost a Victorian Frenchman, who revelled in the progress that horticulture had made, and sought to advance it further. André was sufficiently shrewd to observe that, although the

Sphinxes at Bagatelle. Their faces are sometimes said to have been modelled on the Comte d'Artois's mistress; in fact they were acquired years later by the Marquess of Hertford.

Ferrières (c. 1875), the château seen across Joseph Paxton's landscape park.

cultivation of gardens and the science of horticulture had made great steps forward, the *art* of gardening had scarcely progressed at all. He became a sort of French William Robinson, held in such regard that he acquired several commissions in England, landscaping for the very people who had invented the landscape movement. André's most famous work, and one he considered among his best, was the design of Sefton Park for the city of Liverpool in 1867. His *L'Art des jardins – traité général de la composition des parcs et jardins* (Paris, 1879) is a substantial compendium more than 850 pages long, of the sort so dear to the French. It systematically explores the history, aesthetics, composition and classification of gardens, and lays down a modified landscape style as the ideal.

One garden of which Édouard André wholeheartedly approved was Ferrières, east of Paris, which Paxton designed for James de Rothschild. Paxton was the outstanding personality of English gardening in the period between John Loudon and William Robinson. It was a time when improvements in technical excellence and horticultural craftsmanship kept pace with the fast-expanding wealth of industrial England. Paxton was an exponent of the gardenesque school: he extolled unity of com-

position, contrast and variety within that unity, and a balance of mass and void, which meant, for example, that he understood the need for open lawn between the pleasure garden, the park and the background planting. The application of such principles at Ferrières distinguished it from contemporary French essays in landscaping of the kind ridiculed by Duchêne.

Paxton's first association with the Rothschilds had been the design of the 350 ha (865 acre) park at Mentmore for Mayer Rothschild, head of the English branch of the family. In 1852 James de Rothschild saw the plans for Mayer's new mansion at Mentmore. Perhaps the thought of being outdone by a nephew was too much for him. It is said that he summoned the architect to Paris and ordered him to 'build me a Mentmore, only bigger'. Paxton obliged with a square mansion in the style that was then thought typical of the Italian Renaissance. The Goncourt brothers visited it in July 1858 and did not like it at all. They called it 'an idiotic and ridiculous extravagance, a pudding of every period, the fruit of a stupid ambition to have all monuments in one!' It is hard to agree with this dismissive judgement; the house is certainly Italianate rather than Italian, but it is more than just a stylistic conglomerate. Indeed, the purity of its lines and the homogeneity of its details compare well with many mid-nineteenth-century *folies de grandeur*. The last member of the family to live there, Guy de Rothschild, considers Ferrières to be France's most magnificent example of nineteenth-century domestic architecture.

Paxton laid out the grounds between 1855 and 1859. Although 400 ha (1,000 acres) of the 4,000 ha estate were enclosed by a high stone wall, the house does not have a long approach. The distance from the gate lodges to the house itself is no more than 200 m (220 yd), and the drive is lined with formal gardens, giant urns and sunken pools. Paxton grounded the house in a grand series of parterres below a terrace where huge trees of the hardy palm *Trachycarpus fortunei* were wheeled out for the summer in orange boxes. Broad staircases led down to the lawns: the descent on the southern side is guarded by a monumental pair of lions couchant. Paxton laid out the park in the classical English landscape style, with large clumps of blue Atlas cedars, wellingtonias, hornbeams and copper beeches. It is an eighteenth-century park planted with nineteenth-century trees. An English equivalent would be the garden planted around Fonthill Abbey in Wiltshire for the Marquess of Westminster in 1846. Guy de Rothschild explains that Paxton 'not only planted a great number of rare trees, but also skilfully composed a variety of vistas and landscapes, as only the English know how to do. Several decades later, the walks were an enchantment, due as much to human genius as to the work of nature.'

The lawns run down to a large natural-looking lake in front of the house which Paxton excavated. A group of three Austrian pines *Pinus nigra* at the edge stands like a sculpture of the Graces and provides a focal point for the design. In winter the frozen surface of the lake is covered with russet leaves of beeches and taxodiums. Narrow points are spanned by bridges, made to eighteenth-century designs that could have come straight from Painshill or Monceau. One rather rustic model leads to an Île d'Amour in a prominent inlet near the house. This corner has a picturesque *chinois* air that owes much more to the eighteenth century than the nineteenth. It is set among tufa grottoes and planted with trees of weeping habit – ash, lime and sophora. William Robinson admired the weeping sophoras, but Robinson commended everything at Ferrières, especially the model standards of cultivation and maintenance which he attributed to English influence. Ferrières was 'an oasis amid the dreary fields of this part of

France ... [because] the gardens show an instructive mixture of the best features of the horticulture of both countries'. He particularly praised the fruit garden, whose espaliered trees at 3 m (10 ft) were twice the height usually seen in England.

Others felt that Ferrières was overdone. The Goncourt brothers were quick with their verdict: 'we are just back from Ferrières ...' they wrote in July 1858, 'trees and waterworks created by the squandering of millions ... nothing superlative, nothing outstanding on this land where one man's fantasy has sown bank-notes ...' The Goncourts may not have liked Ferrières, but the Rothschilds had no difficulty in persuading the Emperor Napoleon III to visit them, and he planted a giant redwood *Sequoiadendron giganteum* on 16 December 1862 to commemorate the occasion. The extent and skill of Paxton's planting took a while to become apparent. Guy de Rothschild tells us that, since his ancestors planned to be at Ferrières mostly in the autumn, Paxton carefully selected trees and shrubs whose colours were most splendid at that time of year. 'The grounds then blazed with multicoloured fires: the usual gold and brown of French forests, but also rarer tones – the russet highlights of maples, the gleaming purple of copper beeches which Paxton had "carelessly strewn" here and there, the blood-red of Virginian creepers.'

In England Paxton is chiefly associated with Chatsworth and, in a sense, Ferrières can be seen as the French Chatsworth, the model by which other gardens were judged. None had a greater range of glasshouses, none produced finer fruit or propagated so many exotic plants, none attained such heights of neatness and order. Robinson wrote of the orangery: 'nothing can exceed the health and beauty of the specimens grown in enormous but well-designed tubs, and standing so close together that the dense heads touch, and one seems in an Orange-grove'. Unfortunately, the orangery has recently been destroyed by fire, and remains boarded up. It stands at the end of a double lime avenue which leads the eye to a Temple of Love on the top of the hill. This may have been inspired by the example built at Méréville by Jean-Joseph de Laborde in 1784, which stood first on an island in the river Juine, and later on a dramatic hilltop as at Ferrières; it recalled not only the paintings of Poussin and Lorrain but also the classic Sibyl shrine at Tivoli.

In 1960, Baron Guy, the great-grandson of James de Rothschild, moved with his wife Marie-Hélène back into Ferrières, which had been empty since the

The Emperor Napoléon III planting a giant redwood to commemorate his visit to Ferrières in 1862. The tree still stands.

beginning of the war, stripped and defaced by the Nazis. The restoration of Ferrières to something of its pre-war splendour was a declaration that the Rothschild fortunes were reborn and an assertion of confidence in the future. That bright dawn was marred by the events of 1968, though the Rothschilds lost no time in adapting to the changes. In 1975, Guy removed all the contents of Ferrières to his house in Paris and gave the château with 140 ha (340 acres) to the University of Paris. He built a modern house on another part of the estate and commissioned Russell Page to design the garden. 'The extravagant dream that Guy and Marie-Hélène had created at Ferrières,' Page wrote, 'proved to be just that – a dream.'

After the end of the Napoleonic wars, English colonies grew up in several parts of France. Such towns and cities as Montpellier, Pau, Bordeaux, Aix-les-Bains, Dieppe and Boulogne each had a substantial English presence right up until the Second World War. The modern English preference is for rural retreats in Burgundy and the Dordogne, where there are some good gardens in the making. In the nineteenth century most Englishmen went to France in search of a milder climate or better health,

although it was a love of field sports that drew winter residents to Pau, where foxhounds hunted: 'Leicestershire in Béarn'. The American Edwin Asa Dix wrote in 1891 that four thousand Britons wintered there, so that 'Pau in the season is a British oligarchy ... there are titles and there is money; there are drives, calls, card-parties; dances and dinners; clubs; theatres, a casino, English schools, churches; tennis, polo, cricket; racing, coaching – and, *Anglicissime*, a tri-weekly fox-hunt!' When in 1878 the mayor and councillors, after protracted negotiations, were able to acquire for public enjoyment the landscaped gardens of Parc Beaumont in the middle of Pau, the English colony applied for permission to commandeer a corner for a tennis-court. The best garden at Pau, however, was the Parc Lawrence, which belonged not to an Englishman but to an American.

There was for many years a small colony of English gentlefolk at Tresserve in Savoy. Its members lived in the memory of Queen Victoria's sojourns at nearby Aix-les-Bains in 1885, 1887 and 1890, and included the celebrated gardener and botanist Ellen Willmott, who had bought the Château de Tresserve in 1890.

Tresserve. Ellen Willmott's own photograph of the house which she owned for nearly thirty years.

Her neighbour Sir Henry Bellingham had the largest house at Tresserve; his garden was planted by Gertrude Jekyll. Bellingham was an enthusiastic amateur botanist and gardener, and a close friend of Ellen Willmott; both were devout Roman Catholics, at a time when English papists still preferred each other's company. The park around his house is now conspicuous only for its mature conifers: there are no obvious relics of the Jekyll planting. Villa Bellingham was altogether grander than the Château de Tresserve and it is still privately owned, whereas Ellen Willmott's house has become the *mairie*.

Château de Tresserve was built in the nineteenth century in the style of an alpine manor-house. It sits at the highest point of the village and the garden runs down almost to the edge of Lake Bourget. The climate is continental, despite its proximity to France's largest inland lake: average summer temperatures are several degrees higher than in any part of England, while the winters are notably colder. The range of plants which the climate and the limestone soil will support is restricted, but alpine plants were Willmott's earliest interest. She spent the money a rich cousin gave for her coming of age on creating an alpine garden at Warley Place, her parents' house in Essex. The rock garden she made at Tresserve was designed with a stream and pools bordered by vast boulders, all the better for seeming to occur naturally, and planted with such plants as dwarf rhododendrons, trilliums and primulas. It belongs to the same school of massive stonework as the great rock garden at Wisley made by the Royal Horticultural Society, of which Miss Willmott was a trustee. When planting Tresserve, she bought extravagantly from her friend the Swiss botanist Henri Correvon, who ran the Jardin Alpin d'Acclimatisation at Geneva. Correvon acted as a plant broker on the side, and Willmott authorised him to send her any plant he considered suitable for either Tresserve or Warley.

One of several pergolas at Tresserve on Lake Bourget, photographed by Ellen Willmott at the turn of the century. Here she grew many of the roses for her definitive publication The Genus Rosa.

Ellen Willmott built terraces and steps immediately below the house, but these gave way to a network of straight gravel paths which ran down and across the hillside. Some were enclosed by pergolas and arbours of wood or iron. One splendid length was completely draped with *Clematis montana*; others with honeysuckles, wisterias or roses. Despite these strong structural features – and others which included a Doric colonnade around a well-head where Miss Willmott ate outdoors – Tresserve was a garden of plants, rich in variety. Indeed the plants so dominated the design that the impression was of luxuriance and colour rather than formality. This was increased by Willmott's practice of putting out white-painted tubs and casks for the summer, some with trees 2–3 m (6–10 ft) high in them. She also demanded gardenesque arrangements of tender exotics, with conspicuous cordylines and love-lies-bleeding.

Ellen Willmott is perhaps best remembered for her two-volume study *The Genus Rosa*. It was at Tresserve that she made her greatest collection of rose species and practised the art of hybridising. Vigorous varieties were trained around elegant wooden pyramids in the French style. Her Irish friend William Gumbleton estimated that she grew over 11,000 roses at Tresserve. On another occasion he wrote of an order for 400 cwt (20 tons/tonnes) of bulbs from a nurseryman in Cork: it is clear that Ellen Willmott planted lavishly, even extravagantly. All was maintained for just two annual visits, one at Corpus Christi when the collections of irises and paeonies were in bloom, and the other in autumn.

As well as the many plants named *willmottiae* or *warleyensis* which commemorated the energy and achievements of Ellen Willmott, there was once a verbena with large umbels of rose-pink flowers called 'Tresserve'. It received an Award of Merit from the

Bois-les-Moutiers. Edwin Lutyens set voussoir *tiles into the rendering of the arch to continue the perspectives of the pergola.*

Royal Horticultural Society in 1897 but is now extinct, like its creator's garden. Almost the only relics of Ellen Willmott's work at Tresserve are three venerable specimens of *Fagus sylvatica* 'Tricolor', an overgrown Japanese maple and half a dozen trees of *Magnolia grandiflora*. More poignant is a shrine to Our Lady which she set into the wall of the gatehouse in memory of her parents. It is the sole personal record of Tresserve's occupation for thirty years by one of England's greatest gardener-botanists. The lower parts of the garden are now a football pitch for the village. Housing developments have encroached upon much of the remainder. Trees have been allowed to grow unchecked so that they interfere with the view of the mountains opposite. A meretricious bronze bust has recently been placed in a conspicuous corner of the garden. It is not of Ellen Willmott, but of the French romantic poet Alphonse de Lamartine: it was at Tresserve that he formed his romantic attachment to Julie Charles in 1816.

The English who chose to live at such towns as Boulogne and Dieppe in the late nineteenth and early twentieth centuries often did so for reasons of economy. One exception was the Prime Minister Lord Salisbury, whose holiday house Châlet Cecil overlooked the little valley of Puys about 3 km (2 miles) east of Dieppe. But the best English garden in Normandy was designed at nearby Varengeville by Edwin Lutyens for Guillaume Mallet, a member of the Huguenot banking family, and an enthusiast for painting, collecting and botany. Lutyens fell for Bois-les-Moutiers. 'Oh Emy it is so lovely here,' he wrote to his wife in August 1898, 'so quiet and delicious . . . and the smells are all so good. You will come here one day.' Lady Emily did indeed visit it, and through the Mallets she was introduced to theosophy, the cult that was to have such an effect on the Lutyens's life together.

The house at Bois-les-Moutiers is a rare instance of art nouveau modernism in Lutyens's work. It is first seen from a short brick drive which opens straight off the road. The approach is framed by cob walls, tiled copings and thick mixed borders edged with grass, but the courtyard in front of the house immediately introduces a cross axis. This begins in a formal garden, entirely planted in white, where such shrubs as the hydrangea 'Mme Émile Mouillère' and Iceberg roses are interplanted with white foxgloves, hostas and violas. The long axis continues through two arched gateways – Lutyens set *voussoir* tiles into the rendering to create perspective effects – and passes under a pergola laden with climbing plants to end at a Chinese pavilion which gives shelter to a copy of Donatello's statue of David and Goliath.

Lutyens's inventive genius dominates the formal parts at Bois-les-Moutiers. The park and woodland garden, which run gently down towards the sea, are Guillaume Mallet's own work. Mallet admired the gardens of William Kent and the landscapes of Claude Lorrain and Gaspard Dughet. Every vista in his woodland garden was based on Kent's designs and the drawings of these masters. His sense of colour was refined by observation and reflection: the planting of the rich red rhododendrons 'Alarm' and 'Ascot Brilliant' among the blue cedars *Cedrus atlantica* 'Glauca' was inspired by the colours of the Renaissance tapestries, a borrowing from textiles that Gertrude Jekyll would immediately have understood. Bois-les-Moutiers now belongs to Mallet's grandson Robert, whose additions have been less successful. It is not easy, even for the most anglophile and civilised of Frenchmen, to practise English ideas on colours: the drifts of garish modern azaleas in the park would not have found favour with *la Jekyll*.

None of the English communities in France was to produce an architect or landscaper who designed in the French style, as Cecil Pinsent emerged to serve the expatriate residents of Tuscany. Nor did the influence of living in France create a neo-French renaissance in Victorian England to match the fashion for Italian and Italianate gardens. There are comparatively few examples of French gardens made by Englishmen on either side of the Channel. The gardens of individual Englishmen in France who did not form part of an established colony were often characterised by an excess of Englishness in fiction as well as in fact. Dornford Yates described the garden attached to the imaginary *House That Berry Built*; Bendor, Duke of Westminster, built a house for boar hunting at Mimizon in the Landes, to designs by Sir Herbert Baker, in the Cape Dutch style. Loelia Westminster planted rambling roses and irises which grew surprisingly well in the fine white sand. But not all the English who settled in rural France were rich and snobbish like Yates and the Duke.

Susannah Cooper's family were impoverished Irish gentry, but in 1885 she married a French Quaker Edouard Majolier and went to live with him at Congénies in Gard. Her granddaughter, Nicolette Devas, explained how 'Granny made an Irish garden in Languedoc. Two hectares (5 acres) were stolen from the cultivation of the vine and the olive, and furthermore, walled to assert a *jardin d'agrément*.' Quince trees, almonds, jujubes, cherries, prunes and pears were torn out for a lawn. Mme Majolier made a tennis court, a croquet pitch on gravel, pergolas of roses and a summer-house, greatly to the disapproval of both her husband's Quaker relations and their peasant neighbours. *Le Parc de Madame Suzanne Majolier*, as it was called, was the only garden intended purely for enjoyment in the small agricultural village, in the words of her granddaughter 'a flourish of Irish extravagance and French Quaker money'. Such a garden could not survive in provincial France. By 1971 there were strawberries on the tennis-court and artichokes for market in the flowerbeds. 'Only the lilacs and roses survived where they could,' observed Devas, 'like dispossessed aristocrats.'

English designers made gardens for French owners. The Parc de Clères in Seine-Maritime was laid out in

The rose pergola which the Anglo-Irish Susannah Majolier built in the 1890s at Congénies in Gard; the villagers were shocked by the appropriation of good agricultural land for a garden.

1919 by Avray Tipping, the influential architectural historian and editor of *Country Life*. The château is built on medieval foundations and was restored after the First World War by Jean Delacour (1890–1985), the naturalist and conservationist. Delacour was a sort of French Peter Scott: his garden and zoo were from the start intended for the enjoyment and education of a wider public. Tipping was asked to take into account the needs of free-roaming animals and birds as well as plants; achieving this, while making a collection and pleasing the eye, called for great skill. The result is a cross between Slimbridge and Glyndebourne which has nothing to match it in England. Colette considered it a terrestrial Eden.

Tipping placed a broad formal terrace of stone slabs in front of the house and enclosed it by hedges of yew and box, with pieces of topiary at the corners. To this day, the use of paving rather than gravel strikes the French as a strange and not entirely happy choice of materials. The formal beds within the terracing are planted with such herbaceous plants as ajuga, golden rod and lupins. The whole is strongly reminiscent of gardens in the neo-Tudor style made popular by Reginald Bloomfield and the *Country Life* school of garden designers: Knightshayes in Devon is one that Clères calls immediately to mind. The land drops away below the terrace across a curving sweep of grass to a landscaped water garden whose banks are thick with gunnera. A double border at the side has a massed planting of Michaelmas daisies inspired by Gertrude Jekyll's famous 'aster garden' at Munstead Wood. The main part of the park, where most of the animals and birds range, is laid out in the landscape style to merge with the woods and hills beyond. Despite the vicissitudes of the Second World War, when all the animals were destroyed, the garden and zoo at Clères reopened in 1947 and have lasted better than many of their contemporaries in southern England. It is to the great gardens across the Channel that Clères has to be compared; irony has dictated that one of the purest examples of an English 1920s garden should be preserved in northern France.

Better still is the present condition of another

Pontrancart, near Dieppe. One of the modern parterres designed by Russell Page with blocks of different plants – box, lavender and santolina – in a garden intended to look its best during August.

pre-war designer garden in Normandy – Pontrancart, a handsome brick Louis XIII château in a broad chalk valley near Dieppe. When an Argentine family called Bemberg bought it in 1930 they employed an English garden designer Kitty Lloyd Jones; she was the artist who planted the famous garden at Upton House near Banbury, now owned by the National Trust. The connecting outdoor rooms of yew at Pontrancart are planted with annuals and perennials each in a single colour range. All is planned for a single spectacular season of flower when the family is in residence at the end of August and beginning of September. The modern water garden made by Russell Page on the edge of the lawn fits awkwardly into these surroundings.

THE MOST POPULAR garden in France today was laid out in 1883 by Claude Monet at Giverny near Vernon in Eure. English visitors sometimes suppose him to have been influenced by herbaceous borders beyond the Channel, so familiar does Monet's garden seem. True, the bursting colours of Giverny are far removed from classical French seventeenth-century landscapes, but in fact there is nothing English about his design. Not that the rectangular beds divided by gravel paths belong to the French tradition either, for the formal layout was merely a convenience, as it was for William Robinson at Gravetye. Monet called it his *clos normand*, because he made it from a Norman apple orchard.

Monet stated that his garden was inspired by the tulip fields of Holland, but the principal source of his planting schemes appears to have been the gardenesque tradition of ornamental bedding. The art of planting in bright colours for summer and autumn effect attained marvels of invention and complexity towards the end of the nineteenth century. In England at the time these achievements were already under vehement attack from such critics as William Robinson, who preached a more natural form of gardening. The French, however, had no tradition of cottage gardening or plantsmanship, and tended moreover to treat their gardens as separate from the landscape. This detachment allowed bedding artists to pile on the ornamental effects; the massing of colours became an object in itself. Yet not only did Monet's garden spring from horticultural methods that had peaked in England, but it also initiated a whole school of its own, still admired and emulated in France today.

Giverny was not a garden for demure treasures,

such as are found in the gardens of connoisseurs: Monet liked his flowers bold and exciting. Detail was less important than texture and the effect of concentrated colour; profusion was essential. Every season brought new combinations and compositions; little of the planting was permanent. Winter introduced sheets of snowdrops; with spring came broad masses of irises, all of a single colour; the summer perennials were paeonies and oriental poppies, followed by michaelmas daisies. But annuals and bedding plants were the mainstay. Nasturtiums, for instance, were the outstanding feature of late autumn: they spread across the broad arcaded walk until their trailing tips and large round leaves covered the surface and hid the gravel.

Horticulturists and art historians have always been fascinated by the connection between Monet's paintings and gardening. As early as 1891 the critic Octave Mirbeau wrote that the garden was

an extraordinary mingling of colours, a riot of pale tints, a resplendent and musical profusion of white, pink, yellow and mauve, an incredible rolling of pale flesh tones, against which shades of orange explode, fanfares of blazing copper ring, reds bleed and flare, violets disport themselves, black-purples are licked with flame.

The Englishman Stephen Gwyn was more analytical, on a visit shortly after Monet's death:

The painter ... aimed at ... an effect of the whole. All was a flicker of bright colour; form was given by the use of trees, limes, conifers and one or two Japanese maples, crimson or bronze. Looking close, one could see careful planning; common willowherb had been brought in for its tall shafts of clear colour; they were ranged in clumps at intervals; nothing was left stray, yet the whole effect seemed as carelessly variegated as a wheat field where poppies and blue corn cockle have scattered themselves. All fell together like a pheasant's plumage or a peacock's.

Monet's techniques are more clearly seen if he is compared to his influential English contemporary, Gertrude Jekyll. She also experimented at length with plants and colours, but began her studies from a different standpoint, which brought her to opposite conclusions. Gertrude Jekyll's studies were rooted in Surrey cottage gardens, where plants flowered in artless abundance. Her choice of model was partly a reaction against carpet bedding, although she adapted the principles that had been applied to bedding to give order, form and structure to her plantings. Monet relied upon contrast and repetition to build up his textures and sense of scale. He constructed patterns of often dissonant colours, and amplified the effect by repeating the grouping over and over again. Jekyll placed special stress in *Wood and Garden* (1899) upon gardening for consonance rather than contrast, and variety in place of volume. She maintained that it was important for plants to look happy and at home. 'I try for beauty and harmony everywhere and especially for harmony of colour,' she explained; 'a garden so treated gives the delightful feeling of repose, and refreshment, and purest enjoyment of beauty, that seems to my understanding to be the best fulfilment of its purpose.' Miss Jekyll developed her ideas clearly and authoritatively in *Colour Schemes for the Flower Garden* (1910). She warned that colours could clash, and with disagreeable results. She analysed why one plant sets off another. Jekyll preferred the interweaving of long swathes to the repetition of clumps; she seldom repeated a plant, yet sought to achieve unity. Graham Thomas explains how these sausage-shaped drifts, narrow and gently laid obliquely to the line of the border, each contributed a small area of colour, but when looked at from a distance they overlapped in a medley of graded tints. 'The result is that when a certain plant has spent its flowers, it presents the minimum of a gap in the scheme from either direction.'

The English tradition of gardening with flowers retains a strong following in France, bolstered by horticultural clubs and magazines devoted to idealised English gardens. Enthusiasts find, however, that the range of plants available to garden owners in France is substantially smaller than in the United Kingdom. Moura Lympany has described how in the mid 1970s the neighbours at her cottage in the village of Rasiguères in Roussillon admired 'the million stars' of her *Clematis montana* and the sight of her climbing rose 'The Garland' covering a pear tree 'as if with snow': they had never seen either plant before, and were certain that Moura Lympany would have no fruit from the tree.

The gulf between French and English garden owners is well illustrated by a story, told recently by Sarah Coles in *Hortus*, of meeting a French garden owner (the Duc d'Harcourt) who had designed an attractive 'old' garden and published his own guide to it, *Des jardins heureux*. The book was written in the florid style so popular in France, full of such poetic gems as '*les fleurs portent ce moment d'éternité perçu en présence de l'ephémère*'. Sarah Coles asked the question to which everyone in England, even a

man with a head gardener and five under gardeners, replies with zest: 'How do you feed the soil?' The Duke looked startled, as though she had asked about the plumbing. 'I really don't know,' he said. 'You'll have to ask the gardener.'

Despite the popularity of English-style gardening, many of its leading exponents in France are not actually English. For Princesse Jean de Caraman-Chimay at Château de St-Preuve in Aisne in the 1950s, the essence of making an English garden lay in her choice of interesting plants, so that she succeeded in making herbaceous borders on a hard chalky soil in a continental climate. At Le Vasterival near Dieppe Princess Sturdza has since 1957 made a garden of exceptional originality in its design and use of plants, all the more remarkable for the rarity of those plants and the scale of the entire garden. Le Vasterival manages without architectural or sculptural follies; there are no clipped surfaces, pergolas, or other artifices. Princess Sturdza herself is Norwegian, married to a Romanian, but many of the students who attend her courses at Le Vasterival, and a high proportion of her visitors, are English, learning from a garden that is in some ways more English than any across the Channel.

English garden writers are widely read in France. At the Parc Floral d'Apremont in Berry there is a white garden inspired by Vita Sackville-West's descriptions of Sissinghurst. Artists too look at the possibilities of plants for composition. Prince Peter Wolkonsky is a painter and designer for whom the visual qualities of a plant are more important than its botanical cachet. His garden at Kerdalo in the Côtes du Nord was English enough to inspire his botanist daughter Isabelle to train at Wisley. Kerdalo and Le Vasterival are the two most exciting and 'English' gardens to be made in France since the Second World War.

There are good English gardeners in France too. Wolkonsky's son-in-law Timothy Vaughan has since 1980 restored the Parc de Courson in Essonne, laid out in the landscape style in the mid nineteenth century and now substantially replanted with rare trees and shrubs chosen to combine botanic interest with ornamental potential. The English Baronne Lulu de Waldner has been gardening inventively since she bought Jas Créma in the Vaucluse in 1979: it is within sight of Mont Ventoux, surrounded by cypresses, olives and vines, and has a field of lavender designed to link the parterres in front of the house to the surrounding landscape. In the Dordogne there are many promising gardens, including that created by Mrs Imbiss since 1956 on a site unusual for the abundance of its water supplies. Further south, in the 1980s Francis Egerton worked a green, blue and grey garden among the olive trees of Provence. The structure was determined by the old orchard terraces and included a rectangular pool to reflect the sky. Egerton had learnt from his London garden that foliage is more important than flowers: the colours of the surrounding *maquis* and the heat of summer determined his cool plantings in Provence.

One man dominates garden design in the mid twentieth century: Russell Page, a designer of genius. Some of Page's best work has been in France. He was uniquely at home on both sides of the Channel, introducing English ideas to France and the best of French traditions to England. A tendency in modern English gardens towards introspection, the proliferation of *treillage* and the resurgence of the *potager* as part of the Good Taste English garden are almost entirely due to Page. His only book, *The Education of a Gardener*, published in 1962, remains the most important analysis of the work of a garden designer by a contemporary practitioner. Jane Brown describes it as 'infuriating, entertaining, infinitely wise and inspiring; infuriating because he is repeatedly vague and confusing about the actual garden he is writing about, and hardly ever identifies a place or a garden clearly'. Respect for his clients' privacy may explain this reluctance to name names (except where the client has a grand one to drop, like the Duke of Windsor) but in fact it is not difficult to recognise the gardens of *The Education of a Gardener* when one visits them.

Page drew on many traditions and claimed to have been influenced by Persian, Mogul, Chinese, Japanese and Italian gardens. It is true that elements of most of these can be found in his work but, as one who was reared in England and lived in France, it was inevitably the English and French styles that he understood best and used most in his work. Page admired the way that French gardens extended the formality of the *salon* into the open air. Green drawing-rooms, shade rooms and theatres of greenery for him expressed their nature quite precisely. He admired Le Nôtre, whom he regarded as a great stylist – Page insisted that a garden architect should be vigorous in his search for style – and extolled the inventiveness of Achille Duchêne. 'Measure and clarity are essential to the French garden scene,' he declared.

In learning from earlier masters Page was conscious that 'contemporary styles and techniques are

Moulin de la Tuilerie, Gif-sur-Yvette. Russell Page and the Duke of Windsor in the garden they made at the Duke's country cottage near Paris. The Duke was a knowledgeable and enthusiastic gardener.

sure to make a pastiche of a style borrowed from another period'. Page himself suffered from a tendency to pastiche. Despite his insistence on the importance of style, and of the appropriateness of the garden to the house and to the landscape, he favoured certain motifs as off-the-peg solutions to every problem. Page found, for example, that the idea of lawns and herbaceous borders was irresistible to French clients: 'when one asks them how they envisage an English garden, the answer is always that they want grass right up to the house and the mixed flower border'. And, although Page knew that herbaceous borders were difficult to make well in much of France, he did his best to provide them. He was particularly fond of formal arrangements near the house, narrow beds bright with annual flowers, designed as a simple pattern of squares or rectangles. Other Page features were the avoidance of verticals in the centre of a design, the use of seats and benches to round off or begin a composition, and a preference for simple colours. Red brickwork was another favourite,

Moulin de la Tuilerie, Gif-sur-Yvette. The entrance gate in 1953 when work on the house and garden was just under way.

especially in the north of France. 'Where the winters are long, grey and wet,' he wrote, 'the warm colour of brick paving and a green lawn look far more cheerful than grey stone, leafless bushes and naked flower beds.'

Page's first commission in France, as a very young man in 1930, was for the American architect Ogden Codman at his garden near Melun. Later he practised in England with Geoffrey Jellicoe, a partnership which ended on the outbreak of war in 1939. After

demobilisation he worked in Paris as a designer for the celebrated seedsman André de Vilmorin. Among his many French commissions was the garden of the Duchesse de Talleyrand for the house in the Forêt de Montmorency where Edith Wharton had lived.

Among Page's best work in the English style was the garden of Moulin de la Tuilerie at Gif-sur-Yvette, south-west of Paris, which he made for the Duke of Windsor. There were no brick surfaces here, because the grounds included a sandstone quarry with enough

Moulin de la Tuilerie, Gif-sur-Yvette, 1975. Russell Page lightened the dark corner just inside the entrance gate with Hedera algeriensis *'Gloire de Marengo' and variegated eleagnus and euonymus.*

stone to pave all the garden paths, but he used the garden to develop some of his best ideas for planting. One was the choice of white and purple petunias in a narrow bed at the side of a cobbled courtyard to match the white shutters and purple clematis growing up the stone walls; they were followed by dwarf pompon chrysanthemums in mixed whites and yellows. A dark corner by the entrance gate was brightened by a pattern of variegated leaves: the evergreen *Hedera algeriensis* 'Gloire de Marengo', and variegated eleagnus and euonymus were set off during the growing months by the fresh green and white leaves of irises, grasses, hostas and annual spurges.

The Duke got on well with Russell Page and called him 'a remarkably talented landscape architect and plantsman'. The Duke was an experienced gardener – or '*dirt* gardener' as he described himself – and could claim, with justification, during the 1930s to have transformed Fort Belvedere in Windsor Great Park from a wilderness into a tidy and organised landscape. He said that, for him, the main pleasure

of gardening came from using flowers in relation to their surroundings, seeing them as masses of shape and colour, and conceiving the garden as an artistic composition. It was because of the site's possibilities for making an interesting garden that he bought Moulin de la Tuilerie in the first place. The Duke thought of it as 'a very tranquil place, where one can garden as one should, in old clothes, with one's hands, among familiar plants' and went on to quote Rousseau with approval: 'a garden is a mood', he declared, adding that his mood was one of intimacy, not splendour. He wanted 'an English type of garden, which means green grass and seemingly casual arrangements of flowers ... here I had the perfect framework'.

In their search for style, Page and the Duke took full advantage of the sandy acid soil, the omni-presence of water, and the many outbuildings that gave the garden its best vistas. One of the prettiest was the tool shed, which Page used to illustrate his book *The Education of a Gardener*. The only drawback was the predatory instincts of the Duchess:

she regarded the garden as a source of cut flowers for the house. 'She is my severest critic . . .' wrote the Duke, 'and hers is always the last word.' But he gave her credit for linking the house to the garden with her arrangements inside and her potted plants on the window-sills and terraces outside.

Page turned the old leat, part of the river Merantaise, into a stream garden, and claimed to have planted it 'in a flowery and English manner unusual in French gardens' with gunneras, rheum, irises and day lilies, as well as bright scarlet patches of *Lobelia cardinalis* near the house. He wrote of transforming the formal *potager* into an enclosed pleasure garden surrounding a central lawn. According to the Duke, it was no more than 'a chaos of cabbage and chickens'. An arm of the stream ran slowly through it over three small waterfalls. This was the Duke's idea, inspired by a series of cascades he had seen on a New Jersey golf course: 'I thought of the Merantaise stream . . . and tapped the ball into the creek.' The Duke loved herbaceous borders. These were wider and more varied than usual, because the Duke dis-

liked clipped yew and box. In order to give weight and body to the planting, Page turned to flowering shrubs, including short varieties of floribunda roses in front and tall mounds of *Spartium junceum*, *Buddleia alternifolia* and *Laburnum × watereri* 'Vossii' behind. He discovered that these background shrubs gave the same depth and luxuriance as conventional hedges. The Duke's version is rather different. They planted floribundas in scarlet, crimson, salmon and rose – 'Vogue' and 'Fashion' are the two he mentions – to provide bright colour among the herbaceous plants, right up until the October frosts. The Duke said that he learnt this lesson from Norah Lindsay, who had advised him at Fort Belvedere: 'she specialised in herbaceous plantings and, if you had money, she was the one to spend it. I think now that her use of roses alone was worth the tuition fee.'

There is in fact no contradiction between Russell Page's account of how they made the garden at Moulin de la Tuilerie and the Duke's version. Page worked best with clients who were knowledgeable,

Baronne Gabrielle van Zuylen, friend and biographer of Russell Page, added this small pool to the enclosed rose garden at Haras de Varaville some years after he died.

enthusiastic and perceptive. The ideas came from both designer and patron, and were constantly developed and updated over the years by observation, discussion and reflection. Page put their conclusions into effect: the client paid the bill.

A more obviously French influence prevails in Page's design for Haras de Varaville, begun in 1966 for Baronne van Zuylen. Varaville is in the flat open country behind Cabourg, a landscape empty except for the occasional cider orchard or kestrel. The house is a modern one-storey structure, built on top of a 5 m (16 ft) mound of rubble from its demolished predecessor, the old *manoir* destroyed by fire in 1937. The garden was designed in large part to be seen from the house, which is not an easy one to accommodate. Page planted the banks of its foundations in such a way that the eye is led up to the roof, while the architectural detail (most of it appearing as plate-glass windows) is lost to the line of sight. He divided the old walled garden into rooms by yew hedges, clipped at an angle to match the pitch of the roof of the stables and farm buildings. A broad central lawn leaves two long enclosures to the sides. These are each subdivided by more yew hedging into three smaller compartments. One is planted mainly with roses, including a mass of 'Iceberg' around the small patch of grass in the middle, with ramblers and climbers on the walls. The other has a large central section with twenty-four box-edged compartments: the four innermost compartments are filled with tall square columns of fastigiate hornbeam, and the outer ones have buttresses of different varieties of box. Page intended a filling of tulips and brightly coloured annual flowers, a different variety in each compartment.

Varaville would not look out of place in southern England. The English style exports well to northern France, and there are many good gardens to prove it. The large number of Britons who have bought country houses there in recent years will in due time no doubt produce some further fine examples of the English garden abroad.

References and Further Reading

William Howard Adams's *The French Garden 1500–1800* (New York, 1979) and Dora Wiebenson's *The Picturesque Garden in France* (Princeton, 1978) are useful sources for the landscape movement in France. There is an article on Bagatelle in *Country Life* on 25 June 1938. The English colony at Pau is described in an article called '*Where Hair Curled Better*' by Clive Aslet in *Country Life*, 17 January 1985 and the gardens of the town, such as they are, by G. Anthony in 'Les Parcs et Jardins de Pau' (*Bulletin du Musée Bernadotte*, December 1973). William Robinson wrote of Ferrières in *The Parks and Gardens of Paris*. Monet's use of colour is analysed by Stephen Gwyn in *Claude Monet and his Garden* (London, 1934) and in 'The Puzzle at Giverny' by Fred Whitsey (*Country Life*, 16 July 1981). Nicolette Devas wrote of her grandparents' garden at Congénies in *Country Life*, 16 June 1977. Jas Créma and Pontrancart are well treated in Anita Pereire and Gabrielle van Zuylen's *Private Gardens of France* (London, 1983). Princesse de Caraman-Chimay described her own garden at Ste Preuve in *RHSJ*, November 1973, pp. 499–502, following Alvilde Lees-Milne's piece in *Country Life*, 5 August 1971. Moura Lympany's garden I know only from a short article she wrote for *The Garden* in February 1978. Kerdalo was written up by Timothy Vaughan in *The Garden*, May 1982, and Anita Pereire in *Country Life*, 15 July 1985. Le Vasterival often appears in gardening magazines now; see, for example, Anne Scott-James's article in *The Garden*, June 1980. The Duke of Windsor's own account of the garden at Gif in its early days was written for *Life International* on 20 August 1956.

Chapter Thirteen

NINFA

Within the Walls

NINFA IS A deserted medieval town in the Pontine marshes south of Rome. Spread among the ruins of its houses, churches and fortifications is the most beautiful and romantic garden in the world. It witnesses the English love of landscaping with ornamental plants, applied to the cultural inheritance of the Italian family who dominated the area for seven hundred years.

Ninfa is known to have existed in the first century AD when Pliny described a temple dedicated to the sacred nymphs near the lake, but the ruined town we see now was born, flourished and died in the Middle Ages. At its greatest extension, it had four monasteries and ten churches, and in the largest, Santa Maria Maggiore, Pope Alexander III was consecrated in September 1159. In 1297 Pope Boniface VIII bought Ninfa for 200,000 gold florins as a present for his nephew Pietro Caetani. It was a large sum in those days, but the investment proved sound. The town prospered, partly by levying tolls on travellers along the road to Rome and partly because the abundance of water attracted dye works, tanneries and water mills. The classical River Nymphaeus flowed past the tall keep of the Caetani castle, along the side of the town hall or Palazzo Comunale and through the middle of the square fortified town. Then as now, water was everywhere. It was the key to Ninfa's ancient fame and medieval prosperity: some consider that it is still the key to the garden too.

In 1382, the town was completely destroyed in one of the many civil wars that plagued the Papal States

Ninfa. The old keep of the Caetani castle is reflected in the broad stream which is planted as a magnolia glade.

during the Avignon Captivity and the Great Schism. The sacking of Ninfa, as it happened, coincided with a period of economic contraction and the arrival of malaria in the Pontine marshes. The town was left desolate, still a fief of the Caetani, but no more than a romantic ruin. A few inhabitants crept back from time to time but succumbed to the fever. In the seventeenth century the Viceroy Francesco Caetani arrived in Ninfa from Cisterna to revive its fortunes but returned defeated to the healthy air of the Alban hills, where he acquired renown as a breeder of anemones. For some years Ninfa's buildings were quarried for stone. The historian Gregorovius visited the town in 1860 and declared it 'the Pompeii of the Middle Ages ... its walls, its towers, its churches, its convents all half buried in the swamp and entombed beneath the thickest ivy'. The wild flowers that covered the ruins captivated Ferdinand Gregorovius's German imagination: he was enchanted to discover that

a fragrant sea of flowers waves above Ninfa; every wall is veiled with green, over every ruined house or church the god of spring is waving his purple banner triumphantly ... flowers crowd in through all the streets. They march in procession through the ruined churches, they climb up all the towers, they smile and nod to you out of every empty window frame, they besiege all the doors ... you fling yourself down into this ocean of flowers quite intoxicated by their fragrance while, as in the most charming fairy tale, the soul seems imprisoned and held by them.

(*Römische Tagebüchen* 1852–74, 1892)

Gregorovius was not the only nineteenth-century writer to be enraptured by Ninfa. Augustus Hare visited it in 1874 and extolled an unspeakably quiet scene of sylvan beauty ... where Flora holds her court, where the only inhabitants are the roses and the lilies and all the thousands of flowers which grow so abundantly in the deserted streets, where honeysuckle and jessamine fling their garlands through the windows of every house, and where the altars of the churches are thrones of flame-coloured valerian.

The painter Edward Lear was a friend of the Caetani and stayed with them during his winter travels: one of his sketches, still in the Palazzo Caetani in Rome, shows the ruins of the town entirely open to the surrounding countryside. Ninfa moved even the prosaic diplomat Sir James Rennell Rodd to ecstasy when he recalled a visit in 1902, and babbled that its chapels were 'invaded by wild jasmine and red valerian, and festooned with climbing honeysuckle. Between the lake and the hills masses of broom were golden in full flower, and seaward all the plain was scarlet with a riot of poppies.' His final rapture was to discover that 'only the song of mid-May's nightingales broke the silence of beautiful desolation half-veiled in the ivy of centuries'. The nightingales still sing there, although Rose Macaulay considered that Ninfa was more melancholy by night when 'mist

Ninfa. A plan of the town before it was cleared and planted as a garden in the 1920s.

swathes the phantom town, reptiles and rodents glide about, pursued by rapacious and hooting owls, and the atmosphere is eerily bewitched'.

The garden at Ninfa is the story of three Caetani women: Ada Bootle-Wilbrahim, Marguerite Chapin and Lelia Howard, each more English or American than Italian. When Ada Bootle-Wilbrahim married Duke Onorato in 1867, she was not the first Englishwoman to marry a Caetani: Onorato's own mother had been English. His father, Duke Michelangelo, was said to be 'the cleverest man in Italy', and his formidable intellect passed to several of his descendants. Duchess Ada had other Italian connections: one of her sisters married the Earl of Crawford, whose parents lived at Villa Palmieri in Florence. Ada was immensely high-spirited. According to Lady Paget 'she rode and hunted; she climbed impossible mountains in Switzerland, passing the ridges *à califourchon*; she went up in balloons, telling her husband he must stay below, because it would not do if something happened to both of them, on account of the children'. There were six little Caetani, five boys and a girl: Leone, Roffredo, Gelasio, Livio, Michelangelo and Giovanella. As the children grew up, Ada and Onorato needed a place in the country outside Rome. Ninfa was still considered too dangerous: although Ada insisted that the estate workers should be dosed with quinine, she herself nearly died of the fever one winter. They built a house instead on the lagoon at Fogliano south of Latina.

Ada made a garden at Fogliano in about 1890. It was an English gardenesque monstrosity: nothing more different than Ninfa could be imagined. She planted palms, agaves, pampas grass and eucalyptus among the native stone pines; every tree had a circle of annuals and lamium around the base of its trunk. It is said that she also grew many roses and that when she took her children for picnics among the ruins of Ninfa she brought rooted cuttings of climbing roses from Fogliano to plant against the walls. Old plants of *Rosa laevigata*, *R. bracteata* and 'La Follette' at Ninfa may date from these expeditions. Ninfa itself is so utterly different from Fogliano that to this day you will not find agaves, eucalyptus and palm trees there. They belong to the Afro-Mediterranean tradition, while Ninfa is a garden of the temperate climate. It is greatly to Duchess Ada's credit that she observed this distinction.

When Duke Onorato died, Ninfa was inherited by his son Prince Gelasio. He was perhaps the most remarkable of all the Caetani, a perfect Renaissance man. He had practised as a mining engineer in San

Ninfa, 1919. The ruined Palazzo Comunale at the time Prince Gelasio Caetani began his work of restoration upon the ruined castle and town.

Francisco before the First World War, became an Italian war hero in 1917 when he led the counter-attack on Austria after the disaster of Caporetto, and was to serve as Italian Ambassador to the USA between 1922 and 1924. For some years afterwards, he was engaged on draining the Pontine marshes for Mussolini, a project which was just about completed by the time of his early death in 1934. It employed a labour force of 14,000 men on an area of 70,000 ha (175,000 acres), now among the richest agricultural land in Italy.

Prince Gelasio, part English and part Italian, embodied the old saying that Italians are impelled to restore ruins and the British to create gardens. He commemorated his own work at Ninfa on a plaque in the wall of the grand *salone* in the Palazzo Comunale. 'In the year 1920,' the Italian inscription reads, 'I, Gelasio Caetani, planted the trees at Ninfa and restored this room, which was threatening to fall into ruin.' Prince Gelasio's tree-planting was responsible for the majestic specimens of the black walnut *Juglans nigra* and the American evergreen *Magnolia grandiflora* that, together with several evergreen oaks *Quercus ilex*, help to create the present air of maturity at Ninfa. His most extensive planting was

of the Italian cypress *Cupressus sempervirens*, which has reached great heights and gives Ninfa much of its structure. The grand avenue of cypresses that marches through the centre of the garden follows the route of the old main street of the medieval town: it was planted by Prince Gelasio, although many of the trees are also host to his mother's rambling roses and to such other climbing plants as wisteria and clematis.

During Italy's 1915–18 war, German and Austrian prisoners started to clear the ruins of the town. Most of the undergrowth was of ivy and briars, not the jessamine and honeysuckle mentioned by earlier visitors. Gelasio's restoration at Ninfa was not confined to the *salone*. He adopted the Palazzo Comunale as his country house, rebuilt the tall keep of the Caetani castle, and stabilised the walls of the ruined churches, convents and larger houses within the fortifications of the town. Gelasio was the only one of Duchess Ada's six children not to marry, and she made her home with him after Duke Onorato's death. She continued to plant climbing and rambling roses: the huge specimens of *Rosa sino-wilsonii*, 'Mme Alfred Carrière', 'Maréchal Niel' and 'Alister Stella Gray' which cover the walls of ruined churches and houses

Ninfa. The inner driveway leads along the walls of the old castle, festooned with climbing roses, to the restored Palazzo Comunale.

are one of the features of Ninfa. Ada Caetani also planted large clumps of the popular nineteenth-century tea rose 'Général Schablikine', which recurs throughout the garden and serves to unify the planting.

After Prince Gelasio's death, the estate passed to his nephew Camillo, the son of Prince Roffredo Caetani and his American-born wife Marguerite Chapin, soon to become Duke and Duchess of Sermoneta. Camillo was barely twenty years old, and Ninfa effectively became his parents' home for the next twenty-five years. Roffredo was a composer – his godfather was the Abbé Liszt – and the 'hand-somest man you ever saw'. His sister Giovanella once remarked that before he met and married Marguerite 'Roffredo had only to smile at a girl – and he was always very nice to them – and she thought she had been chosen'. He decided to divert the lake and springs at Ninfa to run through the garden in innumerable streamlets and channels, so that almost every part was filled with the sight and sound of running water. One stream actually runs over

another on a small aqueduct not far from the *palazzo*, before both race into the main river with a froth of white bubbles.

Duchess Marguerite was by all accounts a creature from one of Henry James's novels about Americans in Europe. According to Iris Origo she came to Paris originally to study music with Jean de Reske, and then decided to dedicate her life to all that was most significant in contemporary literature, art and music. She became a great promoter of new artists and was the founder of two important multilingual literary reviews: *Commerce* published some of her cousin T. S. Eliot's work, while the first extract from Lampedusa's *Il Gattopardo* appeared in the pages of *Botteghe Oscure*, as did the earliest version of *Under Milk Wood*, with the title of *Llareggub*. Duke Roffredo and Duchess Marguerite continued to lay out the garden at Ninfa in an English natural style until the Duke's death in 1961. They planted a large number of flowering cherries, crab apples and magnolias for spring colour, more roses, including in every part of the garden *Rosa chinensis* 'Mutabilis', which opens pale yellow and darkens to deepest crimson, and irises in great quantities, among them *Iris japonica*, the damp-loving *I. kaempferi*, and winter-flowering *I. unguicularis*. The ditch along the western side of the town walls was filled with white arum lilies. The novelist Giorgio Bassani summed up the achievement to date in January 1958:

The city, enclosed within its grey-blue fortifications has thus become a garden, the park attached to a house. The streets, the little ruined houses, the scorched apses of the seven churches, the slighted Romanesque bell towers, the little curved bridges of pink stone above the clear fast-running waters of the River Nymphaeus: all have now found a new and secret harmony.

Prince Camillo, to whom Ninfa had belonged since 1934, was killed during the Second World War, and the estate passed to his sister Lelia. In 1951 she married The Hon. Hubert Howard, himself a member of the Anglo-Italian nobility, since his mother was a Princess Giustiniani-Bandini; indeed, Hubert had rather more Italian blood in him than his wife. Both were dedicated to the preservation and improvement of Ninfa, the garden and its estate. Lelia devoted herself to developing the garden, especially after the death of Duchess Marguerite in 1958, and throughout the 1960s and 1970s she intensified the plantings in quantity and variety.

Lelia and Hubert were both English and Italian, but English was the language they spoke to each other, and Englishness determined their interests. They understood the need for conservation long before its imperatives had permeated the Italian consciousness. Eventually they dedicated their lives' work to the restoration of Ninfa and its establishment as a centre for the protection of the environment. Hubert Howard was the founder jointly with Giorgio Bassani of the Italian equivalent of the National Trust, Italia Nostra. Lelia was an artist. Gardens made by artists often merit careful study, and Hubert's brother Edmund Howard has observed how Lelia would 'compose her garden as if painting a picture. Then she would recreate in her evocative paintings what she had fashioned in her garden.' Sometimes she used to paint the garden not as it was at the time of her composition but as it would be in the future. Her paintings allow us to compare her vision of twenty or thirty years ago with the garden as we see it now; they also serve to guide its future development.

The garden is about 8 ha (20 acres) in extent, with an alkaline soil, although it is possible to grow such acid-loving genera as magnolia, crinodendron and rhododendron in a few places where there is a sufficient accumulation of humus. The ubiquitous presence of water allows plants to be irrigated during the dry months that would otherwise not survive the heat of an Italian summer. It also creates a cool freshness and a smell of growth that are unique to the garden: temperatures are often several degrees lower within the walls of Ninfa than outside.

The entrance leads along poplar-lined canals with a hedge of *Rosa roxburghii* on one side, past huge bushes of oleanders and overgrown box hedges as much as 8 m (27 ft) high. The rose is the double-flowered form of *roxburghii* which, due to a taxonomist's impatience to describe it as a new species, is in fact the botanical type. It was introduced to Ninfa by Duchess Marguerite and appears all over the garden, with beautiful pink flowers, long pinnate leaves and a hip covered in prickles like a sweet chestnut. The drive passes through an inner gate and into a courtyard that once formed the main square of the town, with the walls of the Caetani fortress on one side and the Palazzo Comunale at the far end. The walls of the *palazzo* are festooned with white wisterias, the climbing rose 'Mermaid' with its great sulphur-yellow single flowers and red bougainvilleas. A huge bush of the wintersweet *Chimonanthus praecox* flourishes against its western side, and other large specimens have been planted near by to scent the air at Christmas time. Bushes of *Viburnum carlesii* 'Aurora' take over in spring. The main river runs along the eastern side of the Palazzo Comunale and a dramatic staircase descends from the *salone* to a small sheltered area on the embankment. Here, underneath a pergola of honeysuckle, roses and *Clematis viticella* 'Purpurea Plena Elegans' are more sweet-scented plants including Madonna lilies and jonquils.

Immediately to the south of the *palazzo* stretches a small irregular lawn in the English style, shaded by a large spreading cedar. The conical thatched summer-house beneath exactly copies the huts in which the woodsmen and charcoal makers who worked on the estate at Fogliano lived in winter. A bed at the edge of the lawn has 3 m (10 ft) shrubs of *Rosa chinensis* 'Mutabilis', together with a great variety of other roses including the hybrid musks 'Moonlight', 'Vanity', 'Buff Beauty' and 'Cornelia'. All roses seem to flourish at Ninfa: the dwarf polyanthus 'Yesterday' grows to 1.5 m (5 ft). A little

Ninfa. The river runs right through the ruins of the medieval town and provides one of the main axes in this carefully unstructured garden.

further on, round a race of the river drawn into the garden by Don Gelasio's water engineering, a glade of magnolias is underplanted with spring bulbs. The magnolias include *sprengeri diva, sargentiana robusta, heptapeta, sieboldii, stellata* and *kobus*: the effect is as English as it is possible to imagine, if you ignore the tower of the Caetani fortress in the background, bristling with Ghibelline battlements. The nearby beeches and birches reminded Hubert Howard of his native Cumberland.

Ninfa has been planted in the natural style, according to the English taste, and at no time has any attempt been made to Italianise the gardens: there are no straight lines, clipped hedges of box, yew trees shaped in cones, nor any statue, fountain, pool or stone ornament in any part. The ruins of the medieval town are enough to produce extraordinarily charming effects. Every wall and hummock seems to have a rose or other climbing plant draped over it: clematis, honeysuckle, passion flower, jasmine, wisteria, bignonia and tecoma. One of the principal walks is along the banks of the river, which is

spanned by several bridges. If you stand on one of them, admiring the vast clumps of the giant *Gunnera manicata* and look up beyond the limits of the city walls, you see the cliffs of the hill town of Norma as a distant backdrop high in the sky. Another long walk is bordered by a double hedge of English lavender, a tall form of *Lavandula angustifolia* seldom seen in Italy. It passes close to a small rock garden where forms of the bloody cranesbill *Geranium sanguineum* mix with flowering pinks and scarlet salvias from Mexico. A second and larger rock garden, made on the ruins of the outer walls of the town, is thick with verbenas, hebes, salvias, alyssum, annual eschscholtzias and miniature pomegranates *Punica granatum nana*, which flower and fruit in late summer and autumn. The idea of a rock garden is strange to Italian thinking, but stranger still to the English experience is the variety of plants that it actually supports. It is underplanted with cyclamen, including the native *Cyclamen repandum*, which flowers in early April, and autumn bulbs, including the golden-flowered *Sternbergia lutea*.

Elsewhere at Ninfa you find loose hedges of rosemary, a walnut avenue and a long line of American strawberry vines, known as *uva fragola* in Italian, which produce small sweet black grapes that taste unquestionably of strawberries. Then there are the clumps of giant bamboos for which Ninfa is famous in Italy, and a heather garden where lime-tolerant species such as *Erica mediterranea* and *E. carnea* flourish, though *E. canaliculata* and the South African species need to be fed with Sequestrene. And there are groups of *Fremontodendron californicum* grown as free-standing shrubs, banana plants (though they seldom ripen their fruits), and *Viburnum* × *bodnantense*, *Lonicera* × *purpusii* and *Mahonia* 'Charity' to give colour and scent in winter. One of the most striking trees, which never seems to suffer scorch, is a variegated box elder *Acer negundo* 'Variegatum'; it stands near a huge mound of *Rosa bracteata*, one of the parents of 'Mermaid', which has little bracts subtending each white flower. *Tillandsia dianthifolia* is suspended in bands around the lower limbs of *Pinus pinea*.

The gardens at Ninfa contain few plants that are rare or special, and it is in no sense a botanic collection. None of the plants even carries a label, though the competent plantsman has little difficulty in naming most of the species grown in the garden, even if he does not grow them himself. Almost all were bought from English nurseries, Hilliers of Winchester in particular, so that the trees and shrubs, though many are rare in Italy, seem to the English visitor almost commonplace. Thus it is to some extent the selection of plants that makes Ninfa such an English garden, though it also contains many plants that would be considered too tender for England. These include the sweet-scented *Luculia gratissima* and *L. pinceana*, both from comparatively low altitudes in the Himalayas, the rampant climbing *Caesalpinia japonica*, the mimosas *Acacia podalyriifolia* and *A.* × *hanburyana* from La Mortola, such tender species of roses as the Chinese *Rosa gigantea* and forms of *R. banksiae*, and a large collection of citrus fruits.

Ninfa is part of the endowment of a private foundation, set up under the Howards' wills, whose main aim is to preserve the garden and castle in perpetuity. Hubert Howard's brother Edmund calls it 'a unique and delicate legacy'. There is a farm of 500 ha (1,200 acres) but the income of the estate does not cover the wages of five gardeners, let alone the expense of maintenance, repair and improvement, so the garden and castle are open to the public three or four times a month from spring to autumn. Every year 40,000 visitors come, but individuals may not visit the gardens by themselves. They are only admitted in groups which are conducted along a route chosen to cause as little wear and tear as possible to the fabric of the garden. The guides tell them that Ninfa is a special place and demands high standards of behaviour from visitors – always a good point when trying to control Italian crowds – while the guides themselves are graduates of botany, biology and the history of art. Parties are encouraged to see the ruins of the castle rather than the garden, because the effect of large numbers there is less destructive. Indeed, two thirds of the applications to tour the garden are turned down, and permission is only given to school groups if the organisers can show that they have prepared for the visit and done their homework first. A new 2 ha (5 acre) arboretum has been planted outside the walls to relieve pressure on the main garden.

Hubert saw himself as a trustee of the Caetani inheritance, a guardian for posterity. For Lelia, who was by nature more possessive, the garden was a favourite child that needed protection from the rude world outside. Lelia did not like opening the garden to the public; Hubert, by contrast, thought that Ninfa was a message for humanity, partly because he had a greater sense of history and respect for the past, but also because he saw it as a model for others. Even if there was a price to be paid for admitting the public, in terms of wear and tear, it was a price that he believed should be accepted.

Hubert and Lelia Howard appointed their nephew Esmé Howard and a young Italian Lauro Marchetti as trustees of their foundation. Marchetti is the curator of Ninfa; the Howards adopted him as the heir presumptive to their ideas, educated him in their way of thinking and took him on their travels to England. Since Hubert's death in 1987, Marchetti has been responsible for the constant renewal of the garden by replanting and for the introduction of much new plant material. Between three and four hundred new plants are added every year, so that there is a progressive sense of intensification at Ninfa. The guiding principles when making additions to the garden are that they should match the ruins and not create violent contrasts with the existing plants. Marchetti is that rare phenomenon, an Italian who thinks like an Englishman: he understands completely the spirit of the garden. He has been able to keep up a high standard of maintenance throughout the garden, which is better kept than any English garden abroad of comparable size – indeed, it would do credit to the National Trust in England. Ninfa is safe in the hands of the trustees, and safe for the foreseeable future too, but well-endowed private charitable trusts are the traditional prey of Italian politicians and it may be that the Caetani foundation will have to tread delicately to preserve its independence. The garden is maintained entirely without the use of pesticides and, as a result, has great importance for the number and variety of its insects, particularly the larger species which act as predators upon the smaller. Bordeaux mixture, the simplest of fungicides, is however sprayed on the many prunus trees in the garden: it gives a ghostly hue to their trunks. The foundation consistently emphasises the importance of the environment and respect for nature.

Ninfa continues to exercise a strong influence on the creative imagination of visitors. Gregorovius and Augustus Hare have been followed by Giorgio Bassani and the English poet Kathleen Raine. Bassani is said to have based certain aspects of *The Garden of the Finzi-Contini* on the garden. He was a close friend of the Howards and spent six months at Ninfa while writing his most famous novel. Granted that the book's action takes place among the Jewish community of Ferrara, not the Anglo-Italian nobility of Rome, it is still a fact that the Finzi-Contini lived behind the walls of their 10 ha (25 acre) garden isolated from the life outside by aristocratic sensibility. They created for themselves a richly intellectual private world, symbolised by the love they had for their garden. The narrator of this *roman à clef* explained how it seemed to Micol Finzi-Contini absurd 'that there could exist on earth someone like me who did not cherish for trees . . . the same feelings of passionate admiration that she felt. How could I not *understand*?' There are parallels between the Finzi-Contini, vulnerable in a time of political change because they were not wholly Italian, and the English Howards, preoccupied by the garden in which they expressed their values and their creativity. Both faced extinction, despite the opulence of their house and garden, a world that they had created and that might one day be their best or only monument.

Kathleen Raine's principal poem about the garden was 'Ninfa Revisited', written in 1968 at a time of social upheaval. It reflects the pessimism of many who had survived the Second World War only to see its fragile peace threatened by the children of returning soldiers waving the little red books of Chairman Mao. Raine imagined Lelia Howard as the custodian of a second Garden of Eden,

Her only privilege her task,
To recreate felicity,
This ancient garden, ever new,
That some have found, and all desire,
And all believe on earth, somewhere,
Though none knows where, these flowers bloom,
In Persia, India, Avalon,
Whose multitude seems infinite:
Her art to make that legend true.
The rabble clamouring at the gates
Raise slogans of a future age;
They will break in, yet never find
Lost Eden, but the accursèd ground
Of those who live by bread alone,
The thorns and thistles of the waste.
Rose and cypress are the dream
Of Adam awake in Paradise,
And fade into the common day:
No social justice can confer
Beauty's immeasurable gift,
Or touch with silent, secret joy
The crowds that envy and destroy.

For years Ninfa was a well-kept secret. Occasionally a piece about it slipped into the horticultural press: Alvilde Lees-Milne described the garden in *Country Life* in 1956, and the late Lord Skelmersdale wrote – very well – about it in the Royal Horticultural Society's *Journal* in 1969. These articles tended to be written by the rich and famous. Later one heard that the Queen Mother stayed at Ninfa during the 1970s and that the Prince and Princess of Wales had visited the garden. There was never any suggestion that humble visitors would be welcome, or indeed that it was possible for ordinary people to visit it freely. It was a sort of paradise: people were encouraged to believe that it existed, but to be unsure that they could ever gain admission to its delights.

Current rumours that its future is none too secure are fortunately without foundation in fact. The British public understandably confuses one Italian garden with another, and the menace to La Mortola, the same threat from local politicians that has already destroyed Villa Táranto, is transferred in the English imagination to Ninfa. One is told that the river will be diverted for industrial uses, or that there is insufficient funding to keep the garden as good as it was in the Howards' day, or that the curator is an Italian and so the character of Ninfa is certain to change for the worse. Such rumours are groundless, and serve only to prove that the power of Ninfa to provoke the imagination is as strong now as it was in the time of Gregorovius and Hare.

Ninfa is quite unlike any other garden, for the intensely romantic setting of a deserted medieval village has no parallel. The lawns and woodlands appear so natural that it is difficult to realise that all the trees were planted since 1920 and that Ninfa is an abandoned city invaded by a garden rather than a park containing ruins. Alvilde Lees-Milne saw an affinity between Ninfa and Sissinghurst, particularly in the way plants are encouraged to grow naturally and allowed to scramble up trees and walls. She added, 'Sissinghurst was also created among ruins, and both places have an indescribable magic about them.' Yet the scale of the gardens is very different: Sissinghurst is much more densely planted, altogether busier than Ninfa, and the combination of formal design, rare plants and clever planting which sets Sissinghurst in the forefront of modern garden design is not found at Ninfa. It resembles Hever Castle in some of its characteristics – the old castle surrounded by water for example – while the views up and down the river are strongly reminiscent of Mount Usher in County Wicklow. Nymans too comes to mind when one sees the architectural ruins festooned with climbing plants and surrounded by trees, and Ninfa shares with Knightshayes the sense of walking through a magic woodland. Certain corners, with mass plantings of water-loving herbaceous plants, also recall Longstock Park in Hampshire. But the disposition of plants around and over the ruined walls of a medieval village is unlike anything in England, while remaining predominantly English in spirit.

Ninfa is a garden almost without structure. The main paths lead around the ruins, through gaps in walls, across yards and alleys, by bridges and gates that seem to bear little relation to the medieval layout. It needs many hours of exploration to understand how the pieces fit together. The absence of plant labels adds to its Elysian quality, while the exclusion of statues and other artefacts is also an essential part of its character. It is an impossible garden to photograph well, since there are no lines or focal points to give composition to a frame. Views of the river with Norma on its cliff behind contradict the essential feeling of enclosure at Ninfa. Details of roses rambling against crumbling stonework do not convey the sense of being inside the walls of the town, surrounded by buildings whose every surface is covered in climbers. It is a paradox that neither the long shot nor the close-up accurately conveys the genius of the place.

My conclusion is that the essence of Ninfa is its ruins, not the presence of water, although the river is nevertheless responsible for its temperate luxuriance. There is a lost endeavour attached to vanished cities that inspires awe: Ninfa has some of the same spirit that pervades Mistra and Petra. The mystery of these abandoned towns excites the imagination, and elicits such lyrical responses as Gregorovius and Hare were impelled to express. Naked ruins have less charm: the excavated stones of Pompeii do not move the visitor to such outpourings of romantic invention. It is the act of embellishing it with flowers that transforms an archaeological relic into a place of rare enchantment. Such adornment is no part of the Italian tradition of garden-making: Ninfa could only have been made by English owners.

References and Further Reading

Much of my information about Ninfa comes from the library of the Fondazione Roffredo Caetani at the garden itself. Lord Skelmersdale's article in *RHSJ*, June 1969, is the most comprehensive and analytical account of the garden I have found in any language. Alvilde Lees-Milne's article in *Country Life* was substantially republished in *Hortus* in 1988, with but few additions. I have quoted from Sir James Rennell Rodd's *Social and Diplomatic Memories 1902–1919* (London, 1925) and Rose Macaulay's *The Pleasures of Ruins* (London, 1953). Iris Origo's memoir of Marguerite Caetani was published in *Tempo Presente* (March 1965) as '*Ritratto di Marguerite*'.

EPILOGUE

MANY OF THE gardens I have described are beset with uncertainties of continuity and succession. The common problem is that other countries do not understand the history of English gardening, the importance of plantsmanship and the tradition of horticultural administration which we take for granted. It is unfortunate, for instance, that gardens of such international importance as La Mortola, Villa Táranto and Monserrate do not have an English administrator or curator. The argument for preserving English gardens is not a nationalistic one: it is as valid to seek protection for the best examples of English gardens abroad as to afford it to works of art by foreigners in England.

Nevertheless, there is a growth of interest in the English horticultural tradition and with it goes a greater understanding and appreciation. No books are more frequently consulted by Italian visitors to the British Institute in Florence than the works of Gertrude Jekyll. But there remains a great gulf between acquiring an academic interest in English gardens and organising the technical skills necessary to maintain them.

Gardens everywhere are ephemeral and English gardens abroad have proved especially so, for two main reasons. The decline of the British Empire and British influence abroad hastened the decay of particular gardens; and the English tradition of gardening was always uniquely personal. Such gardens are linked to individual lives. Time and again it is the people who shape them: they do not self-perpetuate like Italian gardens in the formal style.

So even when rescued the gardens present problems. Of the few that deserve to survive, fewer still should be preserved as they were in their prime. To the likes of Sissinghurst and Hidcote at home one might add Serre de la Madone and Villa Maryland abroad, but no others – and certainly not La Mortola and Villa Táranto, where change is inherent in their role as botanic gardens.

Yet there have been successes abroad. A small committee of English volunteers, with academic and political clout, has saved La Mortola from despoliation and extinction. Daphne Phelps has decided to leave Casa Cuseni to the Landmark Trust. The decline of Monserrate has been arrested. Ninfa is a paradigm. Meanwhile, expatriate owners, designers and horticulturists are all the time making new English gardens abroad.

The terrace garden at Villa Gamberaia in 1990. Owners of historic gardens in Italy have almost no access to funding for hard structural repairs.

INDEX

6